MARK MORRIS: VETERINARIAN

Mark L. Morris, D.V.M., at age eighty, working among his library of friends

MARK MORRIS: VETERINARIAN

by

Willard C. Haselbush

Printed in the United States of America
by
R. R. Donnelley & Sons Company

With special thanks to Alice Wickham of Naples, Florida. Without her tireless research, her flawless filing system and her support, this book might not have been written.

Contents

1

A Veterinarian Is Born

Mark Loren Morris was born November 18, 1900, a few years after William L. McKinley was elected to his second term as President of the United States.

McKinley, who would die in less than a year from an assassin's bullet, ranked higher as an attention-getting news item than the blessed event in the family of the town store keeper in Henderson, Colorado. The Republican President had just signed the Gold Standard Act of 1900. The gold dollar was the proud keystone of all U.S. currency.

With future national prosperity thus assured, the rural hamlet of Henderson, a whistle-stop on the Union Pacific, 15 miles north of Denver, spent most of November 18 fighting off and talking about the early winter snowstorm. It was so intense that the doctor in Denver scheduled to preside over the birth missed his train and decided against risking the trip in the snow by horse and buggy.

The arrival was handled by Mark M. Morris, father of this first child of his marriage to the town's brown-eyed, good-looking young school teacher two years earlier. It was his first encounter with childbirth. He had a special distaste for snowstorms from that day on.

The early years of the snowstorm baby passed without event. Young Mark quickly learned to walk, holding onto things for support. His favorite training ground was a long row of kegs containing nails of varying sizes along a back wall in the Henderson General Store which his parents operated.

"That youngster is a born mixer," his father was fond of remarking. "He picks things out of one barrel and mixes them in with what's in the next barrel." His voice was itself a mixture of pride and pique. "It's hard to get the little nails back into the keg for little nails, but maybe he's inventing something."

1

The father's somewhat prophetic words gave way to something sterner on occasions in the child's young life; like the time he overturned a big drum of linseed oil and liquid spread out over the general store's wooden floor into a stack of bags of flour.

But mostly, life flowed smoothly and uneventfully for young Mark Morris. From the outset, as the frequently underfoot first born of the man who owned and operated the general store, young Mark Morris got a lot of attention—and did a lot of listening—to the farm customers who flocked in from miles around.

In the early 1900s, and for more than 80 years beyond, Henderson was a wide spot just east of the main highway from Denver leading north to Greeley in northern Colorado and Cheyenne, capital city of Wyoming. Henderson was and remains notably rural with farms of up to 120 acres scattered along the nearby South Platte River, counting on irrigation water to make crops. Larger farms spread out into the drylands on the east.

The Henderson of young Mark Morris sat beside the railroad tracks a full mile east of the Platte River. In addition to the clapboard rail station—where the crack flyers headed to Chicago would stop only if the station master had a passenger and put out a flag—the center of attention was the Grange Hall. It was the Henderson unit of the Colorado Grange, a social and sometimes political organization of farmers.

In 1896, the father of Mark L. Morris and a partner, Robert Curtis, had entered into an agreement with the Grange to build a two-story brick structure located about 100 yards from the Union Pacific station. The second floor was Grange Hall, where farmer members met regularly to hold business meetings or to socialize and indulge in square dancing. The first floor held the general store and a rear living area where Mark's father held forth as a bachelor until he took a bride in 1898. Three more children followed Mark in the back-of-the-store apartment. There was sister Beulah Marguerite in 1904, sister Eulah Esther in 1907 and brother Lester Alfred in 1911. As they grew up, most famous in the family was the daughter of Mark's maternal aunt, Beulah Williams. She was Olympic swimming star and actress, Esther Williams.

The parents of young Mark (called Loren during his school years to avoid the "Young Mark" or "Little Mark" syndrome) came from pioneer American stock.

On his mother's side were Samuel Gilpin and Esther Ann Yarrington,

Mark with his two sisters, Marguerite and Eula Esther, about 1910

who married on July 11, 1865, at Blemont, Iowa, and moved by team and wagon to Rice County, Kansas, where Pruda Mary Gilpin was born in a dugout home with a sod roof on June 27, 1874.

En route to becoming Mrs. Mark M. Morris and mother of Mark L., Pruda Gilpin attended grade school in Dodge City, Kansas, during its cattle drive and gunman days. Later she made the trek to Denver to attend the private Denver Normal School for would-be teachers, a higher education institution unmatched in the Dodge City area. Her first and last teaching job was in the Henderson Grade School north of Denver.

Young Mark's mother kept the books and records at the general store and helped out in handling customers. She also took action to end the vacuum in facilities for Christian education in the farming community. She organized a Sunday school which met in the Grange Hall over the store. Later her name appeared as number three on the list of organizers of the Henderson Congregational Church.

Grandfather Morris was born in 1840 in western Pennsylvania. He moved across mid-America by team and wagon and arrived along the Platte River about eight miles north of Denver in the early 1860s. He fashioned bricks by hand and built a small house which still stands more than a century later on the west side of the Brantner Ditch, a pioneer irrigation system which helped bring farming prosperity to the Henderson area.

Young Mark's father was born in the small brick house and attended grade school at Brantner School, near the Denver County Poor Farm, where the elderly poor of the early 1900s spent their final years sitting in neat rows of rocking chairs along corridors lined with glass windows in winter and open screens in summer under sheltering cottonwood trees. The long-gone Poor Farm has been replaced by an 18-hole golf course as part of the expansive new Adams County Fairgrounds.

At an early age, young Mark Morris was exposed by his father to the intricacies of life in rural Colorado. The father was a member of the school board and later the Board of Commissioners of Adams County, which adjoins the metropolis of Denver on the north and includes part of the city of Aurora, now the fourth largest city in the state. In spite of its proximity to Denver, Henderson clings to its rural image.

As a commissioner, Mark M. Morris and his two counterparts were in charge of matters like county budgets, roads, bridges, and land restrictions. The general store was a community meeting place and young Mark spent endless childhood hours tuning in on conversations about politics and other grave county matters.

The store meetings often dealt with sharing or conserving water for irrigation—the water which made the difference for most of the store's customers between the good life and poverty in a drought year.

Mark's father was an organizer and first secretary of the Wellington Reservoir Company which purchased a man-made lake in the foothills west of Denver and used existing ditch networks to bring more irrigation water to the Platte River Valley. Father Morris handled the books of the reservoir company for years and his son, Lester, took over after his death in 1944.

A two room brick building which had replaced an earlier one room version about a half mile east of the general store was the focal point of young Mark's life between early September, 1907, and May of 1916. It was the Henderson Grade School. Here he got his first taste of education and he liked it.

As a November child, young Mark had a late start in grade school. The minimum age was six and he didn't have a sixth birthday until more than two months after school began in 1906. When he did start first grade, he was just ten weeks short of his seventh birthday.

Mark was the only first grader in his initial year in school. He had new teachers annually until his fourth grade when Lucy E. Green came into his life. She and her brother moved to Henderson for respiratory health reasons from Providence, Rhode Island, and Lucy Green was hired as a Henderson school teacher at $65 a month. She later demanded a raise from Mark's father, a school board member. She didn't get the raise, but young Mark took on the job of school janitor at age 12 to relieve the teacher of the sweeping and cleaning chores. He still held the job when he graduated from the eighth grade in May 1916. Creation of the janitorial job by his father taught him a lesson which he never forgot: when faced with a decision always try to involve the family. Throughout his life, his decisions became family, and sometimes larger committee, or group decisions.

For young Mark, the new school teacher exemplified the fabled East Coast refinements of culture, education and personality.

"When she spoke, she meant what she said," he was to recall later. "There was no monkey business. We were there for work and to learn all about reading, writing and arithmetic. We learned all about it. In that school there was no problem about youngsters who couldn't read or spell."

After eight years of school, Mark L. Morris received a diploma which still hangs on the wall of his office in Topeka, Kansas.

"Be it known that Loren Morris of School District No. 95, in the County of Adams, has completed the course of study prescribed for the Public Schools of Colorado. In testimony whereof this diploma is given under our hands this 26th day of May A.D. 1916. County Superintendent Helen Lamb; Teacher Lucy E. Green, Class of 1916."

With his 16th birthday looming ahead and his legally required schooling complete, young Mark faced his first big decision in the fall of 1916.

The nearest high school was in Brighton, the county seat five miles to the north. There were no school buses and five miles each way was a long daily hike.

There was to be no problem about that.

2

A Scholar Meets the Dollar

Five miles of roadway built for horses pulling wagons and buggies connected the rural hamlet of Henderson, 15 miles north of Denver, with the Adams County seat of Brighton in late 1916.

The direct route between the Morris General Store beside the Union Pacific Railroad tracks in Henderson led into Brighton past the County Fair Grounds and tended to be a sea of mud in spring and a frozen tundra of drifts after winter storms.

The main road lay a mile west of the general store and followed vaguely a path near the South Platte River. In a few years, as autos and trucks began driving horses off highways, it would become part of U.S. 85, the first concrete paved route in Colorado—a high speed, all-weather link which evolved in the 1920s to connect Denver with Colorado Springs on the south and the Wyoming capital city of Cheyenne on the north.

But in the fall of 1916 there was no concrete and the distance between the Morris General Store in Henderson and the area's only high school on the southern edge of Brighton was a full five miles.

"I don't believe the word had become part of the language in those early days of the automobile—but I became a commuter," Mark was to recall much later. "I started out making the daily 10 mile trip between home and school on a bicycle. I soon discovered that bicycles and dirt roads are an unhappy and sometimes unsafe combination. By the time the cold fall mornings started turning into snowy nightmares, I knew that the bicycle was not the key to higher education."

To the rescue came a pair of parents determined that nothing should stand between their first child and the high school classes they were convinced were a first step in a good life for their son.

7

"They gave me a gentle horse, one I could ride horseback in good weather and could hitch to a buggy in bad," Mark is fond of recalling. "On some of the worst stormy days, they even let me use the family's top buggy. It had side curtains and I could sit there out of the weather while the horse figured out how to get me to school and back again."

The country boy who was to become an internationally acclaimed veterinary doctor had no hint in those days of the career ahead. But he had an inborn sense of responsibility for the welfare of animals.

"On the final day of riding the bicycle I checked out the man in charge of the Fair Grounds. He leased me a box stall in one of the barns. It had running water and all I had to do was bring along some grain and hay when I drove the buggy, and the horse that got me through the first two years of high school had a comfortable place to wait while I attended classes."

The walk between the Fair Grounds and Brighton High School was about a half mile. Young Mark decided in his junior year that twice that much walking would be worth it for a more modern mode of transport.

"I got friendly with a pair of brothers of the Johnson family, who operated an irrigated farm west of Henderson," he recalled. "They had to help milk the cows before leaving for Brighton High School in the morning. But they had it good. They got to drive the family's Model T Ford truck into town every morning to deliver their milk to the Brighton Dairy Company. I made a deal and met them each morning on the main road a mile west of our store so they could pick me up for the ride to town."

With three youngsters composing the crew, the old Model T usually had a wild time of it on the road between Brighton and Henderson.

"Cars were few and far between on the road in those days," recalls Morris. "To meet one going the same way was an automatic challenge to a race—and we sometimes won."

A favorite Johnson-Morris method of winning was for one of the three boys to lie out on the ample front fender, one foot firmly planted on the running board, "and tinker with the carburetor air mixture to wring the last mile-per-hour of speed out of the engine."

Young Mark Morris had no plans for college during his four years at Brighton High School.

"It was a time when, especially in rural areas, it was not considered necessary to go to college—unless your parents were rich or you were the son of a professional man duty bound to be the next-in-line doctor, professor, banker or lawyer in the family,'' recalled Dr. Morris. ''I had no such tradition to uphold and, when I bothered to think about the future in those halcyon high school days, I figured vaguely that I'd better pick up enough skills at office work to qualify me for some kind of a job when I graduated—if it ever came to that.''

Young Mark's high school subjects ranged from typing and book-keeping for beginners to the standard English, history and literature.

Experience in grade school had established that Mark L. Morris was not good with numbers. The boy who, some years later, would sign a multimillion-dollar contract of sale for something of his own creation, avoided everything mathematic in high school, except the then mandatory algebra. He admitted he hated even that.

With a total enrollment of under 100 students, Brighton High School was not a power in regional athletics. But it had a better-than-average baseball team and young Mark, who threw left-handed, became one of the pitchers. He was of average height and slender of build—a characteristic that later would enable him to avoid the flab and midriff bulge of middle age—but he played forward on the school's basketball team.

Several facets of life at Brighton High School remained crystal clear in the memory of Mark Morris in an interview more than five decades after his graduation.

One was the rowdy basketball rivalry between the boys of Brighton and their prep counterparts in the then coal-mining communities of Louisville and Lafayette on Denver's northwestern fringe.

''Louisville has become a computer manufacturing center and Lafayette now is a booming bedroom suburb, but it was different when we went there to play basketball.

''The gymnasiums in both towns were small and there were no tall galleries of seats surrounding the court. The fathers, coal miners all, and other older males of the towns crowded around and I remember vividly how husky they were.

''They wanted one thing only—a victory. And every time their team fell behind, especially late in the game, they'd stick out a foot or more as you dribbled by with the ball and tripped you up. The referees were blind to that. It was hard to win.''

Another event which etched itself into the young man's memory was a dramatic demonstration of the importance of discipline and orderly behavior in daily life.

''We had some boys, husky fellows, who specialized in being rowdy and trying to bully the younger and weaker students,'' he recalled.

"It was near chaos, until the Board of Education hired a new principal and gave him orders to straighten things out. The new man was named Baker and I'll never forget him or the straight-forward way in which he handled the situation and restored full order to the school.

"All it took was for Mr. Baker to march a few of the rowdies out of a general assembly by force and make it clear that only the well behaved could stay in school. It didn't take long for everyone to decide he meant it. The school was a better place almost at once."

With school pride still showing more than a half century later, Mark L. Morris outlined in the interview on his recollections of Brighton High School the careers of several fellow students.

"It was a small country school in a small country town, but it turned out some memorable people," he said. "A young lady two classes ahead of me was Irene Neunemaker, editor of the Brightonian, our school paper. She went on to journalism school at the University of Kansas and joined Capper Publications, then a power in the farmbelt, after graduation. Later, she became head of public relations for Avon Products, then just beginning to get national attention in the beauty products field. I remember she told me she took part of her pay in Avon stock. Well, there's a multimillion-dollar building now on the campus of the University of Kansas. She financed it, and it's called Neunemaker Hall."

In the same class was Irvin Hines, Brighton High School basketball guard, who became chief surgeon for the Denver & Rio Grande Western Railroad. And another upperclassman was Russell Merrill, who played guard to young Mark's forward. He "died a very wealthy man" after parlaying a job as county agent in Salinas, California, into a national wholesale produce business.

At some point past the midway mark in his years at Brighton High School, young Mark began to discover that girl students were very much different from male students—and that the difference was nice.

This led to more or less formal dates, during which it was mandatory that young Mark spend money on such suddenly important items as soft drinks and dishes of ice cream.

The first girl in his class to command more than passing attention was Elsie Denhart.

"It seems to me I was attracted as much by the fact she was an outstanding student as I was by her good looks," recalled Dr. Morris many years later. "She lived a mile south of town and it got to be a habit to give her a ride on days when I was driving the horse and buggy. We'd talk about school and then, when we arrived at her house, she often would help me with school book problems. She was a very nice person to know.''

And then there was Mary Merrill, the dating of whom required a certain amount of ready cash.

"I had a number of formal dates with Mary," ran the recollection. "Once I got to Brighton in the evening, by bicycle or horseback, I'd check in with my school chum, Leonard Higgins.''

Young Higgins, who was called "Spec" because of his well-freckled features, often had the use for the evening of his father's automobile—a grand Cole 8 and "just about the finest car in the entire town.''

Young Mark and Mary Merrill would climb into the back seat while Spec Higgins and his date of the evening handled the driving for slow tours of the town and environs and stops at refreshment emporiums.

This sudden need for cash was a minor and brief problem for young Mark. From his earliest years, he had been taught to work. His first assigned task was to sort through the potato sacks in the General Store at Henderson "and pick off the little knobs to seal the kerosene cans." As he grew older, his job was to unload the railroad coal cars which brought coal to within 100 yards of the General Store and place it into bins for measuring out to farmer customers.

No stranger to work, young Mark soon found a spare time job with the Great Western Sugar Co. in his own neighborhood. The sugar giant had introduced beets as an irrigated cash crop in the Platte River Valley north of Denver and had established loading points for the harvest on both the Union Pacific and Burlington railroads located near the general store.

"The farmers dug their beets, cut off the tops with heavy knives designed for the purpose, and then loaded the crop into wagons for the trip to the rail siding," he recalled. "Once there, the load and wagon were weighed and the farmer moved along to drop his load so the empty wagon or truck (there were some in those early days) could be reweighed.

"My job was tare man. That meant it was my responsibility to find out how much mud and dirt was clinging to the sugar beets. The company wanted to pay only for the sugar beets—not real estate. The procedure involved selecting about a half-bushel of beets at random from each load and cleaning off the dirt with a brush. The sample beets were weighed before the cleaning job and immediately after. That gave you data on which to determine the percentage of waste on the crop and to write out a tare ticket which figured largely in the final check for payment of the crop.

"The farmers watched to see that you didn't select dirty beets only, and the station boss kept an eye out for local favoritism. It was a good lesson in diplomacy."

Another spare time job available during summer and early fall in the general store area involved Kuner Canning Co. as employer.

One of the good canning firm's product lines was pickles of all types, generally prepared for marketing in retail stores from ample produce crops of the area. At Henderson, along the Union Pacific tracks near the general store, was the Kuner Pickle Dump where growers brought daily in bushel baskets the 24-hour output of tiny gherkins and cucumbers of varying size ranging up to "slicers" for sale to the company.

A major function of the Kuner Dump at Henderson was to take larger pickles from the field crop and put them through early stages of the conversion into dill pickles.

Young Mark became a "dill man." He supervised filling of the brine vats with a layer of fresh pickles, followed by a layer of dill until the vats were full. Between layers, the job was to don rubber hip boots and prance up and down inside the vat to make room for more pickles and to insure firm contact between pickles and dill.

"It paid well and didn't interfere with high school," the former dill man recalled. "And it was a lot better than picking pickles."

The days of high school passed swiftly and suddenly it was late May and graduation day for the 20-some senior students at Brighton High. The year was 1920 and young Mark Morris, slightly older than his classmates because of his November birth date, was dressed in his finest for the occasion.

"The biggest surprise of my young life happened to me that evening during the graduation ceremonies in the school auditorium. I was handed a diploma and with it a scroll tied with a ribbon.

"I think my hands were trembling as I pulled off the ribbon and unrolled the scroll. It was a scholarship, guaranteeing me free tuition, books and fees for four years at the University of Denver."

Mark L. Morris had finished near the top of his high school class. His scholarship was one of four given in the 1920s to top students in each Colorado high school class. The little scroll wrapped in ribbon was a landmark in his life.

"Until the moment I unrolled that scroll, I had no intention of going to college. I don't know what I would have done; probably I'd have taken some business training and tried for a desk job in an office.

"But that scroll made a big difference. It meant the Board of Education had given me recognition as potential college material. From then on, my future was minus a question mark."

3

The Challenge of College

The scholarship scroll he held tightly in his hand all the way home to Henderson from the graduation ceremony at Brighton High School had the glamour of a key to heaven in the mind of young Mark L. Morris.

A vast but silent earthquake had tilted his world.

"That scroll somehow was like a command sent down to me by an unseen power directing my destiny," he was to recall some 60 years later. "I knew it represented money—a lot of dollars in tuition and fee costs. That was important. But even more important was the fact that the scroll was saying to me very clearly that some unseen force had my future pretty well mapped out and I had no choice but to obey a command. The scroll was an order."

The clear light of the next early spring morning of 1920 took some of the thrill out of young Mark's happy feeling of euphoria. The young man's practical mind began to cope with the realities of the sudden scholarship windfall.

The University of Denver, a solid liberal arts institution operated by the Methodist Church, lay on what in 1920 was the southeastern outskirts of Colorado's mile high capital city.

By any measure, it was nearly 25 miles from the Henderson General Store to the campus on South University Boulevard in Denver. That meant a round trip of 50 miles daily if Mark planned to continue living at home as a commuting college student. He already had rolled up several thousand miles (10 per day, 50 per week for four years) by horseback, bicycle, buggy and Model T truck as a Henderson-Brighton commuter in high school, and enough was enough.

The part-time jobs he held in high school as a sugar company and canning firm worker were not the fiscal answer to financing the cost

Mark, a student at the University of Denver in 1920

of college in Denver. It would take something much more substantial and financially rewarding.

Young Mark came up quickly with the answer and promptly hired an attorney for the first time in his life.

"I realized the only venture I was qualified for by experience was farming," he was to recall. "I figured if I could lease some good land, I knew enough or could get enough good advice to work it and produce cash crops. So I leased some land."

The leased land was a 40-acre plot near the general store tied up in the estate of a family member, his late uncle. Through the lawyer, "so that no one could say it was a family deal," young Mark got temporary but legal possession for a fee and a portion of the profits to be paid to the estate.

The youngster planted sweet corn, cantaloupe, tomatoes and pickles. The crops prospered and young Mark was able to hire some Mexican nationals to help him with the chores of wielding a hoe and irrigating during the summer months. He also acquired a small herd of Duroc Jersey red pigs and a small and much-used Ford truck to transport feed and haul the produce to market.

The fine art of turning a crop of sweet corn, cantaloupe and tomatoes into cash took up much of young Mark's first summer as a farmer. He had negotiated a contract with his former employer, Kuner Canning Co., for the pickle-cucumber crop. But the rest of his leased farm's output was highly perishable produce for which buyers had to be found almost daily during late summer.

The obvious solution was to join other farmers in the Platte Valley just north of Denver in patronizing the wholesale produce market which buzzed with activity each summer dawn on the banks of Cherry Creek at the western edge of downtown Denver.

The wholesale produce market area long since has moved to a rail-served tract at the northern edge of Denver's Broadway Viaduct. But in the 1920s and early 1930s, the Cherry Creek market stood without competition.

From as far away as Platteville and Longmont, farmers driving wagons and light trucks began to pull into stalls on the bank of the creek near Speer Boulevard as early as dusk. Many spent the night huddled in blankets underneath or inside wagons and trucks. Others chose to arrive in pre-dawn darkness.

Long before the summer sun came up, the market began buzzing with activity. Buyers from wholesale produce markets, grocery stores, restaurants and even Denver's top hotels began pacing down the lines to examine the day's offerings from the farm. All deals were in cash and the barter system prevailed.

"The goal was to sell out at a good price," Dr. Morris is fond of recalling. "But it was every man for himself, and I learned more about negotiating for a profit before the sun got up that summer than the average man could learn in a lifetime."

Then came early fall, and young Mark reported to the University of Denver. In 1920 and for years later, D.U. was known locally with affection and for a good reason as "Tramway Tech." Its then compact campus stood at the end of the No. 8 line of the Denver Tramway Company. A turnaround system at the south edge of the campus enabled the tramway cars to reverse directions and head back to downtown Denver.

Route 8 ran straight south from downtown through the city's most populous middle-class working area and its rush hour traffic was so heavy that trailers were hooked to the main car to handle the overflow. The trailers required conductors, and Mark soon had a part time job with the tramway company and a rented room in a private home near the university.

Dominating the campus at the time was the Iliff School of Theology, a Methodist Seminary. Despite the fact his mother was a co-founder and leader of the Henderson Church, young Mark had no leaning toward the cloth as a career. He enrolled in English literature, history, economics and general chemistry. A liberal arts course was all he seemed to need at this point, and "I still had no notions about a career," he said later.

A series of chance happenings which were to play major roles in the young man's life began unfolding at the University of Denver.

"A boy who was several classes ahead of me at Brighton High School named Clyde Miller saw me on the campus and came up grinning to shake hands. I was a stranger amid scores of new freshman students, and I was delighted to see a familiar face."

Miller was a member of the Kappa Sigma fraternity at the University of Denver and young Mark soon was a Kappa Sigma pledge.

He moved into the fraternity house and a whole new lifestyle began to emerge for the farmer boy from Henderson.

"As a fraternity pledge and later a frat brother, I was provided with direct contacts with young men and young women who were members of some of Denver's oldest families," he recalled. "I got more than a passing glimpse at the good life and it made a lasting impression on me. I think my ambition to get ahead and become someone a cut above the average was born in the Kappa Sigma house.''

Young Mark was beginning to develop an understanding about people that would play a major role in later years. He decided that getting to know interesting and talented people was something as fundamental as opening a bank account. You could call on friends for advice in the same way you make a cash withdrawal from a bank account. And it became a two-way street and an integral part of friendship when they called on you for help later.

As his freshman year proceeded, young Mark discovered that his course in general chemistry was the one that appealed to him most.

"My interest first was aroused when I discovered that the chancellor of Denver University, Dr. Wilbur Engle, was teaching the course personally,'' he recalled.

Dr. Engle had resigned a post as head of the chemistry department at Columbia University in New York City to move to Denver for health reasons. Doctors had diagnosed his ailment as tuberculosis and the mile-high air of Denver and the area's sunshine were being prescribed throughout the nation in the 1920s by doctors without the miracle drugs of later years at their command.

"I always have appreciated the opportunity for learning that a professor of Dr. Engle's high caliber represented for this country boy,'' Dr. Morris said of his stint at the Denver University. "He made chemistry not only interesting but fascinating. He awoke in me an urge to know more in this field.''

In his second college year, young Mark elected to continue in chemistry. He decided almost at once that his high school dislike for mathematics was a barrier to learning in the new field.

"I discovered I couldn't handle the complicated formulas which are an integral part of organic chemistry'' he said. "The field was so fascinating to me I decided to do something positive about my weakness in mathematics.''

He enrolled in a downtown night school and hired tutors available through Kappa Sigma from the engineering school. In a few months, thanks to long hours and hard work, geometry and other forms of mathematics posed no problem.

The professor of organic chemistry in young Mark's sophomore year was Dr. Reuben Gustavson, a man whose friendship and accomplishments have been a source of pride to him for some 60 years.

But let Dr. Morris tell about it: "Dr. Gustavson was known to his students as Gus, and he really was one of us. It was evident from the outset of the class that this man had a fabulous mind and great teaching ability. He made the subject come alive. He soon was guiding us through fundamental organic and biochemistry and the area of his special interest—endocrine chemistry and the maze of disorders and even death causes which can stem from the improper functioning of the body's organs and glands.

"It was through knowing this man that I developed my lifelong interest in the direct influence of food on the chemistry of living systems."

For the record, Dr. Gustavson later became president of the University of Colorado, chancellor of the University of Nebraska and vice president of the Ford Foundation. In later years, he semi-retired to Tucson, Arizona to serve as associate president of the University of Arizona and head of that institution's graduate program.

Before his semi-retirement Dr. Gustavson—known for his research work on composition of the atom—was a member of the government's wartime Manhattan Project which produced the world's first atomic bomb.

As his second college year drew to a close, young Mark began for the first time to think in serious terms about what the future held for him.

"I knew I had to give some long and careful thought about a third year in higher education," he was to recall. "I knew I'd be forced to decide on some type of major, such as law, journalism, business, teaching, or even dentistry or chemistry in some form. But nothing appealed to me at that time. I discovered that I had no idea how I could turn the liberal arts courses I was taking in college into real dollars. I was uncertain what to do with my life and it was not a happy situation."

Young Mark already was aware that the good life for many he knew revolved around the farm. And in this field he was prospering. The leased acreage was doing so well he had hired a Mexican family to live on the farm and handle most of the work under his supervision.

"I realized that people always will need food. I decided that must be my field, so I gave up my scholarship, asked for a transcript of my University of Denver credits and decided to get the rest of my schooling in Fort Collins and become an educated farmer."

Fort Collins, some 70 miles north of Denver along the Front Range of the Rockies, was home in 1920 of Colorado A. & M. College (the

A. for agricultural and the M. for mechanical), a state-supported school known widely as Colorado Aggies or "the Cow College." It since has become Colorado State University and has broadened its base.

The veterinary college with its outstanding research program remains front and center in its field.

Young Mark arrived on the Fort Collins campus still not sure about the courses he might take or in which department to register. He "sort of gravitated" to the College of Agriculture. A friendly clerk told him the courses dealt with the problems of crops and farm animals and this seemed suited to his plans and experience.

The leased farm at Henderson by now had been joined by additional leased acreage. Crops included plums, cherries and even apples from a substantial orchard area and Mark's Red Duroc swine had prospered, even winning ribbons for him at the Adams County Fair. By now the Mexican family which had moved onto his larger leased farm had proven it could run both places successfully with a little help and a lot of guidance and decision-making by Mark.

The problem of housing and food was solved easily for Mark in Ft. Collins. Through the college, he found a pleasant room and three meals daily at a price he could afford in the Fort Collins home of a former Missouri farm family named Tebow. They had moved to Colorado to launch a large sheep-feeding operation on the outskirts of the city and, in Mark's words, "Mrs. Tebow was a hard-working, pleasant woman and, being a farm wife, she was an excellent cook."

Life at school wasn't quite that easy. After a few weeks, young Mark had slipped into gloom.

"I felt like I was in the wrong place," he was to explain later. "I had two years of college behind me at the University of Denver and ranked, really, as a junior. But most of my fellow students were freshmen and many of them came from the cities—like Denver, Pueblo and Colorado Springs, and it seemed to me they knew hardly anything about farms, farming or livestock.

"It sort of came to a head with me one day when they held a stock judging class and the rest of the group spent most of the time pointing out things like the feet, tails and noses of pigs to each other."

Young Mark, raiser of blue-ribbon-winning Durocs and expert on both the inner and outer portions of swine, left the class for a campus stroll. He was depressed and in doubt that he had made the right move in leaving the University of Denver.

Strolling toward him through the warm shade of fall on the campus came a strangely familiar figure. He recognized Bert Berthelsen, a veterinary student from Brighton who had spent the summer as an aide to Dr. George Carr, the veterinarian who had been handling health problems of Mark's band of Durocs.

"Hi, Mark," grinned the senior student from Brighton, who had assisted only weeks before as Dr. Carr vaccinated Mark's hogs. "How are you getting along?"

The question was friendly, but routine. Mark realized that, with a smile and a "Just fine," over his shoulder, he could continue his lonely stroll. But something stopped him.

"I had a strange feeling that I had reached a crossroads. I don't know why, even now, but I poured out all of my doubts and misgivings right there on the campus sidewalk and that young man I had run into quite by accident stood there and listened with interest."

"Mark," said Bert Bethelson finally, "you are in the wrong department at this university. Come with me."

It was like walking in a dream. Led by Berthelson, young Mark found himself in the office of Dr. George Glover, dean of the veterinary school at Colorado A. & M.

Dean Glover beamed as Mark's plight and concern were outlined. He made it clear that he had heard stories like this before, that he was interested and that he was willing to help.

In minutes, Mark's background on the farm had been outlined to the dean and in less than an hour credits were transferred and Mark was enrolled in the College of Veterinary Medicine. It was too soon at the moment for anyone to realize it, but young Mark had been launched. He at long last had chosen a career.

From the outset, it was clear that a round peg had dropped into the proper round hole. Mark fitted in perfectly at the veterinary school. It made no difference that he was a junior who already had scored well on basic courses at another college. And it mattered not that in the veterinary school he was relegated to basic freshman and sophomore courses in subjects like anatomy, physiology and pharmacology. And it helped that many of Mark's fellow students were veterans of World War I, serious young men interested only in getting a good, if belated, start in civilian life.

Fully intrigued by his class work, Mark threw himself into his studies so deeply that, years later, he was to admit he couldn't remember the name of the girl he sometimes dated during the next two years at Fort Collins.

"She was a technician in the laboratory and a very nice girl," he recalled. "I remember it was fun dancing a few times and we talked a lot about her work and mine. But like the returned war veterans on campus, I suddenly wasn't in school just for a good time or to fool around. I was studying nights, not dancing.''

Mark's credits in both organic and inorganic chemistry from the University of Denver were accepted at the veterinary school and he was able in his first year to plunge into subjects like histology, the microscopic study of healthy tissues, and both bacteriology and pathology, the science of the cause and effect of diseases.

The fact that Mark had been a student under Dr. Gustavson at the University of Denver had an obvious impression on his professors at the Fort Collins school. In his second year of veterinary studies, he was chosen by Dr. William Feldman, professor of histology, for spare time work in the school's pathology and bacteriology laboratory.

"There was no pay, but the appointment was to have a major bearing on my career," Dr. Morris was to say years later. "The things I encountered and the problems I got to solve as a student assistant in that laboratory had a long-range influence on my career."

"The laboratory handled not only the sectioning, mounting and staining of animal tissues used for both teaching and research at the school, but also the human tissues from the hospital in Fort Collins. My reports very soon were being filed both with the professors of the veterinary school and the physicians practicing in Fort Collins. This opened wide vistas for me.

"Soon I was comparing the impact of tuberculosis on humans with the effects of the same disease in animals. And before long, I was handling cancerous animal tissues being collected by Dr. Feldman from all over the world as he prepared for an advanced degree in pathology.

"I recall that Dr. Feldman's studies soon involved the collection of tissue samples from both human and animal tumors. I was making the slides and, while I was at it, I decided to make a duplicate collection for myself. I soon had the best collection of tumor slides of any student in school."

The laboratory work kindled in young Mark the beginnings of a drive that would lead him into biomedical research. The feel he developed in school for glass slides and microscopes—a far cry from raising vegetables and feeding hogs—would lead in the years just ahead to the field which inevitably set him apart from the other veterinary doctors of his time.

The laboratory work also led to his appointment by the faculty as an instructor in general science during his second year at the Fort Collins college. The combination led directly to a bachelor of science degree which Mark received with the class of 1924.

In Mark's mind, the degree he won after four years in college was a nice but rather meaningless bit of paper. He now was dedicated to completion of his studies in veterinary medicine. So he returned to the campus at Fort Collins late in 1924, after a busy summer of work on his leased farm, and lost himself once again in his studies.

Late in the term while he was at work one afternoon in the school laboratory, a messenger arrived with the word that he was wanted in the office of the dean.

Dean Glover, the man who nearly three years earlier had listened to a young man's tale of indecision and guided him into the veterinary classes, was not alone in his office when Mark arrived.

With him was Dr. I. E. Newsom, professor of pathology who had been a co-sponsor of Mark for the laboratory post and who soon would be named president of the university. Both men were unsmiling and grave.

The scene in the dean's office and the happening that unfolded in the next few minutes still were vivid in the memory of Dr. Morris more than a half century later:

"Dean Glover started talking. But he seemed to be looking up at the ceiling with his eyes closed, and that startled me. What he said—I'll never forget—was that he and Dr. Newsom had been talking about me as a student and they had decided that I should not return to the Fort Collins campus the following year for the final work on my degree as a doctor of veterinary medicine."

Dr. Morris remembers only that his knees seemed weak and there was a ringing sound in his ears. But the voice droned on: "Just relax. Dr. Newsom and I have been in touch with Dr. Veranus A. Moore and he agrees that you should leave here after this semester."

As Mark struggled for normal breathing, his world slowly rolled back to right side up. Dr. Moore, it seemed was Dean of the New York State College of Veterinary Medicine at Cornell University. That was in a town called Ithaca, not far from Syracuse and Buffalo in the state of New York. It was a fine school and it was offering a fellowship to an outstanding student from out of the west to be chosen by Dean Glover and Dr. Newsom. They had made their choice. It was Mark.

"Do you have enough money saved for board and room for one year at Cornell?" It was Dean Glover, smiling now and assuring Mark that the fellowship included all tuition and other costs beyond room and board at Cornell and that "this is the opportunity of a lifetime."

Mark had the entire summer of 1925 to make sure that profits from his leased acres would see him through a year at Cornell. And when time came for the trip eastward, he found a way to spend as little as possible on travel.

"The mid-20s were sort of boom times and a lot of people were on the move in America," he recalled. "Many were coming west to Denver and then staying because they liked what they found. So the Denver *Post* had a special column in its wanted section offering the unused return parts of roundtrip excursion tickets on the railroad at a bargain."

Mark found the ad with time to spare. It offered a ticket good from Denver to Buffalo. The cost was about a tenth of the regular fare. He bought it.

4

The Ivy League—on a Budget

The 2,000 mile journey from his pickle patch at Henderson Colorado to the stately campus of Cornell University on America's eastern seaboard was the longest and most exciting of Mark's young life.

The steam train moved steadily eastward through two nights and three long days. Mark's ticket was on a day coach and he stayed glued to a window except for necessary trips rearward to the dining car, which seemed to be gobbling up more than a fair share of his cash.

Between stretches of silent awe at the sights he was seeing out of the day coach window, a panorama of an America he had known until now only through books and magazines, Mark snatched at sleep and planned the moves he must make to stay solvent at Cornell for the full school year it would take to get a degree.

The booming city of Buffalo in upper New York state was the end of the line for the cut rate ticket Mark held. He had studied maps and train schedules so the switch at the Buffalo station to the Lehigh Valley line that would take him on to Ithaca and Cornell was no problem.

Mark knew that Buffalo was on the eastern shore of Lake Erie and that it bordered on Ontario Province of Canada. Niagara Falls, already a honeymoon mecca and a legend in the mid-1920s was only a few miles to the north. But there was no time for sightseeing, a luxury which wasn't on the brief list of necessities which constituted Mark's budget for the coming school year.

So Mark waited in the station at Buffalo for the Lehigh Valley train to Ithaca. When the call of "all aboard" finally sounded, he found himself in a crowd of chattering young people headed for the line of coaches. This was registration time at Cornell and it seemed that students from all of upper New York State had chosen the train Mark did.

In the clatter and hubbub, a startling fact became clear. Mark's fellow passengers for the most part were a different breed from the students he had known in Colorado. The girls were beautifully dressed and many wore fur coats. Even some of the young men sported coonskin coats. This was the "Roaring 20s" and Mark was about to enter the Ivy League.

From the pamphlets he had studied, Mark knew that Cornell University was unique. It was both an independent Ivy League school and the land grant university of the state of New York.

Mark knew that the phrase Ivy League came into being as the name of an athletic conference which included schools like Harvard and Yale. The ivy part, of course, stemmed from the vines which covered many of the main buildings on campuses of the Atlantic seaboard school. But Mark also was aware that Ivy League had come to mean prestige and upper class in the world of education. He was grateful all over again for the fellowship that made his presence possible on the Ithaca bound train.

"But I got the feeling in a hurry that essentially I was a total stranger, almost like somebody from another planet, among these people," Mark was to say later of his train trip from Buffalo to Ithaca. "Their dress was totally different, and so was their conversation. They talked about racing cars and things like sailing and having fun in Europe. I kept to myself and began to realize I had landed in a different world and would be forced to stay alert if I hoped to survive."

Mark's feeling that he was an unwanted stranger deepened on his first visit to the Cornell campus. He found his way to the registrar's office and was told to wait until "Mr. David Hoy has time to see you."

After what seemed an eternity, Mark found himself standing before the registrar's desk. An obviously angry David Hoy was glowering in his direction.

"You are Morris?" asked the angry man. As Mark nodded, Registrar David Hoy glowered even more deeply. "You must be stupid," he said. "I don't think we can use you here at Cornell. You obviously can't read the English language. The instructions you have been given are very clear. They spell out where and when freshmen should report for registration and this is not the place or the time."

In the foray that followed, Mark tried to explain that he had five years of college behind him, that he held a scholarship for his year at Cornell's veterinary college and that he didn't consider himself a freshman.

"You're new to Cornell and you sign up with the freshmen or

not at all," shouted David Hoy. "Now I suggest you go pack your bags and go back to wherever it is you came from."

Thus dismissed, Mark left in dismay, followed by righteous anger. One thing was certain, he decided: "I'm going to stick it out here."

A few minutes later Mark's upside-down world began to right itself. He found the office of Dean Veranus A. Moore of the veterinary college. His welcome was a warm one.

"Old Davy Hoy is an institution at Cornell," Dean Moore chuckled. "He only appears to be rough and tough. He knew you'd find a way out."

Still chuckling to himself, Dean Moore picked up his telephone and said a few quiet words. Minutes later, a friendly office assistant arrived to open the doorway of Cornell University to the young man from Colorado. In an hour, officially registered for classes at the veterinary school, Mark was ensconced in a room at Cascadilla Dormitory under an arrangement which provided him with rent-free quarters in return for tending the furnace.

That left only the problem of meals still to be solved. There were numerous restaurants on the hill near the Cornell campus, but Mark found them crowded and expensive for a student on a budget. So he continued his search and discovered a perfect answer—a home on a main street near the campus where meals were being served to a group of graduate students from West Point and Annapolis. One opening only remained, the price was right and Mark had solved the meal problem for his year at Cornell.

His fellow diners were newly commissioned officers of the U.S. Army, Navy and Marine Corps doing post-graduate work in engineering and mathematics. Mark found them perfect after-hours company.

"In the classrooms on the campus at Cornell, I found a very cold environment," Mark was to recall. "I was almost an outcast.

"Nobody was rude, but it seemed that everybody was ignoring me. I got the message. It was clear that they regarded me as a nobody from a cow college somewhere out west that had dropped into their class at Cornell and was just so much excess baggage.

"I decided it made no difference to me how these fellows felt. I was here to get a year's training and finish my education. I'd go about my work and they could get on with their socializing."

With that settled in his mind, Mark plunged into his studies. A strange and unexpected problem arose almost at once.

"Two of the professors spoke with an accent I couldn't master," he said. "They seemed to be talking through their noses and many of their words and even parts of sentences didn't make sense to me. I realized that were using the twang of New England, but they might as well have been speaking in Portuguese. I couldn't keep up with them.''

To the rescue came a happenstance of the alphabet. The senior veterinary class was composed of 19 men and one woman scholar. Seating was done by the alphabet and Mark found himself sitting in many classes beside a young man named Peter Olafson.

"He was a brilliant student who was later to become chairman of the department of pathology at Cornell," Mark recalled. "He was friendly and it wasn't long until he was going over my notes with me and helping me fill in the gaps that the nose-talkers created for me. He was a godsend.''

It was Peter Olafson, a native of Iceland and several years the senior of most of his classmates, who spelled out for Mark another classroom enigma which arose: "It was a class in medicine. The professor was the author of textbooks used throughout the world. I was very impressed and paid close attention to everything that man said in class. When I got my grade it was a lowly 65. I'd never had a grade that low in anything since my first day in school and I was shocked. I couldn't imagine where I had gone astray.''

Olafson sat down beside the stricken Mark, rooted to a chair in the otherwise empty classroom and staring at his report sheet.

"Don't fret," he told Mark. "I have figured out this professor and it's actually a simple matter. He figures that nobody in the world knows 100 percent about anything. He figures a student is very lucky if he understands 75 percent.

"So in the case of this professor, a grade of 55 is very good and a grade of 65 is more than good. Perfect would be a 75.''

Before he left Cornell, Mark was getting grades of 75 or near that from the professor of medicine. Once he got an 80. He was more than content.

"I think," he was to recall years later, "that in that class I learned a lot about the theory of relativity.''

Another Cornell incident which stands out in the memory of Mark was one involving a fellow student.

"I hadn't been in class long before I noticed a striking-looking older person who obviously was a class member. He kept to himself and seemed to be some kind of a foreigner. It took me a while to learn that he was Dr. Franz Boenesch from Vienna, Austria, and actually was the dean of the veterinary college in one of the oldest universities in Europe. He also was head of the department of surgical medicine. He was at Cornell studying American methods under a state department arrangement.

"Dr. Boenesch had trouble, as I did, following the lectures of some of those Cornell professors who spoke with a New England twang.

"We became friends, partly because he told me that my Colorado accent was much broader and easier to understand than the through-the-nose lectures of some of the professors. I soon found myself helping him with his notes just as Peter Olafson was helping me."

Dr. Boenesch stood beside Mark one morning during a class in the Large Animal Clinic at Cornell. A small Guernsey heifer, pregnant with twin calves, was about to deliver and her problem had become a class case for senior veterinary students.

"The young cow was ready for delivery, but the presentation was abnormal," Mark recalled. "One calf was presented head first in the usual way, but the other was reversed in a breech presentation. The instructor went into great detail about this and told us it would be necessary in this case to perform surgery and literally to separate the two calves within the uterus of the mother. I felt an insistent tug on my coat sleeve. It was Dr. Boenesch."

"Will you please to interrupt the professor for me and tell him I have an instrument in my room and some anesthesia that can make it possible for these calves to be easily and quickly delivered?"

The man from Vienna clearly was excited and was asking Mark to intervene for him, not trusting his own halting English in this obvious emergency.

Mark quickly explained that Dr. Boenesch had a comment on the case and explained what it was. He and his friend were sent by staff car to the Austrian's room. They returned with a long-needled syringe and instrument which had the appearance of an aluminum pipe with protruding wires.

"The case was turned over to Dr. Boenesch, whose qualifications were well known by all of the staff. He took the long needle and inserted it into the posterior portion of the spinal canal and injected a clear, watery appearing liquid. In seconds, it seemed, the nerves supplying the uterus were anesthetized and the cow stopped straining. With the uterus relaxed, Dr. Boenesch took his pipe-like device which he called a FoeToTome—and quickly performed what is called a dissection embryotomy. There was a wire looped at the end of the cane-like device and within 15 minutes he manipulated the tangled bodies and both calves were delivered and the heifer was returned to her box stall in good condition."

The suddenly silent and wide-eyed audience at Cornell had witnessed the introduction of epidural anesthesia to the United States.

Days blurred into weeks which became months and the graduation time was near for senior students in the veterinary college at Cornell.

"All of the class members were talking about what they were going to do, where they were going and what positions they were considering or hoping for," Mark recalled. "I realized that I had been so busy all winter and spring that I hadn't given graduation a thought. There I was, about to receive a degree in veterinary medicine, and I had not the smallest idea what I was going to do after that."

As in other key turning points of his life, fate intervened once more for the young man soon to become Mark L. Morris, D.V.M.

The dormitory room Mark had rented when he arrived at Cornell was located on a main highway route leading from Ithaca to the rich farmland nearby. Mark's duties as tender of the dormitory furnace kept him close to the house during the chill evenings of fall and winter in upper New York and he always was in his room studying on weekends. He thus was available when either one of the two ambulatory clinic doctors assigned to the veterinary school was called out on a night or weekend emergency.

The ambulatory clinic was designed to give veterinary students in-the-field experience in treating sick livestock.

"One or more students went with the ambulatory doctor, observed and gave what help was necessary and then wrote out a full report on which a grade was assigned as part of classwork," Mark explained.

"Since I lived on the road out of town and was always available on short notice, I got a lot more than my share of experience out in the field on actual emergency cases."

Less than two weeks before graduation day, one of the ambulatory clinicians, Dr. M. G. Fincher, suddenly pulled a letter out of his pocket while he and Mark were returning from a night call in the country. "He told me he thought the letter might represent an opportunity for me, that it had been passed around among the veterinary faculty at Cornell, that there didn't seem to be anyone interested and that he thought I might at least read it."

Mark opened the letter in the quiet of his room. It had been written by Dr. Eldon Loblein, a graduate of the Veterinary College at the University of Pennsylvania. It said Dr. Loblein had decided to sell his practice in New Brunswick, New Jersey, and—addressed broadly "To Whom It May Concern" at the Cornell veterinary

Mark graduated from Cornell University in 1926

college—it suggested that any qualified person with interest should contact him.

Mark was to recall years later that "an urge to act on this" flooded over him as he read the letter.

"There were no details, no mention of terms or price, not even a hint as to why the practice might be for sale. But something kept nudging me. I felt this was important and I felt it was an opportunity."

Mark checked his budget reserve. The balance was fearfully low with the end of the school year in sight. So he studied maps, packed a light suitcase and headed off on foot down a highway leading south from Ithaca amid the pleasant greenery and balmy breezes of spring.

"I hitchhiked every foot of the way to Allentown, Pennsylvania, before dark. Then I caught a train coach to South Plainfield, hitched a ride to Metuchen with a fine old gentleman and took a bus to New Brunswick."

Mark checked into the New Brunswick YMCA for the night and headed by foot the next morning after a quick breakfast down Livingston Avenue to the address of Dr. Eldon Loblein.

"It was a beautiful street, lined with trees and rather fine homes. I began to wonder if I was out of my league."

A "very fine looking gentleman" answered the door at No. 177 Livingston Avenue. He looked the young man over, listened to his explanation of why there was a stranger at his door and slowly said:

"I'm afraid, young man, that there has been a mistake. I certainly did not have a student in mind and I can't imagine how my letter ever was referred to you, as you say. My practice is for sale—but it would take someone older, someone with experience like one of the ambulatory clinicians up at Cornell to handle it. I'm sorry you made the long trip."

Dr. Loblein, smiling but firm, began to close the door.

"Just a moment, sir," said Mark in what he hoped was a voice both firm and friendly. "I've come a long way. I'm a stranger to this part of the country and I'm full of curiosity."

The doctor was listening and Mark rushed on.

"I've had a lot of experience riding with the ambulatory clinicians and I find it intriguing. The train back to Ithaca doesn't leave until this evening and I have the whole day on my hands in a strange town. Would it be all right with you if I kind of stayed around and got the experience of watching a real veterinarian at work for a day? I'd appreciate it a lot."

Dr. Loblein had little room for objection. He nodded his agreement, and a day that was to launch Mark L. Morris, D.V.M., into a notable career had begun.

The first call was at the nearby New Jersey Agricultural Experiment Station. The chore was to vaccinate a group of about 20 young pigs against cholera. Young Mark, raiser of hogs on his Henderson, Colorado, farm and veteran of pig-holding, pitched in to help. The art of convincing a struggling, frightened and squealing young porker that the needle is inevitable and it helps if you quit squirming and get it over with can be acquired only through experience. Mark had experience.

"Well, you handle this like a veteran," commented an obviously impressed Dr. Loblein.

Moments later, Mark asked an interested bystander if the young boar pig he had just turned loose might be a Duroc Red Jersey from the state of Nebraska. The bystander, it quickly became clear, was Professor Skelly, head of the swine department of the College of Agriculture at Rutgers University. He was visiting the Experiment Station to check on a new group of imported young hogs.

"The one I just turned loose looks like he had a lot of Great Orion Sensation in his veins," ventured Mark.

"What makes you think so?" countered Professor Skelly, as an openly intrigued Dr. Loblein halted his work to tune in.

"Well, sir, that little boar has the kind of back I know Great Orion Sensation puts on his offspring. You see, I raise pigs back home in Colorado and I got one of the sons from that famous string in Nebraska only last year."

Out of the shop-talk-among-pig-raisers that followed came a final comment from the professor to Dr. Loblein as he and Mark climbed back into the veterinarian's car to leave: "You know, doctor, you should consider someone like this young man to take over your practice. I know you're set on someone more mature but this fellow has had lots of practical experience. And he's smart. It shows."

Dr. Loblein had no answer. The pair drove off in silence. Mark decided to keep it that way for now.

The next call was Woodbrook Farms at Metuchen, New Jersey, a large dairy with several hundred milk cows supplying certified milk for northern New Jersey and the city of New York. As part of his regular practice, Dr. Loblein was in full charge of the veterinary supervision of the large herd. His certification at regular intervals of the continuing health of the herd was vital to the marketing of the milk.

Some 20 cows were on sick call that morning and Mark pitched in to help. The experience he had gained on the extra ambulatory clinic calls at night and on weekends paid dividends. This was almost identical work.

After lunch, the pair made a series of house calls in nearby Plainfield and Westfield where people in fine homes with sick pets were awaiting them. Dr. Loblein, with offices in the basement of his impressive home in New Brunswick, spent much of his time driving to farms and homes in the area calling on patients. He handled calls at his office during evening hours, but animal hospitals and clinics did not exist in the mid-1920s. Dr. Loblein, like hundreds of his fellow veterinarians, devoted much time on the road dispensing pills, and ointments and occasionally writing prescriptions. Their "bedside manner" was sharpened in stalls, pens and kennels or the kitchens and back porches of people with ailing dogs and cats.

The last call of late afternoon was to Strongheart Kennels near Bound Brook, New Jersey. These kennels were engaged in importing the newly-popular German Shepherd breed from Germany and Switzerland and training the young dogs for sale across the United States.

Mark assisted as Dr. Loblein vaccinated ten of the young dogs newly arrived on a boat from Switzerland. It seemed a routine chore.

On the early evening ride back into New Brunswick, Dr. Loblein broke his idle conversation inviting Mark to stay at his home for dinner. He said he would drive Mark to the station in time to catch his train back to Ithaca.

During dinner, the telephone rang. Dr. Loblein excused himself to answer it and returned to the table with a slight frown on his face. He resumed his dining in silence, then moved to the living room to bury himself in the evening newspaper. The silence persisted and Mark joined him in the living room, thumbing through a magazine.

"Look," the doctor suddenly said. "We've got to go back to that kennel. One of those dogs we vaccinated is dead and it's heavily insured. They want me to do an autopsy and sign the death certificate so they can collect the insurance. It's more than $1,000."

The drive back to the kennel was in heavy silence. Mark was sharing the veterinarian's concern that "this is a hot potato."

The autopsy took place in a shed with Mark holding a sputtering gasoline lantern for light and the kennelman observing. Not a word was spoken until Dr. Loblein suddenly looked up from the table directly into young Mark's eyes.

"Young man, what killed this dog?"

Mark hesitated only a moment. Once again, a benign fate seemed to intervene on his behalf as it had frequently in his young life. A few days earlier, Dr. William A. Hagan, who in later years became the dean of the College of Veterinary Medicine of Cornell, had returned to Cornell after completing a sabbatical leave in Germany studying immunology. Mark was fortunate to attend classes taught by Dr. Hagan and he asked Mark if he'd be interested in reading some material he had gathered in Munich. Mark leaped at the chance and pored through a volume translated from German dealing with the body's immune process.

"The cases in the German translations seemed identical to the problem we faced in the shed at that kennel," Mark was to say years later. "I had no hesitation after that first moment and I told Dr. Loblein I had a pretty good idea what killed the dog. Then I asked him for a look at the bottle which had contained the distemper antiserum we had used that afternoon. Sure enough, the evidence was there and to me it was very clear."

The bottle bore a label which read: "This is a product prepared from the whole blood of immunized horses and is intended for the immunization of dogs against canine distemper and its complications."

Mark held out the label and spoke in a firm voice. "Dr. Loblein, this animal died of shock—anaphylactic shock. His stomach was filled with partially digested horse meat when you opened it a few minutes ago. It's clear that some of the protein derived from that horsemeat was circulating in the dog's system. This product, when administered parenterally, in isolated cases can trigger a mechanism known as anaphylactic shock. It can be fatal."

Dr. Loblein wasted no time. "Of course," he said. "You are absolutely correct and that is my diagnosis. I'll clean up and sign the certificate and we can be on our way."

Mark chatted with the kennelman as Dr. Loblein filled in the papers which would assure the kennel of an insurance payment. He made it clear to the handler that none of the other dogs would be affected nor had been harmed. He said studies in Germany had established that the shock syndrome affects only certain very sensitive and allergic animals when their bodies are in the process of developing substances which interact with a similar substance suddenly introduced into the body parenterally.

"It's like people who get sudden and unexplained reactions from a bee sting or a shot to which they are allergic," he said. The handler was satisfied.

The ride from the kennel to nearby South Plainfield where Mark was to catch his train back to Ithaca suddenly was interrupted when Dr. Loblein turned the car into a small off-the-highway lane and snapped off the ignition.

"Let's have a little talk," he said. "You have impressed me today on several scores. I thought you were much too young to handle my practice when you showed up this morning. But now I can see you have been well trained and that you've paid attention to your lessons while getting a lot of field experience. I think we can work something out for this summer at least."

Long before the train pulled out of South Plainfield, a working arrangement had been reached. Mark would report to New Brunswick immediately after graduation. Dr. Loblein had purchased a lumber business at Point Pleasant, New Jersey and was anxious to take it over. Mark could use the doctor's house and office during the summer.

"Keep books and we'll split the income from the practice next fall," said Dr. Loblein. "After that, I'm sure we'll be able to work out something permanent if everything goes smoothly."

A handshake sealed the deal. Mark rode through the night on a coach. His mind was much too busy with plans to permit sleep. Back in his room at Cornell, he figured up his finances. The budget he had worked out at the start of the school year was slightly overspent.

Mark had $12 left in cash. But he also had very high hopes.

5

Purchased: A Phone Number—
Found: A Bride

He turned on the bare bulb hanging from the ceiling which provided light in the dingy basement room. This somewhat confined and sparsely furnished area of Dr. Loblein's home was to be the center of his new life.

The light fell on the only shiny new thing in the room—the framed license to practice veterinary medicine he had secured only a few hours before from the New Jersey State Board of Veterinary Medical Examiners in Trenton. Its wording still looked a little strange to him: "Mark L. Morris, D.V.M.," it said, had passed the examinations and was "licensed and authorized to practice veterinary medicine."

Still tucked somewhere in Mark's as-yet-unpacked luggage was the crisp diploma he had received—resplendent in a rented black cap and gown—only a few days earlier at the formal graduation ceremony in Ithaca, New York, for the 1926 class of Cornell University. It certified that he was the qualified holder of the degree, Doctor of Veterinary Medicine.

The actual moment he first held that diploma in his hand after six years of self-financed college work stood clear in Mark's mind. But the hectic short days that followed still were sort of a blur.

As he stood there in the harsh light flooding the small room that was to be his office headquarters, at least for the summer, Mark's mind flashed over the events of those immediate post-graduate hours.

His carefully worked out Ivy League budget had run out of cash just before graduation day. With reluctance, but with a burning desire to make a proper start on his career once he arrived in New Brunswick to take over for the summer for Dr. Loblein, he had made a telephone

Mark's father, Mark M. Morris, with Lester, about 17, and Mark, about 29

call to his father in the general store at Henderson, Colorado.

"I need $500," he had said. "I'm sorry, and I know that's a lot of money, but there is no other way for me to get started, you see . . ."

His father had cut him off. No need to explain, he had assured Mark. The $500 would be sent via Western Union. And what's more, Mark's father and mother had talked it over. Mark's mother was coming to New Brunswick by train to spend the summer and help him get launched in his career. No need for thanks or tears of relief. He was their son, wasn't he?

Mark packed his bags, paid his remaining small debts and moved out of the dormitory a few hours after the Ithaca office of Western Union called to tell him his money had arrived. Then it was on to New Brunswick, where his first act was to make a down payment on an automobile.

His choice had been a small Ford coupe. They came in black only in 1926 and the dealer had no reluctance about immediate delivery when Mark explained that he was taking over for Dr. Loblein.

"Dr. Loblein sits next to me at Rotary most weeks," the dealer had said. "He told me you were coming, and I hope it works out. The doctor has his heart set on that new lumber business of his and we'll be needing a good veterinarian in these parts."

Mark, hoping indeed that he would become the new "good veterinarian in these parts," had driven off to Trenton to face the examining board. Now he was back in New Brunswick. His mother had arrived that afternoon by train and upstairs in the handsome Loblein home on Livingston Avenue there were sounds indicating that she was moving some of the furniture around to make the place more suitable to her taste for the summer. Down in the basement with its private entryway from the street, Mark was preparing for the next day—his first as a licensed and practicing doctor of veterinary medicine.

The Loblein family already had moved to the coast for the summer when Mark first arrived from Cornell. Dr. Loblein, anxious to join them and get on with his new business, had given Mark brief directions, put a plain notebook in his hand with assurance that "it's all in here," and left.

The notebook was open now on the table covered with oilcloth which served as an examining and treatment center for dogs and cats brought in as patients. A few chairs, a desk, a storage cupboard and the light globe suspended from the ceiling over the table were the main furnishings.

Mark's mother, Pruda M. Morris, with Mark's sisters, Eula Esther, age about 23, and Marguerite, age about 26

Mark took another rueful look at the notebook, grabbed it and a map from the nearby desk and headed upstairs for a conference with his mother.

"We faced a very difficult situation," he was to recall years later. "Neither my mother nor I knew a single soul in all of New Jersey. We didn't even know the names of the nearby towns, much less how to find them. It was painfully clear from the schedule Dr. Loblein had drawn out for me for the next few days in that notebook that he did business regularly in or near at least a dozen towns in the area. And the telephone already had been ringing with requests that the doctor drop by the next day in three or four places not on the list."

Mark was to find out in the coming days that the range of Dr. Loblein's practice was vast indeed. New Brunswick, in upper central New Jersey, was about 30 miles by highway or train from the skyscraper canyons of New York City. The Empire State Building soon would rise into that skyline to remain for decades as the world's tallest office building, and already in the mid-1920s the New Brunswick area had many commuters.

Many of the commuters were wealthy clients of Dr. Loblein. They lived in small towns in the hilly, wooded areas of New Jersey or on estates which spread in all directions, from New Brunswick to Perth Amboy, New Jersey, on the Atlantic coast. About 18 miles southward on the route to Philadelphia lay the Ivy League college town of Princeton.

Two morning calls were first on the list as Mark formally launched his career the next day. One was to the Woodbrook Farms dairy complex where he had passed one of the first tests during that fateful first meeting with Dr. Loblein. But on the way near the town of Metuchen, about five miles from New Brunswick, was a call to be made at the estate of a family named Johnson. Mark stopped there first and learned that the sick pet dog belonged to the family which had founded Johnson & Johnson, worldwide manufacturers and distributors of bandages and other hospital and medical supplies. His first client, who paid cash for the call via the yardman who watched Mark administer to the ailing dog in the family garage, was Robert Johnson. He later was the General Johnson who became chairman of his family's company and founder of the Robert W. Johnson Foundation.

"I didn't have any idea there were houses like that in America," Mark marveled to his mother that evening over dinner in the Loblein house. "I thought anything that big and that grand would be a castle somewhere in Europe."

The day had been a long one and Mark had been in several mansions in or near towns like Plainfield and Bound Brook which rivaled the Johnson home. All of the calls involved sick pet animals and all diagnosis was based simply on physical examination with medicine dispensed either out of Mark's shiny new leather case or via prescription written to a nearby pharmacy. That was, it seemed, the way Dr. Loblein ran his practice and Mark was obliged to follow the pattern.

Mark discovered his mother had been busy also. A stack of telephone messages awaited him. All were from Loblein clients who wanted "the doctor" to stop by the next day to examine an ailing animal.

As Mark rose from the dinner table he stopped by a window to find the source of a steady buzz of voices and arriving automobiles which had been rising from the front yard for several minutes. Outside, stretching from the basement entry to Dr. Loblein's office to the curbing, was a growing line of people. Each was carrying or leading a dog or cat. It was late bedtime that night before the last of the drop-in trade had been cared for.

That first day, it turned out, was typical. The Loblein practice was what is known even today as a general veterinary practice. The days were spent by Mark traveling among the 20-plus towns ranged in all directions with New Brunswick as a hub. There were stops at regular clients like the Woodbrook Farms dairy and the municipal stables in Perth Amboy and New Brunswick, where Dr. Loblein was under contract to care for the scores of horses used to power garbage wagons in the area. And there always were a dozen or more stops at private residences Mark first had to search out on a map.

But most of the persons who called at the basement office during evening office hours, or, in emergencies, made a telephone call.

The first month was full of double difficulty, Mark was to recall later. "There was the problem of trying to locate the homes where the animal patients lived. Besides using regional maps, I stopped many times to ask directions in those first days. Then there was the fact that most of the calls came to Dr. Loblein's number and the clients expected him. I got accustomed to the strange stares when a young man obviously just out of school carrying a new bag showed up."

The wary aloofness some clients showed at first view of the new doctor was understandable. Dr. Loblein had been in practice some 15 years and had taken over from his father, the area veterinarian for more than 25 years. Dr. Loblein was well known and well liked in towns outside New Brunswick as well as at home. His regular rounds included Perth Amboy, Rahway, Metuchen, South Amboy, Plainfield, Westfield, Bound Brook and many others. He possessed, in Mark's words, "the perfect kennel-side manner" and an outgoing personality which gathered friends easily.

"After a few false starts, I began to fit in and discovered that people were beginning to like and trust me," Mark recalled. "The summer literally flew by and before I realized, it was time for such a thing to happen, I got a telephone call from Dr. Loblein."

The doctor, settled into his new lumber business, had discovered he could operate it from his home in New Brunswick. He was anxious to move his family back into his home before school began and he was anxious to "finalize our deal."

The meeting between Dr. Loblein and Dr. Morris in the basement office was brief.

"I find my new business will take most of my time," Dr. Loblein said. "You seem to have caught on around here in fine fashion and the people I have contacted are very impressed with you. I want to sell my practice and have no further responsibility in connection with it. How about $12,000—after and above my half share of what you've done this past summer?"

Mark, in a daze, explained that he didn't possess $12,000 or even a down payment on a sum that large. This was 1926 and, although the national economy was humming along in near-boom fashion, the average three bedroom home was selling for less than half of $12,000.

"Of course, I realize that," Dr. Loblein said. "You can have two years to pay me off in installments. And if you make it in 24 months or less I'll deduct part of that and make it $10,000."

A handshake sealed the deal. Mark was both in business and in debt. He had no fear of the future. His only concern, he recalled, was that he'd be forced to find a new office and new living quarters at once.

Just three miles away at a junction of the Lincoln Highway linking New York City with Philadelphia, Mark found what he was seeking. A two-story house was for lease in Stelton, a village and a stop on the Pennsylvania Railroad which since has been named Edison, New Jersey, in honor of Thomas Alva Edison, the inventor. The rented home had a basement with an outside entry. In less than a week, Mark had moved to his new headquarters with his mother and it was business as usual.

"All I really bought from Dr. Loblein was goodwill, a few office supplies and the rather dingy furniture in his basement office," said

The first office on Central Avenue, in Stelton, New Jersey, which also served as Mark's residence

Mark. "Oh yes. There was one more thing—and it made all of the difference. I insisted that the Loblein telephone number be included in the purchase. It was no trouble to have it moved to my new office and it was my link with the public. That number—278—had been in service since early in the career of Dr. Loblein's father. People for miles around knew that all you had to do was tell the operator to call 278 in New Brunswick and you reached the veterinarian."

The telephone began ringing in steady fashion after the office move was made. And clients were beginning to ask for Dr. Morris. A torch had been passed without a flicker and Mark was in business, this time for himself.

Only a single problem arose after the move, and Mark handled it swiftly. His mother informed him it was time for her to return to her home and his father in Colorado. He immediately suggested that his younger sister, Marguerite, might be a proper replacement. She had been married shortly before to Eldon Sutton, a young man who worked as operator of a small garage in Henderson, Colorado, along the main highway a mile west of the Morris general store. Mark offered the couple free housing and more income than the garage could produce if they would come to New Jersey and help him. They came.

The couple's arrival as 1927 dawned gave Mark time to catch up on his thinking. With a new year just opening, it seemed proper to Mark that he should assess his position and do some planning for the future. One thing stood out clearly: Mark would not be content to carry on without changing the practice of Dr. Loblein, which he considered to be "strictly clinical."

Included in a mid-1920 letter to his family, young Dr. Morris phrased his problem this way: "I've been giving much thought to the future operation of this practice. If I am going to keep it and succeed in it, I must give some careful thought to building it on a strong foundation and on a long-range basis. This means that changes are necessary."

As young Dr. Morris wrote those words, the art of veterinary medicine was confined mostly to domestic farm animals—the cows that produced milk, butter and meat for a growing nation and the horses which pulled the wagons of commerce and the plows of agriculture. As household pets, dogs and cats were loved and sometimes pampered. Mostly they were fed table scraps and only in obvious emergencies were they taken to an animal doctor. If dogs got ill, it was the general consensus that they suffered either from worms, distemper, or mange, and treatments were basic and simple. Only a few hundred veterinarians were in practice in the United States (versus the estimated 35,000 of 1982 who have graduated from one of 27 veterinary schools in this country) and most of them concentrated on farm animals. It would be decades before the advent of small-animal intensive care units where critically ill pets of the present era often lie in oxygen-equipped padded areas trailing intravenous tubes and electrocardiograph wires. This was an era of barn calls by day and evenings spent treating cats and dogs with problems or diseases that couldn't be identified by casual examination. Young Dr. Morris decided he would base his new practice on tenets he had learned from experts in the classrooms of Colorado A. & M. and Cornell. The first and most important of these, he decided, would be that the ability to make an accurate diagnosis was the key to good medical treatment.

The basic tools of the scientific approach to his practice that Mark decided to introduce were the microscope and the centrifuge. Both are expensive, but he found an answer. His biggest client, Woodbrook Farms, was equipped with an on-premises laboratory in which technicians met legal requirements of the time by rigid testing of milk samples.

Mark asked if it would be possible for him to use the microscope and centrifuge in hours after the technicians had completed their daily chores. Permission was readily given.

Mark promptly added a collection of small bottles to the medicine and instruments he carried with him in a bag on his daily rounds. Into the bottles went samples of feces, urine and even skin scrapings from animal patients. Back in the borrowed laboratory, he began to use the centrifuge and microscope to identify what ailed his patients.

"People thought it was simply amazing that this could be done," Dr. Morris was to recall years later. "I kept explaining that it was dangerous to treat an ailment until it was identified. I even stressed that a simple deworming capsule for a dog was not sufficient. It was necessary to find out first what type of parasite was involved."

"They quickly understood that treatment might be different for roundworms than tapeworms, but they still were amazed that I could identify the trouble by putting something in a bottle and carrying it off with me. They were even more impressed when I demonstrated in several cases that the tests showed no parasites were present and that the sick dog or cat could be made well by a prescribed change in diet or regular use of a prescribed tonic or medication."

"In all of my years of practice experience, I do not know of anything that spread from one person to another as fast as did the story about the new young veterinarian who was collecting samples from sick animals, testing them and then calling the owners on the phone or showing up in person to explain exactly what ailed the animals and exactly what would be done to effect a cure.''

"As the record of cures mounted, so did my practice. The word spread and clients decided that the new veterinarian was a scientist. People liked that. Very soon I was getting more small animal calls than I could handle and still keep up with the work on cows and horses which had been the keystone of the practice.''

It didn't register with him at the time as a major career decision, but Mark took action which would lead to his specialization in companion animals and his lifelong devotion to the then unheard of doctrine that food can function similarly to medicine and that proper nutrition can aid in managing many diseases.

Pushed by an ambition and goal forming deep inside him, Mark took the bold step of offering a partnership in his fledgling practice to Dr. Edward Cushing, one of two ambulatory clinicians and veterinary doctors under whom he had served on after-hours calls at Cornell.

The name was changed to the Cushing and Morris Veterinary Practice and Dr. Cushing and his wife moved into the leased house in Edison which served as the office for the practice. Mark moved into a room in the same house. Dr. Cushing assumed the responsibility for the large animal calls and Mark began to devote full time to the growing small animal practice.

Simultaneously with this burst of activity, Mark's younger sister and her husband, the Suttons, decided it was time to move back to Colorado. Mrs. Cushing was handling the telephone and appointments, but the case load had grown to the point where Mark decided he needed more help.

That simple business decision was his first step to matrimony.

The assistant Mark hired was a boy in his early teens named Fred Weber who lived about a mile from the office. His assignment was to report after school hours, clean the office and then sterilize all instruments and help by holding the small animal patients during the nightly office hours. The boy fitted easily into the routine and Mark found himself becoming fond of the youngster.

It still ranked as a small surprise, however, when young Fred Weber showed up for work one fall evening with his brother-in-law in tow. Ray Lewis was introduced as the husband of Nettie Weber Lewis, who lived just across the street from the office and was young Fred's sister.

His mission, said Ray Lewis, was to invite Dr. Morris to have Thanksgiving dinner with the family "because you're Fred's friend and we know your only alternative in a city of strangers is a lonely meal in a restaurant somewhere."

Mark showed up, grateful and on time, for the Thanksgiving dinner and promptly discovered he was not among total strangers. One of the guests was a young woman he had offered a ride to several weeks earlier when he discovered her waiting for a bus on a street corner nearby on the road to New Brunswick, a route he used several times daily.

That lift to New Brunswick had been followed by several such short trips by the two when Mark happened to find her waiting for the bus. They had chatted about casual things and Mark was not sure he had asked her name. He knew only that she lived in Stelton (later Edison), was a graduate of the New Jersey teacher's college in Trenton and taught fourth grade in the Lincoln School in New Brunswick. Her name was Louise Weber, Nettie's sister, and Mark discovered quickly in this family setting that she was "a very alert and attractive young lady." This was November 1927. Less than one year and one month later, Louise Weber would become Mrs. Mark L. Morris.

The year 1928 "easily was one of the most memorable years of my life," Mark was to say often in the years ahead.

A romance was budding. Mark and Louise were together increasingly as their friendship deepened. It began with dinner-for-two occasionally, then often. It ripened into twosome trips on house calls and long, casual drives through the countryside.

Although she was busy with her teaching duties, Louise soon began to help Mark keep his practice records and often showed up in the late afternoon to help with the telephone and in handling the lengthening lines of clients each evening.

The steady increase in business quickly led the new partners in Cushing and Morris Veterinary Practice into an expansion decision. They agreed the one-room office in a leased house was no longer sufficient. But the alternative was a bold and expensive one.

"We decided to build an animal hospital, the first of its kind in New Jersey and the only such facility in the region outside of New York City," recalled Mark. "The idea basically was mine, since the new hospital mainly would serve small animals, and that was my end of the business. But Dr. Cushing agreed and we bought some vacant land about a mile from our office on the Lincoln Highway, the major route between New York City and Philadelphia."

The next step was to hire an architect and line up a lawyer to help arrange the myriad details. In final design, the Raritan Hospital for Animals—named for a New Jersey river and township—was a three-story structure combining offices, a laboratory, kennel areas for patients, and ample living facilities. Offices, examining rooms, a surgery, an infectious disease ward, a three-car garage and a full basement with room for storage of feed, surgical and other supplies were included. On the second floor was an apartment with three bedrooms, dining room, living room and one and one-half baths. The third floor had a bedroom and a bathroom designed for a kennel or hospital aide.

The construction price tag was estimated at $40,000, a small fortune by the standards of 1928. But Mark, who was nearing a late 1928 payout of his original $12,000 debt to Dr. Loblein in order to achieve the $2,000 discount, was full of optimism. He personally handled negotiations which led to a construction loan of $20,000 from the Jersey Mortgage & Title Co. of Elizabeth. Contracts were let and construction began in early summer. Completion was scheduled for December.

A highlight of his 1928 patient load, Dr. Morris was fond of recalling in later years, involved a client who decided to take her prize-winning black chow dog to the dog show in Cleveland by airplane instead of on the train.

"It was a media event in that part of New Jersey," he recalls. "Nobody had heard of a dog flying and this one was all fitted out with goggles and a helmet because airplanes in those days had open cockpits."

Dr. Morris, who had checked the animal carefully to insure it could make the trip without harm, was on hand at the airport. He posed for the local press with the chow and its special parachute and the story quoted him as seeing no reason why travel via plane by pets as well as people would not become commonplace in the years ahead.

As fall arrived, Dr. Cushing arranged a private conference with Mark to announce he felt the large animal practice he was handling should be separated from Mark's end of the business—including the hospital, by then taking full shape. He said he wanted to move with his wife to nearby Plainfield, New Jersey, to be closer to the dairies which were a mainstay of his practice. He wished Mark well, he made it clear, but he was adamant in a belief both he and Mark would be best served by ending their partnership.

A dissolution agreement was drawn by Douglas Hicks, a lawyer in New Brunswick, and became effective on Nov. 1, 1928.

The new Raritan Hospital which he had built in 1928. Mark and Louise lived on the second floor.

Mark and the lawyer set out at once to untangle the financial problem involving the nearly completed hospital. The original construction loan for $20,000 signed by both ex-partners was converted into a first mortgage. A second mortgage for $15,000 was obtained from the National Bank of New Jersey. A third mortgage for equipment in the form of a promissory note, was endorsed by Anthony Robisek of New Brunswick, owner of the pharmacy on which Mark wrote the medical prescriptions for his growing practice.

"Mr. Robisek is a good friend," Mark explained to his family. "He has faith in my future success."

Amid this flurry of events, Mark and Louise announced their engagement. They had decided that true living is done in pairs. It was to be a church wedding and Louise chose the Livingston Avenue Reformed Church in New Brunswick, part of the German Reformed Church of America where the elder Webers, both born in the "old country" were longtime members of the congregation.

Louise made her own wedding gown and helped her bridesmaids make theirs. Mark rented a formal suit and called on Douglas Hicks, the lawyer who helped him finance the now completed hospital, to act as his best man. The ceremony was held on Dec. 21, 1928.

Mark, who had set up shop temporarily in the garage of the new hospital, arranged for Dr. Joseph Millar of Asbury Park to handle his practice while the newlyweds drove off to Philadelphia for a honeymoon.

It was a one-day honeymoon, since Dr. Millar had to return to his own practice. Among Mark's mementoes is a bill marked "paid" from the Hotel Walton in Philadelphia in the amount of $8.

The young couple moved into the as yet scantily furnished living quarters on the second floor of the still unequipped hospital on their return and promptly were caught up in a round of holiday celebration with the German-born Weber family, to whom a combined Christmas and wedding were cause for special joy.

The year 1928 ended with Dr. and Mrs. Mark L. Morris hunting for furniture for their apartment and planning where the hospital equipment would be placed on the floor below when it arrived.

As far as Mark was concerned, he decided on New Year's Eve, he had it all—love and mission. The debts of the new hospital venture, nearing $70,000, worried him not at all. The venture was certain of success and would pay for itself in quick order.

There was no hint that before another year had passed a collapse of the stock market in nearby New York City would plunge the nation into the Great Depression.

6

The Shaping of a Career

There was nothing haphazard about life with Louise, Mark soon discovered. She possessed a strong and burning desire for order. Life had to have form, she often told him. There must always be a clearly recognizable pattern to living. Even everyday commonplaces had to exist within a well-defined and acceptable frame of reference.

First there was the apartment on the second floor of the new Raritan Hospital for Animals. The first furniture acquired by the couple before their wedding was limited to an unpainted kitchen table, chairs to match and a bed and dresser of uncertain vintage for one of the bedrooms. The living room was decorated by stacks of wedding present boxes.

With Mark in tow as an observer and lifter of the heavier articles, the bride began a round of used furniture shops and family attics. In short order the apartment emerged as a comfortable home and one of her attic finds—a settee and three chairs purchased from a second-hand store by her mother five years before and then relegated to storage—remains a treasured family heirloom.

Up to ten separate coats of varnish somehow had been applied to the original walnut. When Mark and Louise laboriously removed these and had the pieces reupholstered, they emerged as antique gems.

Next on the action list for Louise was the new hospital. In days its furniture and fixtures were moved in, a bookkeeping system was established and Louise took over the telephone and all scheduling of appointments. She also began a patient file system, maintaining a record of each animal treated.

It was necessary for Mark to continue his regular house-call practice at full steam during the early days after the hospital opened. Louise learned to fill in at the office on routine patient calls during Mark's

53

absence, and out of that came an experience the couple was never to forget.

It involved a rural client who came to the hospital with an elderly dog that he said he wanted "put to sleep." Mark was out, but Louise had been introduced to the procedure and had witnessed it on several occasions. Rather than ask the man to wait for Mark's return (not expected for hours) or to come back later, she took on the task.

Mark tells the rest this way:

"I had been using strychnine sulphate intravenously, which would dispose of the aging, incurable animal quickly and painlessly. She took the old dog into the examining room, out of sight and sound of the client, and made the preparations just as she had seen me do several times. She boiled the syringe to make certain it was sterile—(a procedure which was a bit unnecessary since the animal was going to die)—and then she picked up a bottle which said 'strychnine' on the label.

"The only trouble was that the bottle held pills containing only five-hundredths of a grain of strychnine. It was a tonic dose I had made up for an ailing cat. She gave the injection and the old dog merely wagged his tail and began to look better. She had used two of the pills in the first solution, so she tried four. The dog looked even better. She went to six and then more on subsequent shots and the old dog finally stretched out in relaxed fashion and died. She delivered the body to the client, who paid his two dollars and left none the wiser. But Louise never forgot the difference between a five grain tablet of strychnine and a cat tonic pill containing five-hundredths of a grain."

Added Mark: "And that shows you how determined to help me was my ex-school teacher bride."

Louise also spearheaded the big educational job involved in getting the public accustomed to using the new animal hospital, first of its kind in the region, instead of calling telephone number 278 and requesting the "vet" to make a house call.

Louise spent hours convincing clients that pets would be better cared for if they were brought in to take advantage of the many facilities offered by the new animal hospital. She stressed to all animal owners that the alternative to bringing the patient in for examination and treatment was to have Dr. Morris drive the 12 to 14 miles to their home and then return. The cost of mileage would show up on the final bill, she pointed out, and Dr. Morris could use his time better doing what he had been trained for and charging only for actual

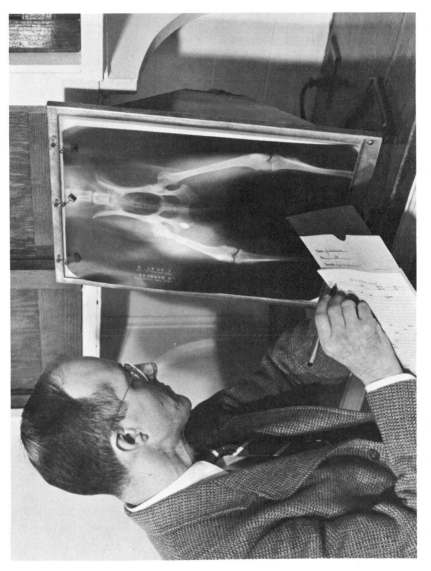

Mark was one of the first veterinarians to use radiographic techniques in an animal hospital.

professional services rendered. The final fillip employed by Louise to convince the still skeptical was that the service was bound to be better at the hospital because of the laboratory facilities and the equipment, "which he can hardly carry with him."

The year 1929 whizzed by with business mounting daily for the Raritan Hospital for Animals. Mark and Louise—whose smile made every day a sunny one for the young veterinarian—had expanded the laboratory in the original operating room of the new hospital in recognition of its growing contribution to his reputation as a scientist-veterinarian and its growing impact on business. A new operating room was equipped in the basement of the hospital.

A man commonly known by everyone as "Pop" Nelson was employed. He was a member of an old Danish family that lived in the area, and his services were greatly appreciated. His duties were varied—he was chiefly on night duty at the hospital, answered phone calls, fed and cared for the animals at night, and mixed quantities of dry ration with hand tools. (It was this mixture that was used in preparing the various dietary foods which at that time were being fed to patients in the hospital.)

Pop was a thoroughly honest and reliable individual, and was liked and respected by everyone that worked with him. He loved the animals, took excellent care of them, and was loved by them in return.

The historic crash of the stock market in October, 1929, at first left the Morrises untouched. They owned no stocks and their main link with banks was the pile of notes and mortgages they had acquired and were paying off.

But as 1930 unfolded, so did what would go down in American history as the Great Depression. Its impact on many of Mark's wealthy estate-owner clients with ties to Wall Street was quick and vast. People with reputations of substantial wealth began closing their large homes and moving into the servant quarters on the grounds. Unemployment was on the rise in the cities and towns of New Jersey, as across the nation. Bill-paying slowed.

At times, in the years of the Depression, Mark and Louise were hard pressed to meet payment deadlines on some of the notes involving hospital equipment.

At one point, a bank threatened to foreclose on one of the notes. Mark sought an audience with the president.

"If you people think you can get your money by trying to operate an animal hospital better than I can," said an angry Mark, "you are welcome to try. But I think you'd stand a better chance of getting your principal back if you let me run the hospital and pay you the interest regularly until I can fight my way clear and start working on the principal."

The banker decided Mark was right. There were no more threats.

"This is a period when it is absolutely essential to produce exceptionally good service for the people who own pets," Mark noted in a letter to his parents. "Pets have, in fact, become luxuries."

But income records of the Raritan Hospital for the 1930s show that business increased steadily each year. They also show that Mark methodically widened his sphere of influence, drawing new clients from both New York City and Philadelphia, from Long Island and even from depression-proof Westchester County as well as suburbs of Philadelphia.

It was during this period, in the early 1930s, when a new member was added to the staff—Clarence Johnson, D.V.M., previously employed by the state of New Jersey for field work testing cattle, etc. He came to Raritan Hospital to assist in the clinical work, surgery, etc. He was especially proficient in dealing with the clients, as he had an exceptionally nice personality.

However, a rather serious problem arose. It was discovered that powdered nembutal could be purchased directly from a wholesale distributor, dissolved in the laboratory at Raritan by mixing it with grain alcohol. The end product was used intravenously for anesthetizing dogs or cats. This was working well until it was suddenly found that this anesthesia solution was not taking effect. The wholesaler was contacted, as it was thought the nembutal powder was defective, and they asked that the powder be sent to them, together with the grain alcohol we were using, so they could test them both in their laboratories. This was done. To the surprise of all concerned, their results showed that the grain alcohol sent them was nothing but distilled water! Nembutal is not soluble in water; therefore the solution had no effect as an anesthetic. The balance of the grain alcohol on hand was tested and the entire stock was found to be nothing but distilled water.

After investigation, Clarence Johnson admitted that he had been substituting the distilled water for the grain alcohol, which he was using to make "bath-tub gin." He was embarrassed and ashamed, and asked to be retained on the job with promises to discontinue his "side-line." After consideration it was decided to keep him on, and he was with the hospital for some time before moving on—a little older—and a little wiser!

"It was our increasing application of scientific methods in diagnosing patient problems that increased the reputation of the Raritan Hospital,'' Mark was to say often in the years that followed. "We were producing results for pet owners and that counted.''

As his practice expanded despite the economic turmoil sweeping the nation, Mark's determination to delve deeper into the medical mysteries that tantalized him grew stronger.

"We've got to do better,'' he told Louise. "We must learn to go farther than the routine examination of a skin scraping or a fecal sample. There are too many unanswered questions. We don't know now why some dogs consume large amounts of water, continue to vomit and then die on us. And we've got to do something about the fact that when cats get sick and they are brought in to us, too often they just die.''

Mark once summed up his problem of the early 1930s this way: "We had been able to diagnose and manage certain diseases through physical procedures quite efficiently, but we had many things affecting dogs, cats and other pets which were baffling and for which we had no answers.

"We could get no further information from colleges of veterinary medicine, because virtually all of those colleges in America were devoted to the diagnosis, treatment and prevention of diseases of domestic animals such as cows, horses, swine and sheep. There was almost no research going on in the field of small animal medicine, the field in which I had chosen to specialize.

"One of our best sources of information at the time was to talk to the salesmen from pharmaceutical firms who came around and carried information from practice to practice. They passed on from veterinarian to veterinarian the case histories of new drugs which were proving effective. We would buy some of the medicine, possibly something the salesman particularly wanted to sell, and try it out. The drug might or might not work, but we were depending on the pharmaceutical industry to do our research.

"To me, it became obvious that we would be forced to work out some means of doing the research ourselves if there ever were to be major breakthroughs in the treatment of small animal ailments.''

Mark's attention was drawn at this time to the Schilling Blood Charts, a system for the classification of human blood cells then being introduced in the field of human medicine. The system, still in use in the 1980s and developed by a German pathologist, already was recognized as a major aid in diagnosing a variety of human ailments.

Mark's problem was that nobody seemed to know if the Schilling charts and techniques had any application in animal medicine.

"I asked several experts, and they said they didn't know," Mark recalls. "I came to the conclusion that no one knew and I had to find out."

Mark began to collect blood samples from most of his canine and feline patients and turn them over to a clinical laboratory used by physicians in the New Brunswick area. Reports on the animal blood were returned in all cases without comment from the pathologist. He told Mark he had "not the slightest idea" whether there was any connection between Schilling findings on human disease and those of animals. He told Mark that "any interpretation is up to you."

In desperation, Mark turned to James B. Allison, Ph.D., who was teaching physiology and biochemistry at Rutgers University in New Brunswick and a man who was to become one of Mark's closest friends. Dr. Allison spent days pouring through various medical libraries and contacting known experts on the Schilling method. His final report was emphatic: "There is nothing, absolutely nothing on record which shows the blood values of canines or felines. You are in an uncharted sea."

Mark continued his work, confident that eventually he would be able to draft charts of his own which would show as clearly as in the charts being used in human medicine when an animal patient was beginning to suffer from an infectious disease or other specific ailment.

As part of his practice, Mark routinely performed necropsies on as many as possible of his animal patients which died. His goal: to pinpoint, if possible, exactly why the animal died and did not respond to treatment.

The necropsy routine had been difficult when Mark was an on-the-road practitioner treating most of his patients in barns or garages or on back porches and in kitchens. But after opening the Raritan Hospital, the rate of necropsies performed with client permission increased and Mark began to learn more and more about some of the darker mysteries of small animal medicine.

But Mark, who easily admitted to a constant curiosity about the reasons and the possible cures for any animal ailment he encountered ("I guess I was born with an inquisitive mind—I always had an urge to hunt when there seemed to be no answers to something"), took his necropsy work a step beyond the ordinary. Dr. William Feldman, one of his professors at Colorado State University's veterinary college, had joined the staff of the Mayo Foundation for Medical Research at Rochester, Minnesota. The two had been keeping in touch through occasional letters and Dr. Feldman volunteered to help Mark in his necropsy work by examining tissues, preserved in Formalin, shipped to Rochester when Mark's examination at necropsy had failed to pinpoint a cause of death.

After a series of such shipments, Dr. Feldman wrote a suggestion that Mark make a trip to Minnesota. He said he was confident an arrangement could be made to provide more Mayo Foundation assistance to Mark in his pioneer diagnostic work. Mark leaped at the chance and traveled to Rochester a few days later.

He returned with a new employee added to the payroll. Dr. Feldman and his chief at the Mayo research complex, Dr. Jess Bollman, had advised Mark that he was on the right track in his diagnostic work but had reached the point where he needed technical assistance. They offered to make available the services of an animal medical technician then completing his training at the Mayo Foundation. His name was Al Adler and Mark formally hired him at a conference in Dr. Feldman's office. Adler became one of the first of a new breed—the veterinary clinical pathologist—to be employed in a private animal hospital in the United States.

Life at Raritan Hospital for Animals quickly settled into a routine of mounting patient work and long hours in the laboratory after Adler joined the staff. Mark had become a father on April 4, 1930 with the birth of a daughter, Ruth. The newcomer quickly became the center of the universe for both Mark and Louise and the proud father quickly added a housekeeper to the staff to ease the workload on his wife.

Another staff addition was a 16-year-old youth named John H. Whitlock, who had just graduated from high school. His parents were owners and operators of a restaurant in Highland Park, near New Brunswick, where Mark and Louise were frequent diners. They learned that young John was going to enter veterinary school at Iowa State University in the fall and was eager to earn some pocket money by working with animals during the summer. He joined the hospital staff to feed the animals, clean kennels, help change dressings and supervise such chores as the bathing and clipping of canine patients.

Years later, the ex-cleaner of kennels at Raritan Hospital had some comments about his experience there in a letter written on the letterhead of the department of preventive medicine at Cornell University, where he was named professor emeritus after a long and distinguished career as a veterinary parasitologist. The comments:

"The Morrises lived in an apartment over the hospital and, for part of the time, I had night duty. My chief chore was to keep the dogs quiet so the Morrises could sleep undisturbed and the neighbors would have nothing to complain about. Dr. Morris was brusk, energetic, arbitrary and a good teacher with a very short fuse. Mrs. Morris was a very pleasant, gracious lady.

"One of the things I learned while working for the Morrises was that pet owners in that day, as a group, had more than their share of neurotics and psychoneurotics. I enjoyed working with the cats and dogs; I couldn't stand the owners."

Among the hundreds of persons who visited the new Raritan Hospital in the early 1930s was a motorist who dropped in and asked for a brief tour. He was Dr. John V. LaCroix of Evanston, Illinois, on his way to New York City on business, and owner-operator of a newly opened small animal hospital in Evanston called North Shore Animal Hospital. Dr. LaCroix also was owner, editor and publisher of the NORTH AMERICAN VETERINARIAN, a leading national veterinary publication in which regularly appeared the newest research findings of the profession.

Mark's laboratory was the focal point of the LaCroix tour. He expressed interest when Mark demonstrated his work in the application of blood and urine studies to the more accurate diagnosis of the diseases of small animals. Before he left, he had made arrangements to publish in his NORTH AMERICAN VETERINARIAN the first of a series of reports by Dr. Mark L. Morris on his pioneer work. A lifelong friendship had begun.

Mark's spreading renown in mid-New Jersey as a veterinarian with a scientific approach led to another lifelong contact in an unexpected and rewarding way.

One of the frequent drop-ins at the Raritan Hospital was Lyman Peck, who was employed in a new department of Merck & Co., at Rahway, New Jersey, less than 10 miles from New Brunswick. Peck's job involved the development of a line of minerals and vitamins for use in fortifying feeds for poultry and livestock.

"I have a hunch you could help Merck with a problem we have," Peck remarked one day to Mark. "I'd like you to come to the headquarters with me and meet a few people."

Mark decided it would be interesting at least to see the inside of the pharmaceutical complex. He quickly found himself in the office of the company president, George Merck, who subsequently observed that "I was wrong; I thought all veterinarians were horse doctors."

Mark was hired as a Merck consultant and worked with Dr. W. D. Engle, head of the department of organic chemistry at Merck, in the development of a topical lotion called Canex, marketed by Merck as a treatment for demodectic mange in dogs.

The Canex study took many months, during which Mark also aided as a veterinary consultant in the design of the animal quarters of the Merck Institute of Medical Research.

Meantime, in his own laboratory, Mark was making definite progress with his new clinical pathologist, Al Adler, in the never-give-up campaign to turn examination of blood and urine samples into a dependable method of diagnosing diseases in animals. The reports on findings he was making public through the pages of Dr. LaCroix's NORTH AMERICAN VETERINARIAN attracted wide attention and Mark suddenly found himself invited to present a paper at the 1932 convention of the American Veterinary Medical Association at the Palmer House in Chicago. Mark prepared carefully for his debut as a speaker at the national convention of his profession. He assembled clinical and laboratory data and recorded it on projection slides to illustrate the address he had rewritten a half dozen times.

The big day finally arrived and Mark took the podium at a general session of the convention. In the audience of 700 persons, there was only a scattering of small animal practitioners. The majority of veterinarians present were dairy practitioners or specialists in equine and other domestic animals, veterinarians from the Federal Bureau of Animal Industry, Department of Public Health and other federal agencies and a host of executives and salesmen from pharmaceutical firms.

"There was little interest in the group as a whole in the changes in blood counts in sick dogs and cats which I had discovered and was demonstrating on slides and explaining in my speech," Mark was to recall. "My methods were entirely new and I was aware that hardly a person in that crowd ever had heard about the techniques I was telling them about. I knew that the methods I was proposing were not being taught in any of the veterinary colleges.

"To say the least, my presentation did not bring down the house."

When Mark finished talking, the session moved on to other business. The applause seemed more to reflect relief that Mark was sitting down than approval of his speech.

Mark stayed in the background as the general session ended, preferring to slip out unnoticed when most of the crowd had gone. As he stood near the stage, only one of the delegates paused to shake his hand.

"It sounds to me like you have hit on something very valuable," said this man. "I'd like to make arrangements to visit your hospital in New Jersey and find out more about it. Perhaps you could help me set up a similar laboratory in my own hospital."

The man was Dr. Arthur Theobald of Cincinnati, Ohio. He was to become one of Mark's close professional friends and a national leader in small animal veterinary medicine.

One of the key medical discoveries outlined in the Chicago presentation was that dogs previously thought to be suffering from gastroenteritis, or stomach and intestinal disorders, actually were victims of failing kidneys.

"After trying all sorts of medical treatments aimed at relieving the disturbed digestive tract, we gave up on that traditional approach to stop the vomiting and excessive drinking of water," Mark had told his Chicago audience. "We relied instead on laboratory reports from the Mayo Foundation which began to show clearly that these sick dogs had degenerated kidneys.

"We switched to methods then being employed in humans with kidney failure and uremic poisoning, and adapted these methods to dogs. We introduced the intravenous use of saline and dextrose fluid therapy, withheld oral water and—in a very few days—we were able to pronounce these animals much improved."

The implied yawn with which this was greeted by most of the Chicago audience did not apply to Dr. LaCroix, the veterinarian-publisher who had given space to Mark's work in his nationally circulated veterinary magazine. He published a special report on Mark's Chicago speech weeks before a similar report appeared in the official JOURNAL OF THE AMERICAN VETERINARY MEDICAL ASSOCIATION.

"Interest in the subject began to grow across the country almost from the day of publication," Mark was to recall years later. "There was a sudden demand for clinical laboratory technicians to work side by side with veterinarians in small animal hospitals and, you could say, that out of the poorly received speech in Chicago grew the beginning of interest in the new discipline of veterinary clinical pathology."

Professional praise would replace in short weeks the silence which originally greeted Mark's appearance in Chicago, but he suddenly was too busy to brood about the temporary silence. A telephone message from Dr. LaCroix greeted him as he returned to his room. He was invited to a meeting.

The meeting at the Palmer House, held while the convention proper was winding down its business, turned into an explosive near free-for-all and catapulted Dr. Morris, from New Jersey, into national prominence in his profession.

The session was called to discuss a proposal advanced months before and quietly promoted by Dr. LaCroix. His suggestion was that

The founding members of the American Animal Hospital Association were honored at the organization's 35th annual meeting in 1958. Left to right, Dr. Joseph A. S. Millar, Deal, New Jersey, the 1958 president; Dr. J. V. Lacroix, Evanston, Illinois, who conceived the idea for the organization; Dr. Stanwood W. Haigler, St. Louis, one of the original members; Dr. Mark Morris, first president; and Dr. Arthur Theobald, Cincinnati, the first treasurer.

the time had come to create some type of organization to devote time and group thinking to the betterment of the growing number of small animal hospitals in the United States and to, coincidentally, take combined steps toward the improvement of methods used to treat small companion animals.

"This is a proposal for which the time has come," Dr. LaCroix said in a brief talk setting the tone, he hoped, for the session. "It is time to draw up some standards for small animal hospitals in America and to provide an organization for enforcing those standards. It is time also that the small animal practitioner come into his own.

"The current view on small animal practice is that it is a nuisance. Critics say such practices cater only to the hobby types—people with pets—and make no contribution to the food supply of our country or to public health."

"There are several well-planned and well-equipped small animal hospitals in this country, but a lot of our fellow professionals have put up signs giving hospital status in the public eye to facilities in barns, to garages equipped with a few cages, to outside kennels and even to basement offices. We owe it to the animal-owning public to bring some order out of this chaos."

The small animal veterinarians in the group applauded. Not so other members of the American Veterinary Medical Association who had come out of curiosity after hearing a rumor that a rival organization to A.V.M.A. might be in the making.

"It got very heated," Mark was to recall. "The doctors began to mill around and voices were raised. There were shouts that 'You can't tell me to shut up' and yells that 'This is an outrage.' There was some language that professional men would use only in the heat of rage. Somebody had to do something."

Mark did something. He walked to the microphone, asked for quiet, got it from the crowd surprised to hear a calm voice over the general hubbub, and then said:

"No one is here to ruin our profession. Nobody is seeking to divide and conquer. It appears this is not the time or place in which to accomplish anything.

"I move that our chairman be authorized to appoint a committee to develop an organizational structure and report back at a later date. And, gentlemen, I also move that we adjourn."

Cheers and applause—notably lacking a few hours before when he had spoken—greeted Mark's proposal.

In the moment of silence which followed as Mark returned the microphone to the chairman, a veterinarian's voice rang out. Mark never learned who made the motion, but it carried. Mark L. Morris, D.V.M., was named by acclamation as temporary president "of the new organization under consideration."

Out of the stormy session came, in the months ahead, the American Animal Hospital Association with Dr. Mark L. Morris as its first elected national president.

The association, long since headquartered in its own building in South Bend, Indiana, still works full time to carry out several goals laid down by its founders: Drs. John V. LaCroix of Evanston, Illinois; Joseph A. S. Millar of Deal, New Jersey; Stanwood W. Haigler, St. Louis, Missouri; Arthur Theobald of Cincinnati, Ohio; and Mark L. Morris of New Brunswick, New Jersey. The goals are:

1. To provide the best possible veterinary service and hospital facilities for the care and treatment of dogs, cats and other pet animals.
2. To advance the professional interest of the veterinarians engaged in hospitalization of small animals.
3. To establish and maintain a high standard for the hospital, the equipment, the personnel, and the methods employed.
4. To disseminate helpful information among owners of small animals to neutralize the ill effects of widely circulated misinformation on the health of small animals and the treatment of their ailments.
5. To cooperate with the section on small animal practice of the American Veterinary Medical Association.
6. To cooperate with colleges in elevating the standards of veterinary education.
7. To encourage progress in and cooperation among small animal hospitals.

A key point in the original by-laws of the association was a requirement—dropped in 1978 as outmoded and perhaps in violation of new legal interpretations—that members of the new group first be members in good standing of the American Veterinary Medical Association.

The importance of that gesture is underlined in a 1981 statement made by Dr. Ralph Ruggles of Moline, Illinois. He was a board member of the hospital association for 23 years, served as president in 1951-52 and as treasurer from 1954-64. His statement:

"I believe the most important action of the founders was to require that A.A.H.A. members first be members of A.V.M.A. In doing this, and requiring it down through many years, the A.A.H.A. has made other veterinarians on the sidelines realize that all of us are first veterinarians, and then are encouraged to specialize.''

Back home after his heady experience in Chicago, Mark had among his first callers a pharmaceutical salesman who earlier that day had called on the veterinary staff of the University of Pennsylvania.

"I'm not one to spread tales," began the salesman, "but I regard you as a friend and I think you should know who your adversaries are. I just overheard the director of the small animal clinics, a full professor at the university, make a little speech about his having heard your presentation at the Chicago convention.

"He said he was going to spread the word among practitioners that there is nothing valid in your blood test theories. He said everyone knows there are no grounds for belief in such theories and that it would be his recommendation that you be psychoanalyzed and perhaps confined in an institution for treatment.

"He practically came right out and said you are crazy."

7

New Horizons and a Cow in Little America

Mark spent little time worrying about being branded as crazy.

"Everyone is entitled to his own opinions," he told the salesman who had brought him the news. "I have a hunch he's dead wrong, and perhaps a little crazy himself on the subject of blood tests. And I'm willing to wait for time to prove who is wrong."

With that, Mark dismissed the matter from his mind and got back to work in the laboratory at Raritan Hospital for Animals.

The hospital routine itself was going nicely. The capacity of the kennel area had been raised to 100 animals and the cages usually were full. Louise directed the day-to-day affairs of the hospital. Ray Lewis, brother-in-law of Louise, had been employed and had grown into a major asset. Ray learned not only to do all of the routine clinical things, but became almost indispensible in his working with the animals. He was very patient and came to be a capable assistant to the young veterinarians. He quickly learned how to check ears for mites, check skin and coats for parasites, and the many routine clinical procedures required. His natural abilities were such that he enjoyed the work and became very skillful in inserting a needle into the vein so the technician could collect blood samples. He had a very steady hand and developed to the point where he could put a needle into the vein of the neck of even a small kitten.

Ray fully recognized that he was a layman and never overstepped his position, so the young veterinarians became very dependent on his assistance and they were all very fond of him. He was with the Morrises for many years.

In summary, he proved to be one of the most proficient lay

assistants that had ever been employed at Raritan Hospital for Animals.

Despite the steady buzz of activity and the prosperous practice it reflected, Mark was not content. He was spending more and more time in the laboratory and he was worrying. It seemed to him that progress was slowing down in the laboratory efforts to convert the running of blood tests and blood chemical studies into an exact science for identifying animal diseases. His clinical pathologist, trained at the Mayo Foundation, was an expert in his field, but research now underway was probing into fields beyond his or Mark's expertise.

"Things are beginning to get out of hand," Mark confided to Louise. "We're probing into some of the complexities of medical biochemistry and Al Adler (the pathologist) and I are in over our heads. It's going to require someone with greater knowledge of biochemistry if we're going to accomplish our goals in finding the true causes and the differentiations of these diseases."

Louise pondered the situation, then suggested that Mark take it up with Dr. James B. Allison at Rutgers University, the expert in biochemistry and physiology who already had been helpful to Mark and was becoming a fast friend of the Morrises.

Dr. Allison agreed that more needed to be known about the chemical metabolism of the sick dogs and cats with which Mark was working, and a deal was struck.

Under the terms of the agreement, Mark would seek out a young man with a master's degree in biochemistry who was anxious to continue his work toward a Ph.D. degree. This young man could work in Mark's clinical laboratory, equipped to perform the complex tests on the altered blood chemistry of sick animals. And, through a fellowship which Mark and his Raritan Hospital would establish, the young man could carry out at Rutgers University the studies needed to acquire an advanced degree in biochemistry.

The only remaining problem was to find the right young man. Mark turned almost automatically to his former teacher and friend from his University of Denver days, Dr. Reuben Gustavson. Dr. Gustavson replied to Mark's inquiry in less than a week. He recommended a newly married graduate student at the University of Denver who filled every qualification and was eager to combine paid research work in an animal hospital with formal studies at a university like Rutgers.

So David Green and his young wife, Virginia, arrived in New

Brunswick on June 30, 1934, and moved promptly into quarters Louise had found for them. David Green went to work in Mark's laboratory the next day.

Looking back over his career years later, in a 1982 interview, Dr. Morris considered his 1934 decision to add a biochemist to his laboratory staff as a "major event in the history of animal medicine." His work with David Green, he said, was the beginning of a new approach to animal medicine in which nutrition and the diet of dogs and cats would play a major role in their health.

Out of David Green's dual role as a graduate student at Rutgers and a laboratory biochemist at Raritan Hospital there grew a close working relationship between Dr. Morris and the university.

As the Morris-Green laboratory work expanded, information was being uncovered which both men found it difficult to interpret. As a graduate student working on a Ph.D. and specializing in studies on kidney functions in ailing dogs and cats, Green began to seek help from his Rutgers professors.

"We quickly determined that often it was difficult to find ready answers to the emerging problems on subjects ranging from bacteriology to zoology," Mark recalled. "This led Dr. Allison and me to start thinking about how we could effectively use the knowledge and training of professors at Rutgers schooled in specific disciplines. It was obvious that the answers couldn't be gleaned casually from men in the department specializing in biochemistry alone.

"What we were looking for, perhaps without knowing it at first, was a sort of forum where specialists could get together and try to solve problems they all shared by pooling their knowledge."

The problem was a favorite subject of conversation on weekends when the Allisons and the Morrises would get together socially.

"Allison's wife, Dorothy, and Louise would start chatting together, and Jim and I would retire to the living room to talk about the kind of research program we really hoped to achieve," Mark recalled. "Jim Allison was a very important man in my life. He was a great man, a very humble person, but a man of great stature as a biochemist and physiologist. It was Jim Allison who kept insisting that we needed the impact of a carefully chosen group of highly specialized people—good scientists schooled in various disciplines—who could mull over the laboratory findings and combine their knowledge to give us proper interpretations."

It was decided that the university—Rutgers—had a fine group of such men. On the staff were experts in bacteriology and virology, persons well trained in zoology and parasitology, and several specialists in the field of agricultural biochemistry with knowledge of the nutritional needs of both farm animals and pets.

The two men decided during their weekend sessions that there was a definite need for some type of organization which would make it possible for experts at Rutgers to work with Mark and his staff in furthering both animal and human medical knowledge.

"Our goal was to tie together somehow at the research level an animal hospital with a busy laboratory and a great university," Mark explained. "We agreed, Jim Allison and I, that the best route would be to recruit department heads at Rutgers and form them into something like a committee of the whole. We spent quite a few weekends and weekday evenings perfecting the plan, making sure in advance that it was functional and would work.

"This, of course, required clearance and approval from the top administrators at Rutgers. We got that approval."

In due time, after a long series of organizational meetings and as a result of the strong capable leadership of Dr. Allison, the Rutgers University Bureau of Biological Research was created.

Five specialists on the Rutgers faculty were named as original members of the new bureau. Dr. Allison, as professor of biochemistry, was one and later was to become bureau director. Other members were Dr. William M. Cole, professor of physiology, who served as the initial chairman of the research committee; Dr. Walter Russell, who represented the New Jersey Agricultural Experiment Station; Dr. James Leatham, a specialist in endocrinology, and Dr. Alan Boyden, a bacteriologist.

One of the first subjects addressed by the new bureau was protein biochemistry. The object was to identify proteins with high biological value. An early discovery was that whole egg protein had the highest value in canine diets and was capable of providing a means of almost miracle recovery for dogs threatened with death from kidney failure.

"This immediately spawned tremendous interest at the academic level," Mark recalled. "At the Raritan Hospital we established that a sick dog on low intake of high quality protein, such as egg, could recover from kidney failure; it was of wide scientific interest.

"The question that arose at Rutgers was how all of this fit into the field of human medicine. Uremia occurs in man and the experts at Rutgers immediately wondered how the roll of proteins would impact the treatment of mankind. At the time, chemists were developing protein hydrolysates. They are hydrolyzed proteins that can be given by stomach tube or intravenously, but the values had to be established, and it all had to be done working with dogs.

"This, in turn, led to the idea that conferences on the character, the quality and the utilization of protein in man should be conducted to create a better understanding. And this led to the formation of what was known as the Rutgers University Protein Conferences, which were attended by scientists from all over America, plus some from Europe."

During the hectic months of the formation of the Rutgers research bureau, Mark and his new biochemist, David Green, were busy in the laboratory working on an assignment Mark had received from Merck & Co., the pharmaceutical firm, to aid in development of a medicine to help cure demodectic mange in dogs.

The laboratory work centered around a product known as Rotonone. The problem was to find a way to make a Rotonone compound which could be applied to the coat of a dog and would immediately penetrate the hair follicles to attack the mites.

Mark already knew that the demodectic mange was caused by a tiny mite which buries itself in the skin of the dog, living off the animal tissue. This type of mange was not responsive to dipping the affected animals in sulphur solution, the standard cure for onslaughts of another type of mite which causes scabies or mange.

The work to find a treatment for demodectic mange was tedious and time consuming. Mark and his aide tried numerous solvents in their efforts to hit on one which would cause Rotonone to penetrate.

Their task involved making diagrams of laboratory dogs, then treating one area with one formula and another with a second or third experimental solution. Often the treated areas would become bald, a setback for both the dog and the researchers.

Out of the research evolved Canex, a patented formula for which Merck eventually found a worldwide market.

Much of the work which resulted in the development of Canex as a mange cure was done in connection with the new Rutgers University Bureau of Biological Research. And out of this effort came a major biological discovery. This is how Mark described it:

"We took the normal, healthy beagle dog to start this work. They were standardized at the university laboratory and put on protein-free diets, then on minimum levels of various proteins, to determine their exact requirements. To our surprise, the beagles in which protein reserves were depleted due to eating the protein-free diets mysteriously came down with demodex.

They had absolutely no observable symptoms of the disease prior to the protein studies, yet certain dogs—and not all of them—started to scratch and quickly became victims of the demodex mite. We determined that the mites had been present all the time in these dogs but were not activated until we changed the dogs' diet and depleted their protein reserves.

"As a result of this work at Rutgers, we established that there was a direct relationship between diet and the management of demodectic mange. We started out with chemical control of the disease and discovered that proper diet also was a key to the cure.

"It is now common practice for veterinarians to put dogs with early symptoms of demodectic mange on a high protein diet."

Out of this early work with Merck & Co. came new assignments for Mark and his Raritan Laboratory. David Green played a role in much of this, notably in one unique case which underlined the importance of animal research in the field of controlling human disease.

Here is Mark's account:

"One morning David Green came to the clinic and asked if I could please go to the laboratory with him as he had a specimen under the microscope he wanted me to examine. I looked at the urine specimen and could see some unusual-looking tiny crystals, not a rare find, it seemed, since we had learned that dogs frequently form crystals which show up on urinalysis. But Green pointed out to me that these were not mineral crystals; they were crystals of protein. I had never heard of protein crystals appearing in samples of canine urine. I hadn't seen anything like this while I was in college, nor had I seen it in my previous laboratory work. We decided it could be a rare and important find and proceeded to seek more information."

The two men joined in further tests on sophisticated equipment in the Rutgers University laboratory and came to the conclusion that the dog from which the sample had been taken was a victim of a rare human kidney disorder called cystinuria. The disease was believed to be hereditary and research on its origin and treatment were in an early stage on the national medical scene.

"This disease had never been reported in an animal, according to our information, not anywhere in the world. After doing some more checking, we found that the top authority on cystinuria was Dr. Erwin Brand at the College of Physicians and Surgeons at Columbia University. We notified Dr. Brand that we had an Irish terrier dog in our laboratory with cystinuria. He drove out from New York City the next day and confirmed our findings. The crystals we had discovered, he said, were without doubt cystine crystals. But to make doubly certain he took his own sample of the dog's urine back to New York and called a few days later to say there was no doubt—this was a confirmed case of cystinuria and the finding was of major medical importance. There never before had been a living model for further study of this hereditary disease, he said, and he asked if we could trace this dog's background and try to find more dogs from the same family.

"I decided to go to the owner of the dog, Hans Flues, a member of the staff of Merck & Co. as well as a client of mine. A check of the breeding papers showed that the Irish terrier was registered with the American Kennel Club and I drove into New York City to check out the dog's family history at the headquarters of the AKC. I found it had its origin in Massachusetts and took off by car to go on an Irish terrier buying spree. Louise and I had the name of the original breeder, but the venture had to be handled with great tact to get the cooperation of the dog owners.

"We found several owners of offspring of the same family group and managed to buy one male and two female dogs from the same litter. We explained that the family line had a hereditary disease and we needed to know a lot more about it and it would be necessary to obtain some of the dogs so the disease could be studied and a cure found—not only for dogs, but for humans.

"The dogs we bought were moved to nice kennels on the Hudson River north of New York City, where the Columbia College of Physicians and Surgeons was located. An intensive study of cystinuria was launched and the findings were published in the Journal of Biological Chemistry by Dr. Brand of Columbia and David Green and myself as co-authors.

"As a result of this work, much of the mystery surrounding cystinuria was removed and advances were made in the control of this hereditary and deadly ailment, both in dogs and humans."

David Green remained a key person in the Raritan Hospital laboratory for five years. In mid-1939, armed with his Ph.D. from Rutgers University, he joined the staff of the animal science department at the newly-opened Merck Institute at Rahway, New Jersey.

For Mark, there were two memorable breaks from the laboratory-hospital routine in 1934. One was the birth of his son, Mark L. Morris, Jr., his hopeful successor to carry on his work. The other was the arrival of a radiogram from the South Pole. The radiogram was from the Byrd Antarctic Expedition, then encamped at Little America on its historic venture. Here are the texts of radiograms and telegrams exchanged:

"N57 Radio via Mackay Radio, Sayville, New York, Little America, September 18, 1934. To Dr. M. L. Morris, Raritan Hospital for Animals, New Brunswick, New Jersey.

"Please advise treatment for cow slowly weakening during winter night.

"Calved on ship December 19. Brought to Little America early February, no exercise possible until October. Now dried up. Has lost much weight. Legs very weak. Either stands up or lies down for several days at a time. Latter recently resulted in two bad frostbites right flank—one healed, other suppurating freely, two inches in diameter, considerable swelling. Urination is difficult. Apparent retention. Other two cows wintered nicely, milk production quality is good. Please keep confidential. Appreciate your suggestions. Answer by Mackay Radio. Regards. Professor Edgar Perkins."

(The signature of Professor Perkins took the mystery out of the sudden message from the South Pole. The professor, prior to his assignment to the Byrd Antarctic Expedition, had been on the faculty at Rutgers University in New Brunswick and knew of the close association of Mark and the Raritan Hospital with the Rutgers Bureau of Biological Research. When the cow sickened and needed the help of a veterinarian, he turned via radiogram to a veterinarian he knew.)

"New Brunswick, New Jersey. September 18, 1934. To Byrd Expedition, Little America, via Mackay Radio.

"Prepare solution as follows: 18 grams of sodium chloride, 200 grams of dextrose, add to 4000 cc boiled water. Give 1000 cc intraveneously at 105 degrees F. every 6 hours. Continue for 3 to 4 days. If dextrose not available, prepare from table sugar by dissolving 200 grams in one liter of water. Add 3 drops of concentrated hydrochloric acid, boil 15 minutes, neutralize with soda bicarb, make up to 4000 cc with sterile salt solution. Please advise temperature, pulse, respiration, appetite, bowels, vaginal discharge, and if open or pregnant. Check specific gravity of urine, test for albumen, pulse rate, check chest or thoracic region for presence of foreign body in stomach or heart sac. Give one-half grain of strychnine sulfate in one pint of warm water by mouth every 12 hours. Clean up wounds with Dakins solution and dry. Apply 5 percent tannic acid in 70 percent alcohol. If no tannic acid, use equal parts strong boiled tea and 70 percent alcohol. Do you have calcium glutamate? If not, calcium chloride and lactic acid. Advise quality and strength. With kindest regards to you and best wishes for success of your expedition. Signed: Dr. Mark L. Morris.''

''Postal Telegraph—from Expedition Little America via San Francisco, California, September 29 and 30, 1934. Dr. M. L. Morris, Raritan Hospital for Animals, New Brunswick.

''Your reply deeply appreciated. Am delaying injections until absolutely necessary. Have not yet tested for albumen, do not have calcium glutamate or lactate. Wounds healing. Temperature 101, pulse 62, respiration 12, bowels free. Appetite poor. Eats hay, beet pulp and Laro dairy feed. Not pregnant, no discharge. Regards, Perkins.''

''Via Postal Telegraph and Cable, New Brunswick, New Jersey, November 6, 1934. Mr. Edgar Cox, Byrd Expedition, Little America. Cow is not getting sufficient moisture. If intravenous method previously described not possible, proceed as follows: place cow on her left side, shave area two inches square on right flank, paint with iodine, insert an 18 or 20 gauge hypo needle into the peritoneal cavity. Attach rubber tubing 3 or 4 feet long to the needle; use funnel on other end of the tube. Pour two gallons of the following into the funnel and allow to enter the abdomen through the needle: 225 grams of dextrose or glucose to each gallon of water, boil to sterilize. Cool to 105 degrees F. Boil the needle, tube and funnel before using. Give two gallons night and morning in this manner for 3 or 4 days and advise results. Do not give Epsom salts to the cows for a laxative if water is not plentiful. Use mineral and castor oil. Keep water before cow at all times. Reduce proteins in ration to a minimum.

''Increase carbohydrates by giving syrup or molasses on the feed, one-fourth to one-half pint daily. If bowels become too loose, stop syrup. If practical, put the cow in a sling for a few hours daily to change position; at least keep her turned frequently. Do not hesitate to treat cow in this manner. You will do no harm if directions are followed. Massage the legs with hot Epsom salts solution and rub dry. Keep comfortable with ample bedding and blankets. When possible procure calcium glutamate. Examine feed carefully, especially hay, to avoid feeding foreign bodies. Signed Dr. Mark L. Morris, New Brunswick, New Jersey.''

"Byrd Antarctic Expedition II, Little America, Antarctica, January 10, 1935. To Dr. M. L. Morris, Raritan Hospital for Animals, New Brunswick, N.J. Dear Sir: Just a line to extend to you my sincere and warm greetings from a cold country and to thank you for the assistance you rendered the expedition. Signed Edgar F. Cox, Admiral Byrd Expedition.''

With the "down under" cow on her way to full recovery near the South Pole, Mark received a visit a few weeks later from a delegation representing the Purebred Guernsey Breeders Association. They offered Dr. Morris an expense-free trip to New Zealand to meet the Bear of Oakland, the ship which would return members of the Byrd Expedition to Boston.

The plan being promoted by the Guernsey Association was for Mark to return with expedition members aboard the Bear of Oakland and, presumably, pose with expedition members and the recovered bovine upon the arrival in Boston harbor.

"The idea was to spotlight the Guernsey breed as hardy suppliers of milk," said Mark. "I was in favor of that, but I had to tell them I was too busy running my hospital and raising my family to take that much time off from my work."

The word "busy" was hardly expressive enough to describe the days Mark began to put in as his laboratory work expanded. Bit by bit he was establishing beyond reasonable doubt that there was solid merit in his program of differential diagnosis of animal diseases through clinical, pathological and laboratory techniques.

Mark reported many of his discoveries in technical papers published in veterinary journals. He began also to make speeches at meetings of the American Veterinary Medical Association.

An insight into his spreading reputation is contained in a 1982 report on his "early days" association with Dr. Mark L. Morris written by Dr. Harlan Jensen, who became a leading veterinary ophthalmologist.

"Originally, I knew little about Dr. Morris except that he had helped organize and had been the first president of the American Animal Hospital Association," Dr. Jensen wrote. "Then a friend of mine told me about the laboratory work. He said Dr. Morris had set up norms and interpretations of the different blood tests and had outlined how to use them in diagnosis and prognosis for various con-

ditions in animals. I was fascinated and wanted to learn more. Then
my friend, Dr. Elliott Beamer, mentioned that Dr. Morris was looking for a veterinarian to add to his staff in the hospital. Immediately
I knew that I wanted to go for at least a year. I had spent four years
building up a practice in Galesburg, Illinois; I wondered how my wife
would feel about leaving our new home and a thriving practice. That
night I told her of the opening while we were dressing to go to a wedding. By the time we returned home late that night, we had decided
to sell our home and practice if Dr. Morris would hire me.''

Dr. Jensen sold both his practice and his Galesburg home the
following morning.

"Our friends and clients in Galesburg begged us to reconsider,''
Dr. Jensen wrote. "They were certain that I had taken leave of my
senses. My wife and I did not waver. Here was a veterinarian far ahead
of his time and this was a chance to learn. Within two weeks I had
called on all of my clients to smooth out the transition, sold our furniture, packed our belongings in our Studebaker and we were on our
way to New Jersey.''

Dr. Jensen's report says that Mrs. Louise Morris came out as they
entered the driveway of the Raritan Hospital and told the arrivals that
she had lined up quarters for them in the home of a new widower
and his two children. That, he said, was a blessing which removed
a final lingering fear that the move to New Jersey might have been
a mistake.

"At the hospital I soon learned the significance and value of the
laboratory work,'' the report continues. "Ray Lewis, brother-in-law
of Mark and Louise, taught me how to recognize and interpret the
visual signs. Ray never erred in his judgment. Whenever he said 'An
angel is sitting on that cage,' I knew that we must warn the client
that the dog wouldn't make it. Occasionally, at first, it was hard to
believe when the dog seemed to be responding to treatment.

"About four months after my arrival, Dr. Morris began enlarging and remodeling his hospital. He put in all stainless steel kennels.

"The more I learned about Dr. Morris's pioneer work in blood
tests and animal nutrition, the more I marveled that, at that time,
his own state of New Jersey seemed to be ignoring him as a speaker;
yet he was on a growing number of national programs.''

Mark and his new assistant from Illinois, the report adds, made
regular monthly trips to New York City to attend meetings of area
members of the New York City Veterinary Medical Association. At

one of these meetings, Dr. Jensen recalled, the technical speaker was Dr. Gary Schnelle of Angell Memorial Hospital in Boston. He outlined in detail the case history and laboratory report of an unusual case. Two weeks ahead of the meeting he had sent the full case history to each member present that day to enable an individual a leisurely study of the facts. Each case history mailed was accompanied by a warning that the member would be called on after Dr. Schnelle's talk to "present your own diagnosis and be prepared to defend it after I reveal the confirmed diagnosis."

Dr. Jensen said he has "vivid recollection" of that meeting. "During the talk, Mark turned to me and asked what it was all about," he reported. "He had not had time to look at the history, so I handed him the sheet and he studied it briefly as the talk ended.

"Many of the recognized small animal veterinarians of the New York City area were there. Dr. Schnelle asked each man for his diagnosis and each responded. Finally he asked Mark, who told him he thought it was a tumor of the pituitary. Nearly everyone laughed. There had been many different diagnoses from those in attendance, but none of them had mentioned tumors and none had singled out the pituitary or any other gland. Mark just smiled at the laughter and asked Dr. Schnelle to read the pathology report.

"It said the confirmed diagnosis was tumor of the pituitary gland. Although I never was sure Mark could tell automatically what ailed an animal after a routine clinical examination, I knew he was never wrong after he looked at the laboratory workup.

"He made a lot of converts that evening."

8

Thirsty Dogs—and a Blind Man

Canine patients for which the water dish held a special lure turned the attention of Dr. Mark L. Morris to the problem of proper dog diets in the late 1930s.

"We already have established that dogs with a tremendous thirst and a seemingly unending appetite for water were victims of kidney ailments," Mark reported in an early paper on "the uremic complex." He had developed a routine of intravenous feeding of fluids to keep such animals alive. But in the late 1930s studies in the Raritan Hospital laboratory began to pinpoint a new medical fact: without fail animals suffering from the uremic complex and inevitable kidney failure had been eating a large amount of poor quality protein.

"We began to trace the origin," Mark recalled. "The trail led directly to such things as animal gelatin—some of the meat by-products in dog food on sale at that time which contained portions of hide or hoof, pig snouts, lung tissue and other questionable ingredients.

"We established beyond doubt in the laboratory that these were some of the things that were causing stress on the kidney and resulted in the condition we call kidney failure in dogs."

The problem, Mark said, was that table scraps had dwindled as an easy source of food for pet animals during the depression and both canned and dry dog foods had taken their place. In the late 1930s, cans of dog food were stacked on the shelves of most grocery stores for a few pennies—usually less than a dime—per can and the average dog owner found it easy and simple to fill his pet's dish with it.

"We discovered that essentially most of those cans held nothing but by-product waste," Mark reported at several American Veterinary Medical Association and American Animal Hospital Association meetings. "People were feeding that stuff to their dogs, but the

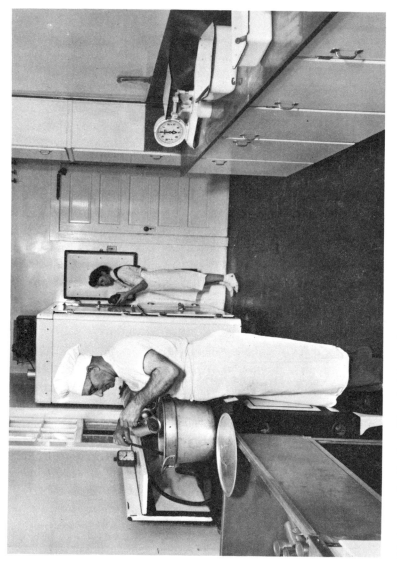

Kitchen at the Raritan Hospital for animals shows the early preparation of Specialty Diet foods for dogs and cats. Mark insisted properly prepared rations were essential for care and rehabilitation of sick animals.

nutritive value was very low, as was the energy value. The number of calories in each can was also very low, and dogs forced to subsist in this manner naturally were candidates for any viral ailment that came along. Sooner or later, kidney trouble developed and, by the time the dog began to consume outlandish quantities of water, the problem was shoved into our lap.

"Dogs put on therapy at the Raritan Hospital and then fed a balanced diet as they felt better, quickly perked up. But when those canine patients went home, their owners would go to the store and buy more cans of dog food. The kidneys were not able to manage the waste, so in a few days the clients would show up back at the hospital with their pets, now suffering from vomiting and diarrhea. We then would give them intravenous feeding and enemas to get them back on their feet. It became a vicious and expensive circle. It was apparent that the food was at fault."

So out of the Raritan Hospital came what Dr. Morris began to label as "Raritan Ration B" for want of a better name. It was a dry meal-type dog food in packages, blended from cereals and other ingredients. All that was necessary was for the clients to add a specified amount of cottage cheese, bacon fat, cooked eggs and scrap meat at home to maintain the ex-patient as a healthy pet dog.

Before long, production of Ration B required the full-time attention of an employee hired originally to watch over the kennel area at night and make certain the patients were comfortable at all times. He was affectionately called "Pop Nelson."

"That first ration we worked out was simple but effective," Mark said. "It was a basic mixture of wheat and corn flakes, bone meal, yeast and powdered milk, and we put it up in pasteboard cartons with a rather crude label at first. At home, the dog owners would add some fresh protein of good quality. The mixture we had prepared would take care of all the minerals, vitamins and energy requirements, except for the protein items added at home. It worked."

Mark's growing interest in dog foods was sparked in intensity by the creation in 1936 of a committee on foods appointed by the American Animal Hospital Association, the professional group he had aided in founding and had served as the initial president.

Aim of the committee was to discover which of the dog foods available to the public and widely advertised actually met the basic requirements of nutritional quality. In 1939, following a study of this program by the executive board of the American Veterinary Medical

Association, the A.V.M.A. joined the A.A.H.A. in the studies and a Joint Committee on Foods was set up to handle a testing program and issue a "Seal of Approval" to dog foods which were found to be of good quality.

The joint committee named Mark as its executive secretary and to serve as a testing expert. He quickly established a special kennel and laboratory near his Raritan Hospital, with a trained staff in charge.

In 1943, because of wartime dislocations affecting food production and the scarcity of essential ingredients needed to maintain the nutritional quality of prepared dog foods, the Joint Committee discontinued the "Seal of Approval," sold the kennel and laboratory facilities at Stelton, New Jersey, and adopted a revised program of using independent laboratories to test commercial foods for the information of members.

Another milepost in Mark's steady swing toward using diet as a tool to manage disease was his association with the Mayo Foundation for Medical Research in Rochester, Minnesota, where his initial connection had been Dr. William Feldman, one of his professors at Colorado State University and now a Mayo Foundation staff member. During a session at the Mayo Clinic with Dr. Feldman on analysis of animal tissue, Mark was introduced to Dr. Wilder, a physician who was in charge of the diet program for Mayo Clinic patients.

"It was from Dr. Wilder that I learned about liquid diets, soft diets and matters like low and high protein diets," Mark reported later in a letter to a friend. "He was very kind to devote his time to confer with me and explain the principles involved in the dietary management of the complicated Mayo Clinic patients—people with no stomachs and some with hardly any intestines.

"Before I left Rochester on that trip, Dr. Wilder provided me with full copies of the diet manuals of the Mayo Clinic. Included were all of the diet applications in use at that time at the clinic for the management of special patients. I began to use those manuals as a reference in my hospital and laboratory work in New Jersey. The dietary management of a sick man with gastric ulcer and with most of his stomach removed is a different problem than treating a sick dog with diarrhea and an unusual thirst for water, but some of the basic principles set forth in those Mayo Clinic manuals were invaluable to me in the modeling and developing of diet foods that could be used to nourish sick cats and dogs.

"I already had found in my laboratory studies that some basic

Raritan Laboratories, Inc., near Metuchen, New Jersey, became the site of his first large group of research animals for nutritional purposes. It was located in an isolated area to avoid possible contamination from outside sources and provided good drainage so parasite control could be maintained.

correction had to be made in the diets of animals suffering from poor kidney function and allied gastric ailments. I could see that the chemistry of the patients in my hospital was wrong. But at first I didn't know how to explain it.

"Then came the explanations from Dr. Wilder on the impact of diet in management of human ailments. I knew I had the beginnings of the answer I was seeking and that's why I began to prepare special diets in our hospital kitchens for my canine patients. It was a start."

Another association Mark developed at the Mayo Clinic gave him a major boost by adding liver problems to his growing interest in proper diet as a tool in medical treatment. This involved Dr. Jess Bollman, associate director of the Mayo Foundation, who was introduced to Mark by his friend, Dr. Feldman.

"I soon learned that some really outstanding work had been published by Drs. Mann and Bollman," Mark said in recalling the association. "Dr. Mann was director of the Mayo Foundation and he and Jess Bollman were doing experimental work on liver functions of the dog. One of their experiments, outlined to me, involved removal of large portions of the liver of dogs suffering from cancerous growth. They had established that the livers in all cases regenerated and built new liver tissue. This had been unknown until their discovery, and it meant that, if a cancer had not penetrated an entire liver, up to two-thirds of the organ could be removed in surgery to get rid of the cancer and the liver would regenerate.

"I also learned from those two experts that carbon tetrachloride, then being used by some veterinarians in capsules to kill hookworms in dogs, was actually an agent which could destroy the liver.

"I also picked up some of the laboratory methods being used at the Mayo Clinic to evaluate the liver and took them back to the Raritan Hospital for Animals, along with the Mayo diets.

"I learned in Rochester that the most important test in the evaluation of liver malfunction was to determine accurately exactly how much uric acid was being eliminated by the kidney of a sick patient each 24 hours. That led us at Raritan Hospital to put in a metabolism cage which enabled us to confine dogs and trap all eliminations and measure them. We could relate the uric acid output to the weight of the dog, correlate it with dietary intake and have an accurate measurement of the liver function. This sounds pretty complicated, but it is related to the treatment of arthritis, stiffness of the joints and several other symptoms.

"The facts I learned at the Mayo Clinic, along with veterinary applications, were duly published in our professional journals for the benefit of others. As for myself, the information brought into focus canine health problems which lead to elimination of large amounts of uric acid. Since that meant problems with the liver, I reasoned the entire problem must be related in some way to the dog's intake of food."

Mark's research into the problem led him to an examination of foods fed to animals with a known relation to uric acid elimination.

"I found on the list of foods fed animals a whole group of glandular meats such as shellfish, bovine horns, hoof material and gelatin which were widely used at the time by commercial manufacturers of pet foods for both dogs and cats. Both dry foods and canned foods at that time were using any kind of offal from packing plants and this was accounting for serious stress on the liver cells of countless animals, many of which were ending up as patients at Raritan Hospital.

"The cells of the liver of animals fed this stuff had to try to convert it so the body could use it. All of this made it even clearer to me that I had to formulate diets of my own for use in my hospital if I intended to establish that proper food is good medicine."

As Mark and his staff continued their experiments on the impact of food on disease treatment, the war which had been flaring for several years in Europe suddenly erupted into world conflict with the sneak attack by Japanese bombers on Pearl Harbor in Hawaii.

The fact America was at war initially had little impact on either Mark or his staff.

Mark had just turned 41 years of age when the bombs fell on Pearl Harbor on December 7, 1941. As a married man and father of two young children, he was not of interest to his draft board. But as a professional, Mark proceeded to do what he could to further the effort.

His first direct contact with the national problems of wartime was a telephone call from Sidney Coleman, president of the American Humane Association with offices in New York City. He invited Mark "for a discussion based on your experience and growing reputation in the field of canine diets."

In the Manhattan office of the American Humane Association Mark heard from Coleman the facts surrounding a national problem then in the rumor stage.

The fact, said Coleman, was that government leaders were worried about the wartime consumption of hundreds of tons of meat, fish and meat by-products each week by the country's millions of pet dogs and cats. Foodstuffs of all kinds—including meat, chicken, fish, fats and sugar—were being rationed and were in short supply. There were rumors that a wholesale program of euthanasia was in prospect under government supervision to "put to sleep" thousands of dogs and cats to help conserve the nation's food supplies.

"A euthanasia plan is being officially considered," Coleman told Mark. "This is causing some hysteria among pet owners and that hysteria could spread. I want you to know that the American Humane Association already has stepped in with strong objections, but the U.S. Public Health Service brought up another problem. It says there are threats of child starvation if people are permitted to keep their pets. They claim that even families with children will divide their meat, fish and other rationed food with their pets."

Mark was forced to agree with Coleman that mass hysteria was a distinct potential under the situation. "People will not give up their pets," he said. "What can I do to help?"

The answer came quickly: "We need a satisfactory war ration so people can maintain their dogs and cats properly for the duration," Coleman said. "It must be a meat-free diet, or as close to it as possible, so as not to infringe on the health of America's civilian population under the point rationing system. Can you do it?"

Mark said he could try and he was named at once to head the American Humane Association project to develop a diet to maintain dogs during wartime on meat-free diets. To conduct the needed studies a new kennel was built adjoining his hospital in New Jersey.

The diet project was little publicized by a government caught up in war, but an article appeared in the October, 1943, edition of American Magazine, complete with a photo of Dr. Morris of New Brunswick and one of the Irish terriers employed in the project. The title was "Feeding Dogs in Wartime" and the article said: "America's number one authority on dog dinners is Dr. Mark L. Morris of New Brunswick, N.J. He is now busy planning diets to keep the 15 million dogs and countless cats of this nation healthy and happy in spite of wartime food shortages."

"For people who are having difficulty getting Bowser to eat dehydrated foods, Dr. Morris advised the owner to make a thick broth of chicken feet, fish heads or butcher's scraps to pour over the dry rations. Pets do not need fresh meat, he says, but can get their proteins from rejected eggs, unsalable fish, soybeans, or even sour milk."

Mark's formulations were distributed widely across the nation by both the American Humane Association and the War Food Administration.

"I was not quite sure the food we concocted for pets was good enough, without some supplementation, for dogs under stress, particularly at the time of reproduction," Mark said. "But the general public was not too concerned about reproductive efficiency in dogs at that time. They were just worried about keeping the pets they were very fond of."

His experience with the wartime no-meat diet for pets caused Dr. Morris to take a dim view of a new development in the pet food industry which surfaced in the late 1960s. It was the effort by a pet food company to convince a new generation of pet owners that an all-meat diet is essential to the health of dogs.

Thousands of dollars were spent on advertising claiming dogs could not do well unless they had an all-meat diet. The company later changed its advertising to alter the "all-meat" advocacy. "The so-called all-meat diet is mostly meat by-products," said Dr. Morris. "The by-products are leftovers after all human food has been removed from the carcass, including the lungs, intestines and udders. The so-called all-meat diet dog food consists of items that cannot be used for human food, but the public often thinks it's buying hamburger or real meat. They are not, and when I remember that in wartime thousands of dogs in this country were kept alive and healthy on diets of cooked cereals and vegetables fortified with soybean meal, the effort to lure the American public into feeding pets an all-meat diet consisting of meat by-products is ridiculous."

During his work on a wartime diet for pets, Mark also was drafted into a $1-a-year federal post with the War Food Administration. This involved almost steady commuting between New Brunswick and the W.F.A. headquarters in Washington, D.C.

Discussing this phase of his wartime life, Mark recalls his gratitude over the fact he had "excellent commuting facilities on the Pennsylvania Railroad."

"I tried to set aside one day each week when I would go to Washington for conferences with people in the War Food Administration," he recalled. "This related to several aspects of wartime nutrition, some of it involving diseases of animals as they might be transmitted to man. Some involved my program of meatless animal diets with the American Humane Association. Most of it involved an endless round of conferences with men and women of the War Food Administration to help determine policies and procedures and the relations between animals, man and the war. I can still remember the huge room with dozens of people at typewriters and various types of communications media who were processing information.''

Another wartime project into which Mark was drafted was a series of far-ranging studies by the Merck Institute for Medical Research in Rahway, New Jersey, aimed at finding a treatment and devising preventive measures against a strange tropical disease.

The ailment is known as filaria and troops stationed in the South Pacific were falling victim to it. The ailment involves slender, threadlike worms which invade the blood and tissues of humans and animals as parasites. It commonly is called heartworm.

Mark's assignment was to cooperate with Hans Molitor, M.D., who was medical director in charge of all animal facilities at the institute. His specific chore was to secure hundreds of dogs which could be used in experiments to help find preventive measures against the parasites and make life safer for U. S. troops in the South Pacific. The work was carried out in cooperation with the department of parasitology of Johns Hopkins in Baltimore. The studies, still on-going when World War II ended, were to have major impact on military health later in the jungles of Vietnam and Cambodia.

One of Mark's World War II experiences had little impact on the final outcome of hostilities but left with him a never-to-be-forgotten impression. It involved a client and friend, Dr. Edwin Kemmerer, his wife, Rachel Kemmerer, and his wife's hobby.

Dr. Kemmerer was a professor at Princeton University, not far from New Brunswick and the Raritan Hospital. He was a famed economist and noted as a banking and financial consultant. He had at one time delivered a short economic lecture to Mark during a round of golf on the Princeton course. Its gist: "Any country which has the full right to run a printing press and turn out money which is not backed by a stable substance as gold could be in serious trouble." (Mark was to comment years later, at a 1981 interview, that he still was not convinced the Princeton economist was wrong.)

Mrs. Rachel Kemmerer's hobby was the raising and showing, especially at the Westminster Dog Show, a line of small dogs she had imported from France.

"It is a very small breed and its name, papillon, is French for butterfly," Mark recalled. "The papillons have lovely butterfly-shaped ears, and Mrs. Kemmerer consulted with me frequently on the problems of raising and feeding these tiny, fragile animals.

"She found little competition at the dog shows, and had set up breeding kennels in Princeton in an effort to expand the breed here.

"Her final shipment from France—a pair of papillon puppies—was aboard a liner headed for America through the submarine-infested North Atlantic just after America entered the war in late 1941. The passenger ship was torpedoed off New York harbor, but all aboard were rescued by nearby ships. One freighter, approaching the sinking liner, sighted a small basket floating on the ocean and picked it up. Inside, shivering and frightened, were the small puppies.

"Somehow, the pups were taken to the New York headquarters of the American Kennel Club and personnel there immediately identified them as papillons, and probably the property of Mrs. Kemmerer, the only listed papillon breeder in the country.

"Mrs. Kemmerer claimed the little dogs and rushed them to my hospital. We pulled them through, none the worse for shipwreck, but the memory of those tiny puppies floating in an unfriendly ocean sort of symbolized to me the innocent victim side of war. I'll never forget that."

As the war drew to a close, Mark was finding more time to work on the problems of canine nutrition. He wrote a summarizing report in the early 1940s which said in part:

"The research work has pulled together many details on a purified diet for dogs which should become a control standard. Information coming out of the programs of the Bureau of Biological Research at Rutgers University essentially is related to the requirements of the normal dog or cat. It now is possible to establish the minimum protein requirements or minimum calcium and phosphorus needs under certain conditions for healthy dogs.

"But what about the sick dog? Little work is being done, other than that under my supervision, for the specialized needs of dogs with various types of illnesses. We need to learn how best to feed the dog with degrees of chronic kidney disease, how to nutritionally manage the dog with damage to the liver, how to help the dog with chronic pancreatitis, how to use proper food to restore health and guard against future ailments.

"All of these problems need careful research. The information flowing from the research bureau at Rutgers and even the Joint Committee on Foods of the A.V.M.A.-A.A.H.A. supplies only fragmentary bits of data that apply to what I regard as the major problem."

Mark's Raritan Ration B for canine patients with kidney ailments had become a fixture at his hospital with consumption growing weekly, but he recalls that he was far from satisfied.

"I was determined to make available to the veterinary profession and the animal-owning public a line of specialized dietary foods. But it became increasingly obvious that if I was to succeed in this aim a great deal of careful research had to be done. We needed to establish beyond doubt, through carefully monitored tests on sick dogs and cats, how to properly nourish sick animals and not withhold nutrients that were really needed to maintain the body. But at the same time we had to establish the identity of nutrients, which for reasons of organic disease could not be effectively utilized by sick animals and whose excess in the diet would only place a burden on the animal's tissues.

"At this time (late 1944) Raritan Ration B was functioning well as 'the kidney diet.' But there was no feasible way to run tests on the product to channel it into a broader market without fear it might produce nitrogen deficiency in some animals and nitrogen excess in others. This would involve careful research.

"We knew if a project of expansion was undertaken, we must undergird it with an effective program of research and development, plus full quality control. Feed testing in the market in various parts of the country would be necessary. I had learned, for instance, that there were ailments in some parts of the country which were not a problem elsewhere.

"The final decision I was forced into was that we needed an expanded laboratory, an ultra-modern testing laboratory with a staff."

In October, 1944, Mark took the plunge and officially established the Raritan Laboratories. The first move was to enlarge facilities at the hospital to make more room for the laboratory.

One staff addition at the time was Dr. Frank Nakamura, a Japanese biochemist with a background in protein evaluation studies. He had been on the staff at the University of Illinois but was glad to make the change into more friendly surroundings because of widespread anti-Japanese sentiment in much of the country during the war.

A building on a lot next to the animal hospital was purchased from the Joint Committee on Foods, which was winding down its work. It was used to house the first dozen animals.

"My original idea of devoting full laboratory time to development of what later emerged as Prescription Diets was partially derailed,"

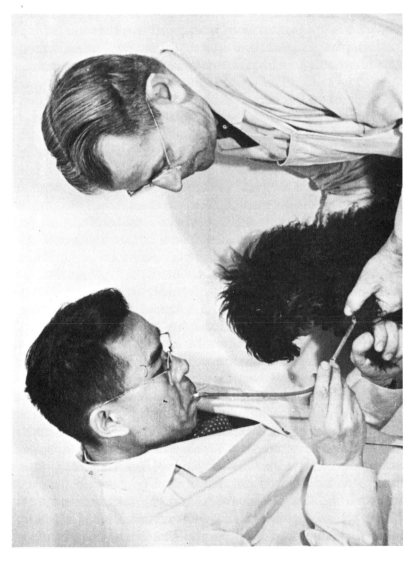

Frank Nakamura and Ray Lewis collected blood samples from dogs so laboratory diagnoses could be made. Mark was one of the first veterinarians to run blood tests on dogs.

Mark was to recall. "From the outset there was a big demand for the services of Raritan Laboratories in the industrial field. We begin testing foods and pharmaceuticals, using dogs as test animals under controlled conditions. Our work ranged from studies on dietary maintenance requirements for mature dogs and studies on dietary requirements of dogs for gestation and dietary factors in the growth of pups to items like the vitamin values of fish by-products, the relation of certain iron salts to hemoglobin formation and studies on the more efficient use of yeasts and the nutritive value of certain poultry products.

"In a few months our staff included a Ph.D. biochemist, two veterinarians, one secretary, an accountant, three laymen and a medical technician. Our client list grew to include the Borden Company, General Foods, Swanson & Sons, Anheuser-Busch, Bristol-Meyers and White Laboratories. It was time for another expansion."

Mark's decision was to move the laboratory and its test animals completely away from the hospital. He found an 18-acre tract near Metuchen, New Jersey, four miles from the Raritan Hospital. The site was ideal and the property was in the hands of the town treasurer, apparently for non-payment of taxes.

"The treasurer's office told me they would be happy to sell the land for development since that would put it back on the tax rolls again," Mark recalled. "I offered $1,800 in cash, a sum of $100 per acre, and the deal was closed immediately."

A flurry of construction followed. A well was drilled at the site and a kennel building with outdoor exercise yards erected for housing 30 animals. At the hospital a large, new garage building was added and the old garage was expanded to house a new food kitchen and chemistry laboratory.

Mark decided the new Raritan Laboratories was a major benchmark in his career and arranged for an elaborate dedication ceremony as construction was completed. The ceremony was held on the afternoon of April 19, 1946, and nearly 100 persons attended. Mark's files yielded a copy of the short address with which he opened the festivities:

"Just 10 years ago the American Animal Hospital Association organized a Committee on Foods to bring some action to bear on the problem of improving dog foods through study and research and perhaps by establishing federal standards.

"On the first committee appointed were some of our guests today. First, Dr. J. V. LaCroix, treasurer of the American Veterinary

Medical Association, editor of the NORTH AMERICAN VETERINARIAN, and a well-known small animal practitioner from Evanston, Illinois. Also, Dr. Charles Bower of Topeka, Kansas, past president of the American Veterinary Medical Association. Doctors LaCroix, Bower and I constituted the first Committee on Foods of the two veterinary associations.

"In addition, several nutritionists were invited to cooperate with the committee in formulating a testing procedure for dog foods then on the market. The group's first meeting was held in the Alumni House at Rutgers University. Among those who attended was Dr. Walter G. Russell of the New Jersey Agricultural Experiment Station, who is with us today. Another member of the group was the man who is to speak to us today.

"Before I introduce him, I would like to explain that this new laboratory is the outgrowth of a decade of work on trying to improve the diet—and the health—of companion animals, the pet dogs and cats most people take for granted. On this tract we propose to construct additional animal housing units similar to the ones you have toured here today. On the site where we are sitting we shall build the new administration building for Raritan Laboratories. The driveway will enter from the paved road from Metuchen over which we drove to arrive here."

Mark then introduced as a "friend, colleague and always willing helper," the main speaker of the day. He was Dr. George R. Cowgill, faculty member of the Yale University School of Medicine and editor of the Journal of Nutrition. Dr. Cowgill had taught Mark how to detect vitamin deficiencies in animals.

The rosy future for Mark's work on canine diets predicted that day by Dr. Cowgill and others at the ceremony still was years away, but the new laboratory complex was a major step forward.

The milepost of Raritan Laboratories is ranked high in importance by Dr. Morris in his career—and his creation of the eventual line of Prescription Diets for animals, now marketed around the world. But Mark ranks just as high in overall importance the first luncheon he ever had with a blind man and his dog.

Mark's years-long association with Morris Frank of Seeing Eye, Inc., and with Buddy II, Morris Frank's guide dog, began with a phone call from Dr. J.V. LaCroix.

"I'm dropping in on you to say hello tomorrow morning on my way to Morristown for a session with some of the people at Seeing

Buddy, the guide dog for Morris Frank of Seeing Eye, Inc., Morristown, New Jersey. Buddy was the dog for which the original Prescription Diet k/d was prepared by hand and later canned.

Eye," LaCroix said. "How about taking a few hours off and riding over there with me? They've invited me and a guest for lunch and I'd like you to be the guest."

The year was 1939 and Mark, aware of the pioneer work being done by Seeing Eye in providing guide dogs for blind persons, accepted the luncheon invitation. He told Louise that "this is a chance to learn more." There was no advance hint that the blind man he was about to meet would play a role in creation of Prescription Diets and even in the founding of Morris Animal Foundation.

"This was my first experience of its kind," Mark told Louise later. "It was a strange feeling, entering that big dining room at Seeing Eye and realizing that most of the people at the other tables were blind and that each one had a large dog lying at his or her feet. It was weird, except that when I closed my eyes the hum of voices and even the bits of conversation I could hear seemed perfectly normal."

Discussion at the table occupied by Mark, Dr. LaCroix, Morris Frank and staff members centered around what Dr. LaCroix might be able to do through his publication and others he was connected with "to encourage more knowledgeable care on the part of veterinarians for the Seeing Eye dogs being brought to them in numbers by blind persons." The emphasis was a claim by Morris Frank that "a lot of the vets we're doing business with don't seem to understand how to deal with blind people and their dogs and all we are asking is that someone like you give us help in putting out information along this line."

It was Mark's first impression that the young blind man, Morris Frank, knew what he wanted and how to get it. It was an impression that time would prove eminently correct.

Frank, 31 years old when Mark met him, had been involved with the Seeing Eye movement since he was 19.

It was in 1927, the year after Mark graduated from Cornell and began his practice, that a youthful Morris Frank had taken pen in hand to write a letter of destiny to one Dorothy Harrison Wood Eustis. Mrs. Eustis, who would become founder of the Seeing Eye on January 29, 1929, had written an article for the November, 1927 issue of the *Saturday Evening Post* magazine telling of the happy experience of blind German veterans of World War I in using specially trained dogs as guide animals. Mrs. Eustis, member of an old Philadelphia "mainline" family and described widely as "an aristocrat imbued with the work ethic" was the owner of Fortunate Fields, a plush kennel operation in Switzerland which had been breeding German shepherds for work with police, border patrols, prisons and the military. The *Saturday Evening Post* article was the result of interest by Mrs. Eustis in guide dog work by German shepherds which would lead within two years to her founding of Seeing Eye in New Jersey.

Morris Frank had been born in Nashville, Tennessee, in 1908 as the third and much the youngest son of well-to-do parents. His mother had been blinded by an accident and young Frank lost one eye in a horseback riding brush with a tree limb and the second at age 16 in a schoolyard fisticuffs mishap. The youngster, whose earliest memories were of guiding his blind mother, was himself totally blind as a teenager.

Frank, an outspoken rebel at times, had turned down a job making brooms to become an insurance salesman at age 19. He had taught himself Braille and was accustomed to hiring young blacks in Nashville to act as guides. One of them had quit suddenly during an argument with Morris Frank over a raise and had left him stranded on a busy street just before he learned of the article on guide dogs in the *Saturday Evening Post*.

Morris Frank's letter to Mrs. Eustis about her article entitled "The Seeing Eye" was rambling and almost without punctuation, according to facsimilies of it published later in a history of Seeing Eye, Inc. The Frank letter drew this further comment in the history: "Its opening sentence gives the wrong title for the article ("The Seeing Eye") and although the writer mentions that he would like to 'forward this work in this country' this could hardly be considered a pledge of commitment, especially in the context of the structureless sentence in which it appears."

But the Seeing Eye history, written by blind Peter Brock Putnam and published in 1979 by E.B. Dutton of New York City under the title "Love in the Lead," continues to this conclusion about Morris Frank and his letter:

"For some reason, Dorothy Eustis, herself a stickler for clarity of expression, sensed something special in this garbled message from a nineteen-year-old in Nashville.

"Was it second sight, dumb luck, or Divine Providence? Whatever it was, it is certain that of all the people who had written her, no one was so well equipped for the role he would play in the creation of The Seeing Eye as Morris Frank."

Mrs. Eustis eventually met Morris Frank and decided that "he wants a dog, not only for himself but for all blind Americans—and he is willing to work for it.'' She financed a trip to Switzerland for young Frank so he and Buddy could be trained together. And when Seeing Eye was founded, Morris Frank became its official roving ambassador. Until his retirement in 1956 from the school he had helped found, Morris Frank traveled tens of thousands of miles each year across the U.S. and Canada helping to build Seeing Eye. The history calls him ''a brash rebel who broke down barriers.'' It says his one constant goal was to aid in ''a stampeding of people who had been locked up in the dark and now were rushing for the light, the freedom of movement and the changed lifestyle a guide dog could give them.''

Mark knew little of the remarkable background of Morris Frank as he joined him for lunch. Here, he quickly decided, was a bright and brash blind man who knew what he wanted and appeared to be confident of getting whatever it was.

''He showed no sign that he was worried about a handicap,'' Mark told Louise later. ''He seemed to view Buddy II, his dog and the successor to the first seeing eye dog in America, as the great equalizer.

''It was an amazing thing in that dining hall to see this group of dogs stretching out comfortably under those tables with no difficulties between any of them. They all behaved perfectly while these blind people were eating their lunch. As lunch ended, we got up and Morris Frank suddenly told Dr. LaCroix that he wanted a good veterinarian to examine his dog, Buddy II.''

Dr. LaCroix asked what the trouble was and the answer was quick and complete. ''He doesn't seem to be working right on the harness. He seems to be less strong on his back legs than he should be. And as I feel his back up there, his skin and hair, something just doesn't feel quite right.''

Dr. LaCroix, a celebrated small animal veterinary expert in his own right, led the way into a hall and swiftly examined the guide dog. Then he turned to the blind man with a smile and said:

''Morris, I cannot advise you what's best for this dog because I do not have enough information on the animal to speak intelligently. But standing right here beside you is a man who can find out exactly what is wrong and what needs to be done. I can't.''

Morris Frank seemed to ponder for a moment, then turned to Mark with a small bow and flipped salute and said, ''If Doc LaCroix says you are the man, you are the man. What shall we do?''

Mark told Morris Frank about his Raritan Hospital for Animals a few miles away and his laboratory work, with Dr. LaCroix inserting sentences of praise for Mark's pioneering accomplishments. The blind man said his wife was sighted and could drive him and Buddy to the hospital that afternoon.

When the couple and the guide dog arrived, Mark explained he would require several hours for the examination.

"I told them it would involve a check on the volume of urine and its specific gravity and that I would need blood samples to see if the dog was storing nitrogen due to kidney inefficiency. I explained that I had one of the few laboratories in the country where that kind of work could be done."

Pressed by Morris Frank, Mark finally said that it would be best if he kept Buddy overnight at the hospital to insure the thoroughness of the needed tests. The reaction was instant and angry.

"I can't do that," snapped the blind man. "The hell with that. I won't leave Buddy in any hospital. We have to find a better way."

Mark carefully went over once again the details of the examination he planned and the steps it would require. Morris Frank listened carefully, asked if the tests could be speeded in any way, then finally said:

"Well, I'll sleep right here in the kennel with Buddy. Fix me some kind of a bed and I'll stay right here with him."

Mark, realizing that he faced an iron stubborn will, offered a compromise. "We have a spare room upstairs," he said. "The dog can sleep right under your bed. All I need to make sure is that the dog has not been out overnight. We'll start on the blood analysis now and take a urine sample in the morning. It really is quite simple and this should work out perfectly."

It did. The Morris Franks dined with Mark and Louise, retired early and were given the verdict the next noon. Buddy II was suffering from failing kidneys.

"Is that a death sentence?" Morris Frank was blunt.

"You've come to the right place," Mark answered in his best professional tone. "This hospital not only is among the first in the country to work out this test, but it also has the medical answer to your problem."

Mark explained that the medical profession had found no drug or potion which would be of the slightest use in treating Buddy. He said the problem was to remove stress from the kidney and aid it in handling nitrogen. He explained that after months and years of experiments he had perfected a dry, basic type of dog food to which the owner could add at home specific portions of cooked whole egg, cottage cheese and some form of meat. The Franks and Buddy II left with several five-pound bags of Raritan Ration B, the cereal mixture which Mark soon would evolve into Prescription Diet k/d®.

The blind man was back in less than a week.

"Buddy seems a little better," he acknowledged. "But if you think I'm going to keep on doing this, you are out of your mind, just crazy. In the first place, my job requires that I do a lot of traveling. And in the second place, I can't see to mix this stuff. If it must be mixed, doctor, you are going to have to mix it here yourself."

Mark broke the silence that followed. "I'm glad Buddy seems to be better. And, yes, this stuff, as you call it, needs additives to make it a complete diet. If we do the mixing here, we end up with a moist mixture and that would spoil quickly if you took it on the road with you. Cottage cheese, eggs and meat need refrigeration."

The blind man thought that over briefly, then asked quietly if there was any solution to the problem Dr. Morris could come up with.

"Well," said Mark, "if it was canned it would keep."

"All right," Frank said, "you put it in a can."

It wasn't an order. It was a challenge and Mark agreed at once that he would see what could be done. Within days, canned Ration B was being turned out in the hospital kitchen in glass mason jars by Mrs. Louise Morris and a helper, using the same procedure Louise had learned from her mother for canning tomatoes.

Morris Frank, at first delighted with the new arrangement, began to complain a few months later when several of the glass jars arrived in cracked condition at hotels in distant cities where he was touring and making speeches on behalf of Seeing Eye.

"This arrangement is not working," the blind man announced on a sudden visit to Mark and Louise. "I'm going to poison that dog or feed it ground glass by mistake. I can't see, remember? You've got to start putting this dog food up in tin cans so it can follow me around the country and be in perfect shape when Buddy needs it." Mark countered this thrust as best he could.

"This country is at war," he reminded Morris Frank. "Tin is rationed. I can't get any tin cans. I don't have any legal right to purchase tin cans as containers for pet food."

"Don't worry," replied Morris Frank. "If that's all that's stopping you, I'll get you the tin cans and some canning equipment as well. No problem. We've got to quit using that damn glass."

In a few days a semitrailer truck backed up to the back door at the Raritan Hospital for Animals. It bore New York plates and the driver quickly unloaded several thousand tin cans, a small, manually operated canning machine complete with instructions. There also was a pressure cooker of the size used in institutional kitchens. The shipment was courtesy of Morris Frank, the driver said. It came from a national corporation based in New York City. Morris Frank and his dog Buddy were friends of the company president.

And thus did Dr. Mark L. Morris become a canner of prepared diets for dogs. He began with a single customer and one guide dog and has remarked that "It's true, the blind shall lead."

The original canning machine long has been on display in the offices of Mark Morris Associates, in Topeka, Kansas, headquarters for new product research and development and quality control of Prescription Diets. It is a sort of monument to the genesis of a multimillion-dollar product line. The little pressure cooker is still being used to sterilize small batches of experimental formulations of new dietary foods for dogs and cats.

9

The Making of a Market

Time for one of the major decisions of his life arrived in the summer of 1948 for Mark L. Morris, Veterinarian.

"Things are getting out of hand," Mark confided to Louise during an early summer dinner-for-two at the Buff and Blue Tearoom in Highland Park. Mark had arranged for a few hours off from the busy rounds of Raritan Hospital for Animals for the two of them. He was troubled, and it helped to talk things over quietly with Louise. The world always looked a little easier to handle afterwards.

"We're working that little canning machine and that pressure cooker around the clock now," Mark continued. "We've got three shifts a day in the canning area, and it isn't enough. The demand is getting bigger than anything we even optimistically can hope to supply. We've got to make up our minds whether we're running an animal hospital or a canning plant. And I don't see any way we can do both."

There was no way they could handle both enterprises at one time but the realization of that lay ahead. At the moment was the problem involved in the fact a clientele of one blind man and his dog had grown beyond belief for Mark's new canine kidney diet.

The original Raritan Ration B, developed as a dry mix to which cottage cheese, eggs and meat could be added, had become first "kidney diet" and later k/d in the lexicon of staff and kitchen workers at Raritan Hospital. A newer product of Mark's laboratory work, originally called Ration C, also was in production. It was a high-protein mixture designed for growing puppies, pregnant female dogs and canine patients with a need for a rich diet. It was named p/d® for "puppy or pregnancy" diet. By this time the phrase Prescription Diets had evolved to describe the two food products. They were available only on the recommendation of Mark or one of a growing number of veterinarians who learned of canine health results stemming from the products and had prevailed on Mark to make a supply available to them and their clients.

"It all began—the steadily-rising demand for k/d and p/d—after patients at Raritan Hospital were sent home," Mark often explained. "Their symptoms had vanished and, without exception, the canine patients we released were back in good health and looking every bit of it. But more and more, the patients with kidney problems would start failing in a week or so after returning to their homes, and their owners would bring them back to the hospital in bad shape, vomiting and with diarrhea. It was easy to pinpoint what was happening."

The problem, Mark and his laboratory aides were able to establish, was that the average dog owner of the time was feeding the pet canned commercial dog food then available on grocery store shelves at less than 10 cents a can. Tests by the Joint Committee on Foods of the American Animal Hospital Association and the American Veterinary Medical Association had established that much of this commercial food was made largely of leftover packing house waste material such as snouts, gristle and skin and contained little real nourishment.

"We'd get these repeat kidney patients back into shape and when we sent them home we'd send the original dry Ration B food home with them," Mark said. "When we started putting the refined Ration B into tin cans for Morris Frank and Buddy II, we started sending spare tins home with dog owners, and repeat business began to climb."

Then there were veterinarians on the staff of the Raritan Hospital who started recommending first k/d and then p/d to their veterinary friends. Repeat business stemmed from these sources also, and a snowball effect was the result.

"We have tons of raw ingredients in our hospital basement and we're mixing that stuff with a cement mixer to keep things rolling," Mark told Louise at the let's-talk-it-over dinner. "There's no way we can expand on what we're producing with the space and tools we have. The time has come. We must do something."

Louise, ever calm when those around her showed signs of losing their cool, hesitated only briefly. "All you need is a specialist," she said. "Look at it this way. You're a doctor, a veterinarian skilled in the fields of nutrition and diagnosis. You are a specialist, but not a packing house executive or even a trained food distributor. You have a choice. Either learn a new business or get some help from an expert in food canning and food distributing."

There was a solution—and Louise made it sound easy. The first attempt to line up a packing plant to produce k/d and p/d came unexpectedly at a meeting a few weeks later of the American Animal Hospital Association in Atlanta, Georgia, which Mark attended.

A fellow delegate was Dr. William Irwin, a Tulsa, Oklahoma, veterinarian who had become a major customer of Mark's limited output of therapeutic canine diets. Orders for cases of k/d and p/d had become even more frequent in recent months since Dr. Leroy Atkinson, after several years as one of Mark's colleagues at the Raritan Hospital, had left to join Dr. Irwin's staff in Tulsa. Mark confided to the two veterinarians of his plans to turn production over to a qualified packing house, if he could find one.

"We may have just the man for you," Dr. Irwin announced. "I'll set up a meeting."

The meeting was held in the lobby of the Atlanta Hotel after the convention adjourned. With Dr. Irwin was a veterinarian, Dr. Pedrick, from the Tulsa area, who had given up his practice to devote full time to canning and distributing a horsemeat-type dog food he had developed for the general commercial pet food market.

"The man seemed to be interested, but he showed little grasp of exactly what I was talking about," Mark recalled. "I explained to him that I had the formulations, the specifications, and all of the information needed for marketing the products. I told him all I needed was a plant which could can the food according to my specifications and then, having put it in containers, get it into packing cases and put it on a dock so I could have someone pick it up."

Dr. Pedrick said he would think it over and arranged a second meeting with Mark and Dr. Irwin for a few days later in Tulsa. He said he had little appetite for the big marketing job such a venture might require, but it sounded interesting and he would "think about it."

Mark was packing his bag for a quick trip to Tulsa when the telephone rang. It was Dr. Pedrick on the phone. He had been to Washington, D.C., after the meeting in Atlanta, and had signed a contract with the federal government to pack horse meat for shipment to Greece under the Marshall Plan. It would require all his facilities. Mark had struck out.

A death in the family called Mark back to the Denver area of his native Colorado before he had time to fret about the lost potential contract with the Oklahoma canning company. After the funeral, he decided to return home via Topeka, Kansas, and "take care of a chore I had been postponing as executive secretary of the still active Joint Committee on Foods of the two national veterinary associations."

The chore involved a detailed inspection of the Hill Packing Co., an organization which carried the tested-and-approved designation of the Joint Committee on the labels of its popular brand of commercial dog food. Mark's job was to check sources of supply for the horse meat which was a prime ingredient of the dog food, verify sanitation measures at the packing facility and inspect laboratory work.

Mark worked through the morning, then accepted an invitation to lunch in downtown Topeka with Don Hogue, a vice president of Hill Packing Co. and an engineering graduate of the University of Kansas. Hogue was in charge of personnel at the cannery and packing house, which was slaughtering up to 250 horses per day at the time in addition to the dog food production. Most of the horse meat was being sent directly to Europe for human consumption in the wake of World War II.

With Hogue were C.V. Black, executive in charge of merchandising for Hill Packing Co., and two aides in the Hill marketing and distribution department.

"It was a pleasant lunch, and it dawned on me gradually that this was the opportunity I had been looking for," Mark told Louise later. "I found an opening in the conversation and mentioned, I hope with a casual little shrug, that I was looking for an organization that could pack a limited amount of specialty foods for animals that I was preparing in my hospital in New Jersey for a few veterinarians. They seemed to show interest, so I laid out my entire plan. I remember, I assured them they probably could turn out enough k/d and p/d in an hour or two at the end of any day to last me a month."

The luncheon ended with a pledge from Hogue and Black to "take it up seriously with Mr. Hill." They asked Mark to outline his proposal in writing and turn it over to them before he left Topeka.

"They made it very plain that Hill Packing Co. actually was ruled by one man, founder Burton Hill," Mark told Louise. "They said it should be called Mr. Hill, Inc. But they also said he was fair in business dealings and that they believed it could be worked out."

Back at the Raritan Hospital, Mark began to watch the mail as days passed following his return from Topeka. Then one morning came the awaited letter from Don Hogue of Hill Packing Co. Yes, Mr. Hill was interested. The plant did not make it a practice to engage in con-

Burton Hill, founder and president of Hill Packing Company, who agreed to produce, can and market Prescription Diets according to specifications of Dr. Morris

tract packing and canning work, but Mr. Hill was willing to make an exception in this case. Mr. Hill, the letter said, felt that the veterinary profession had been very good to him in the matter of his nationally marketed dog food and if a product of the sort I outlined was needed by the veterinary profession he would be glad to help. The letter also made it plain that Mr. Hill was especially pleased that the new product would be marketed only through veterinarians and thus would not show up on grocery shelves in competition with his own brand of dog food. Mr. Hill, the letter concluded, was ready to look at a proposed contract for production between Mark L. Morris D.V.M. and Hill Packing Co.

Mark promptly called on the biggest artillery of his knowledge in the legal profession. He asked Judge Klemmer Kalteissen of New Brunswick, a friend and a jurist and lawyer of renown in the New Jersey-New York area, to handle the job for him.

By the time Mark presented the contract to Burton Hill for signature "it was a classic," in Mark's words. "Judge Kalteissen had studied my situation carefully and he knew exactly what I desired. He also seemed to be tuned in on what Mr. Hill's interests might be and what he would and would not agree to."

Many millions of sales dollars and more than thirty five years later, the original contract drafted by the New Brunswick judge was still in force with only minor, updating revisions over a span of three separate ownerships of Hill Packing Co. Its original unique thrust remains intact.

"That thrust was that Prescription Diets, as we agreed to call the line, were therapeutic and not merely dog food," Mark explained. "Prescription Diets would be sold only by or on the prescription of a licensed veterinarian. The product at no time would be sold in grocery stores or pet shops. There would be no confusion. The products p/d and k/d and others to be developed, would be marketed solely through veterinarians."

There were other classic provisions in the contract. To Mark was delegated the exclusive right of research and development of new products. Mark also retained the critical power of quality control. And to him was left the task of making certain in any manner he wished that the veterinary profession was educated in the use of the products.

"The Hill people agreed not only to can Prescription Diets to my specifications, but to handle the distribution" Mark said. "This opened up an immediate potential national market, since Hill already was selling its own brand of dog food across the country. They also agreed to handle basic advertising and promotion, using anything we came up with from the veterinary angle as well as their own methods. It seemed to be a perfect setup.''

A key clause in the contract specified that Hill Packing Co. would not only handle distribution and sales but would be responsible for all collection and would pay Mark, who signed the contract as an individual, a specified royalty on every can sold.

"I knew these royalty payments would be very small at first," Mark said. "I was counting on the future—and I was right."

With royalty checks of any size still far in the future, Mark took on personally the task of supervising the initial production run of k/d in the Hill Packing Co. plant in Topeka, Kansas. It was mid-October 1948.

"Burton Hill had assigned his plant superintendent, a man named D. H. Phillips, to work with me, Mark recalled. "Phillips made it plain that, at least at first, we'd be better off approaching this as a hand-work job than trying to use the plant itself. I agreed and we mixed that first batch in metal tubs, using scoop shovels and an old platform scale."

When the initial freshly-cooked batch of k/d started flowing into waiting tin cans, Mark could tell at a glance that something was wrong.

"The stuff was sticky and it wouldn't flow properly," he said. "My mind flashed back to the early days when we first tried putting the diet up in glass jars for Morris Frank. We ran into the stickiness problem then, and it got so bad that it adhered to the roof of the mouth of the dog we fed it to. I'll never forget his contortions as he tried either to swallow it or spit it out and found he couldn't do either."

On that hectic occasion, after Mark had solved the dog's problem by using his fingers to recover the food, basic changes had been made in the formula. Now, obviously, something was missing or something new had been added.

"It took three runs, two of which we had to throw away before I was able to adjust the formula to the Hill Packing Co. equipment," Mark remembers. "But after that it settled into a routine and we got into production. The first shipments went from Topeka to the following: Morris Frank at Seeing Eye, Inc., which was using large amounts of k/d to ensure the health of its numerous guide dogs; Raritan Hospital's clients; Bill Irwin in Tulsa, Oklahoma; and Dr. Joseph

Bogue of Wichita, Kansas, to whom we had been sending hand-packed food from the Raritan Hospital.''

Then followed a hectic series of years indelibly engraved in the memory of Mark L. Morris, D.V.M.

For a brief time after signing of the Hill production contract and the beginning of shipments, Mark held to a belief that it would be possible to operate his new dog food business by remote control.

''The center of my attention was in New Brunswick and that area of New Jersey,'' he explained. ''My family was there and so were my hospital and my fast-growing Raritan Laboratory operations. It seemed to me that I could more or less limit my part of the food production to routine testing for quality control. I arranged for regular sample shipments from Topeka to my laboratory. I believed the Hill people could fill the orders and mail me my royalty checks. It wasn't that simple.''

First came nightmares revolving around leaky tins and spoiled merchandise. Then there were mounting problems of product quality. Soon it developed that there might be errors in bookkeeping. And always there was the problem of convincing the veterinary profession that a can of dog food could be used to help cure a sick animal.

''There were problems about trademark registration, problems about advertising, problems about distribution,'' Mark recalled. ''And, of course, there was the problem that our operation was just a small nuisance to most of the Hill people.''

By comparison to the already growing output of Prescription Diets, the regular business of Hill Packing Co. in 1949 was a giant trying to babysit with an infant. Thousands of cases of horse meat packed for human consumption in Europe were rolling out of the plant weekly. The dog food production for the commercial market far overshadowed Mark's operation. The attitude was growing that ''this may be more trouble than it's worth to us.'' But the Morris-Hill contract was solid and production of Prescription Diets continued.

In August, 1949, Mark's worries over the new food business in Topeka were put on a back shelf for the moment by an invitation for a trip to Europe because of his Raritan Laboratory Tests. Forrest Mars, the industrialist who headed the successful Mars Candy Company and owned a major rice company, had begun manufacturing pet food in England. He asked Mark to join him in London for a conference on possible use of whale meat and the flesh of other fish as a source of protein in his pet food line.

"He offered free transportation for me and my wife as part of the consulting fee, so we accepted," Mark said. "We flew to England, where Mr. Mars put us up on an estate outside of London and gave us the services of a chauffeur. It was pretty grand and when my work with Mars was completed, we decided to fly to Germany."

Mark's reason for the Germany trip was a visit to the villages of Oberzell and Argenstein, the childhood homes of Louise's mother and father. The couple flew to Frankfurt in what was newly West Germany in 1949, then boarded a train. Mark described the trip this way in a letter to relatives:

"The best we could do was third class and we had to get on that train before daybreak. We finally arrived in the little town of Schlictern and ran into an old chap with an even older automobile who agreed to drive us the fifteen miles over country roads to the little village of Oberzell. We bounced over the hilly roads of Hesson, an area which adjoins Bavaria, rattled over a shaky bridge and down a winding street covered with cobblestones. The driver knew our destination and finally pulled up in front of a two-story house where members of the Baier family, Louise's kin, still lived.

"I'll always cherish a photo we have of Louise's grandmother herding a flock of geese with a cane. The homes in that village were very close together, and always the barn either was under the house or right beside it. This served to create a blend of odors which clings in my memory. We saw overturned locomotives and heavy bomb damage on our way out of Frankfurt, but in the country there was no war damage. But the war had left its mark. Most of the homes were occupied by women and children only."

Mark went on to describe daily life in Oberzell in 1949.

"The old church still stands, untouched and in good repair both inside and out. On Saturday, the townspeople brush the streets clean with handmade brooms made of twigs from the plentiful trees. On Sunday morning, the wooden shoes so practical for the cobbled streets and rough hills are set aside and everyone puts on American-type shoes for going to church.

"The cattle, geese and goats are housed in the village and driven twice daily, back and forth, to the pasture land across a brook and up the hillside. The swine are housed beneath the houses or in barns beside them, as are rabbits and poultry. The people of Oberzell make their livings mostly from the soil, using the cows both for work and to produce milk, cream and butter for the family. Bread, made at home and called swatzbrod, and the meat, a German wurtz, are the basic diet.

"Veterinarians, who live nearby in larger towns, come to the village to care for the animals. They make the trip on motorcycles with their instruments and equipment strapped to their backs. I doubt that many American veterinarians would be capable of conducting a practice in this manner."

Returned from Europe, Mark and Louise plunged once again into the busy routine of operating an animal hospital, a fast-growing testing laboratory and a food packing business hundreds of miles to the west in Topeka. Mark soon was to envy the veterinarians of Oberzell in West Germany. They rode their motorcycles only a comparatively few miles each day on their rounds. Mark was becoming a weekly commuter to Kansas and back and soon the demand for travel would increase.

Sales of Prescription Diets were mounting steadily. But problems were piling up just as swiftly, most of which required his presence in Topeka. There were questions about product quality which had to be ironed out at the plant. There were questions about labels, product trademarks and registration in various states where sales were being made. And there were problems of bookkeeping and of making certain that Mark's mounting royalties were based on actual sales.

But most of all there was a growing realization that a continuing program of education was needed to spread the facts about Prescription Diets and their role in animal health to veterinarians not only across the United States but in neighboring Canada as well.

"There was a serious professional hazard with the rank and file of veterinarians which we did not anticipate," Mark recalled of this period in the early 1950s. "Veterinarians in general still did not realize that a can of dog food labelled Prescription Diet was something they could use on a therapeutic basis. To many of them, our approach seemed way out and ridiculous. They had been taught to treat sick animals with pharmaceuticals, biologicals and with nursing, rest, some fluids and, in most cases, endless enemas. They had no knowledge of the application of nutrition to the management of disease.

"To make it worse, the canned dog food industry of those years had anything but a shining image with professional veterinarians. They knew that the market had been filled with a lot of very poor quality products. What it amounted to was that packing companies were filling out their day by running tankage and scraps through and calling it dog food.

"Consequently, for us to go into the market and try to start selling a quality product with a price tag several times higher than grocery store canned dog food was difficult. And when we told them our higher-priced product had curative and therapeutic value in addition, it sounded to them like the promotion of a veterinarian who wanted to make a fast dollar.

"We did not have these barriers with the few customers we had at the outset. They were veterinarians who had worked with me in the laboratory or who had full knowledge of the research that had gone into Prescription Diets before we started mass production. These people really believed that miracles could be accomplished in animal health through proper, scientific nutrition.

"But we were finding out that the rank and file of the veterinary profession, the very people we were counting on as a market, thought this Prescription Diet business might be a bunch of hokum. To put it very frankly, some of them believed that they were being hoodwinked for a fast buck. And they were saying just that."

What to do? Mark's solution was simple and direct. He and Louise decided to take their message into the field, to meet with veterinarians and veterinary students and educators wherever and whenever they could and "spread the message."

Mark tried out his grass roots plan at a meeting of the Westchester County Veterinary Medical Association in New York. Both k/d and p/d were available in the area through Hill Packing Co. distributors, but acceptance had been slow.

Mark, personally acquainted with many veterinarians in this area, managed to win a place on the program to talk about the use of dietary animal foods. His brief talk was followed by an endless stream of questions from the veterinarians. Mark fielded all of them and realized that he had found a way to break down the resistance to his products by spelling out to fellow professionals how and why the foods had been developed and adding specific case histories of animal illnesses he personally had conquered with proper food instead of pills and fluids.

"Out of that session came a realization," Mark said. "We needed to develop a professional literature program and, to do it, we needed to contact in person as many veterinary professionals across the U.S. as was humanly possible."

Within weeks Mark was booked almost solidly for personal appearances at local and state veterinary meetings. He visited veterinary

Mark hit the road, speaking to veterinarians and explaining the philosophy of nutritional therapy and therapeutic values. Photo was at White Plains, New York, on August 10, 1950. He always carried a small audiograph with him for recording questions from the practitioners. This information later was incorporated into a question-and-answer booklet.

colleagues in all parts of the nation, talking to students and faculty groups of any size. He spent hours with salesmen of Hill Packing Co., educating them and helping them answer the questions of skeptical veterinarians they were calling on regularly.

Between speaking engagements Mark made it a practice to tour sections of the country by automobile, stopping in central towns to talk to veterinarians personally. Louise took time off from her duties of running the hospital, supervising laboratory work and handling everything from payrolls to supply orders to join Mark on most of his trips.

"One of our favorite activities was to arrange an informal dinner in a major town for all the veterinarians of that area," Mark recalled. "Always I managed to deliver my story and to ask for questions. And always the questions came in a flood. We made it a practice to use a recorder at most of the meetings and were able to take down most of the questions and answers. From this we started producing a booklet which was eventually called '174 Questions and Answers,' a carefully edited collection of the key questions being asked out in the field, with answers for all of them."

At one point Mark wrote home to Louise that "We've found there is nothing a veterinarian likes better than questions and answers."

The sales curve continued to crawl upward, but Mark was convinced that the upward movement was not swift enough. Files of his correspondence of the early 1950s show many letters to Burton Hill, head of the packing company. Excerpts from the letters show clearly the urgency and persistence with which Mark was carrying on his campaign to create a national market for Prescription Diets:

"February 28, 1950 to Mr. Hill: We now have had sufficient experience in the marketing of Prescription Diets that some estimate can be made on the volume that should be sold very easily on a monthly basis in the United States. A study of the records shows that a conservative estimate would list at least 100 animal hospitals which should be averaging at least 50 cases each per month, or a total of 5,000 cases. Conservatively, there are at least 500 more animal hospitals which should be ordering at least 20 cases each per month, a total of 10,000 cases.

"The mailing list in your office at present contains the names of 2,000 veterinarians who have shown an interest in Prescription Diets and have requested bulletins. If we deduct the 600 listed above, that leaves 1,400 veterinarians who should be using 10 cases each per month. If we add another 1,000 cases per month for miscellaneous veterinarians who should prescribe but do not hospitalize patients, we have a total market at the moment of 30,000 cases per month.

"Each of the 30,000 cases would contain 24 one-pound tins for a total of 720,000 pounds of Prescription Diets sold per month. But if you examine the report for the most recent month, you will find that total sales amounted to 2,712 cases or 65,000 pounds. What plans do you have in mind for effectively servicing the market outlined above?"

"March 1, 1950 to Mr. Hill: On March, 9, Mrs. Morris and I plan to leave New Jersey by car and drive via Topeka to San Diego, California, up the coast as far as Seattle, back to Denver for the national meeting of the American Animal Hospital Association, returning to Topeka in early May after attending several regional meetings of veterinarians. I should be in Topeka March 18-20 and would appreciate the opportunity to spend some time in conference with you."

This letter listed nine topics to be discussed, most of them dealing with future sales and merchandising plans on the part of Hill Packing Co. Two of them went directly to the point: "What further plans do you have for effectively selling these products to veterinarians and their clients?" and "How long will it be before an effective and efficient job of merchandising can be done?"

"July 17, 1950 to Mr. Hill: I received a letter from Clarence Black (Hill Packing Co. vice president) regarding the appointment of Carpel's Inc. as distributor in the Baltimore-Washington, D.C., area for Prescription Diets.

"I spoke to Joseph Carpel in Baltimore to ascertain what plans had been formulated to follow the sales work in his area. He said Mr. Black had sent a letter to all veterinarians in the region announcing that Prescription Diets now were available through Carpel's. I asked what plans they had in mind for contacting veterinarians. He said they had none and were counting on Mr. Black's letter to do the job.

"I told him I had a lot of experience in following the results obtained by distributors and that I knew the Black letter was only their introduction, a mere announcement of their appointment. I said it was their signal to get busy and sell, to start calling on veterinarians. I told him about the success produced by personal follow-up and our question and answer service in New York and Philadelphia and suggested that he take a day off and come to New Brunswick so we could go over the Prescription Diet program in detail and he could become familiar with the problems he might face and the answers to those problems. He agreed to do this, and we have an appointment for July 29.

"The distributors need help. A letter announcing their appointment is not the answer. A definite plan should be worked out so that distributors can have more help from the home office.

"Also, I hope that before long it will be possible to do something about rusty tins. The shipments still contain a large number of cans with rusty tops."

As the months rolled by, problems kept mounting with sales and Mark found himself spending more and more time in Topeka. Quality control was a continuing problem and Mark felt also he could use the time he now was spending on commuting between New Jersey and Kansas to better advantage in the development of new products.

During the many periods of absence of Mark and Louise while they traveled around the country in their efforts to educate the profession in the use of dietary foods, the operation in New Jersey was essentially left in the hands of Edna Druiett.

Edna had worked for Mark Morris as secretary and office manager for many years; she was very capable in running the office and handled the banking, necessary correspondence, telephone calls, and made regular reports to Mark and Louise during their periods away from New Jersey.

In January, 1951 the Morris family moved to Topeka after leasing the facilities in New Jersey on a temporary basis. For a time the family was forced to "camp out" in a motel, but a house finally was found. Mark and Louise settled into the new lifestyle quickly. Daughter Ruth was a journalism student at the University of Colorado in Boulder, near Denver, and took the move in stride. But young Mark, Jr., was in the middle of his junior year in high school. For him the uprooting from the New Jersey scene and the friends who had been with him through grade school and junior high into high school was a disaster.

"Mark registered in Topeka and started school for the second half of the school year," his father wrote to friends at the time. "He came home the first day a very disappointed and disillusioned boy."

But the father's letter made it plain the tragedy of uprooting was only temporary for Mark, Jr.

"He had learned to play the saxophone pretty well and we suggested he try out for the music program in the Topeka High School," Mark, Sr., wrote. "They had a music director who was outstanding

Mark and Louise at home at their residence at 1500 MacVicker Street in Topeka in the fifties so young Mark applied for admission into the band, but they told him the alto saxophone chair was filled. The only opening was for a tenor sax. We asked Mark if he could switch. He said he could, so we traded in the alto sax and got him a tenor.''

In his senior year at Topeka High, Mark, Jr., was student director of the school symphony orchestra and was elected drum major of the marching band, which toured most of the state. He won the second lead in the senior class presentation of Brigadoon, the musical comedy, and finished with high grades. As his father put it: "He really fit in."

The move to Topeka, near the geographic center of the United States, proved to be a happy one also for Mark and his Prescription Diet business. It was easier to handle production, quality and sales problems from an office near the packing plant and Hill headquarters. It was also a good central point for Mark and Louise to make trips into the field for speeches at meetings and private sessions with area veterinarians.

Together they crisscrossed the nation by automobile, bringing to veterinarians the word that proper laboratory analysis combined with emphasis on proper nutrition could work a miracle in their practices. They covered many tens of thousands of miles on these trips and were rewarded by the steady upswing in Prescription Diet sales. The skeptics who at first were reluctant to view a can of dog food as a therapeutic agent were beginning to respond. The questions and answers, along with advertising of Prescription Diets by Hill Packing Co., in veterinary magazines, were beginning to score.

But Mark was formulating plans for opening a new campaign to break down the crumbling resistance against his nutrition credo in the veterinary profession. Bit by bit he gathered knowledge about the then new profession, public relations, born no one knows exactly when or where but emergent after World War II as an almost magic way to spread the word about something new, influence public opinion and generally promote any desired image in chosen right places.

In November 1954, Mark signed a contract with the Denver based firm of William Kostka & Associates, at the time an unchallenged leader in public relations headed by a former New York City newsman and ex-editor of *Look* magazine, aided by a young and aggressive staff.

The unique contract specified that work by Kostka & Associates on the Prescription Diets account would be centered around Ruth Morris, Mark's daughter, who had been working for a California

After moving to Topeka, the family usually returned to New Jersey in the Christmas season to visit Louise's relatives and to check on the hospital which they still owned and leased to another veterinarian. At time of this photo Ruth was working in Denver, Mark, Jr., was in Cornell University and Louise and Mark were living in Topeka in the fifties.

newspaper following her graduation from the University of Colorado with a degree in journalism—and a campus beauty crown won as an undergraduate. She was eager to learn the new field of public relations and equally eager to join the family business as a full-fledged working partner.

The Prescription Diets account was assigned space in the Kostka headquarters office on downtown Denver's California Street and chosen to supervise was Claude Ramsey, former executive of United Press International. He had returned to UPI after a World War II career which he began as an army draftee and ended with Ramsey as a decorated captain on the staff of General MacArthur on the Pacific Front. He recently had resigned a post as head of news coverage and bureau operations for UPI in South Texas and its Lower Rio Grande Valley bordering Mexico to seek a new postwar career in the field of public relations.

The assignment of Ruth Morris and Claude Ramsey was, as Mark wrote to a friend at the time, "rather large and involved." The main goal was to make more veterinarians feel kindly toward k/d and p/d but, in Mark's words, it was to include "development of a whole new area of professional and public relations as it may relate to veterinarians."

10

The Founding of a Foundation

"I believe that sums up pretty well the aims, the goals, we all have been talking about for months now," Mark said. "It adds up to a lovely dream, you know—but I think that working together we can make it come true. What do you say?"

Mark put the last page of his notes on the desk in front of him, leaned back in his chair and surveyed the group gathered in his office at the Raritan Hospital for Animals. Louise, his wife, smiled at him and nodded her head. The others seemed wrapped in thought. The sudden silence, Mark thought, was a good sign. He had them thinking.

It was early fall of 1948. The meeting in Mark's office had been called as a final prelude to the formal formation of a non-profit foundation to underwrite research into diseases threatening the health and life of America's pet population. Those present, in addition to Mark and his wife, were Dr. James B. Allison, Morris Frank, Agnes Fowler and Judge Klemmer Kalteissen.

Dr. Allison, Director of the Bureau of Biological Research at nearby Rutgers University, was a long time friend of the Morris family and had seen a key figure in the research program of animal nutrition conducted by Mark.

Morris Frank was the blind roving ambassador of Seeing Eye, Inc. of nearby Morristown, New Jersey, whose vocal demands for his guide dog for a diet he could carry safely around the country with him on speaking tours had led to the initial production of Mark's k/d Prescription Diet formula in tin cans.

Agnes Fowler was a board member-trustee of Seeing Eye, Inc. who specialized in overseeing the breeding program to keep the Seeing-Eye organization supplied with healthy German shepherds. Mark had worked closely with her for years on breeding-farm health problems. Miss Fowler was a vocal advocate of "more research into the ailments our dogs are picking up in the field."

Judge Kalteissen of New Brunswick was a friend of Mark's who was working with him on final wording of the soon-to-be-signed contract which would turn the Hill Packing Co. of Topeka, Kansas, into a producer and distributor-marketer of Mark's patented Prescription Diets for dogs.

The brief silence in Mark's office was broken by Dr. Allison. "I'm overwhelmed, Mark," he grinned. "You've done a great job in outlining a final form for the thinking we've all been doing. I think we should move ahead."

Similar comment erupted from the others. Mark's plan was adopted by unanimous voice vote and the Buddy Foundation was born.

"We agreed to name the foundation after Morris Frank's guide dog," Mark explained in detailing what had happened. "After all, it was Morris Frank who sort of shoved me into the Prescription Diet business. And it was Morris Frank who first started hammering at me not only about making k/d and p/d available to the thousands of dog owners across the country and around the world, but to join him in doing something about the fact nobody was doing much about the obvious shortage of scientific data for the diagnosis and treatment of the diseases of dogs. He said Seeing Eye, Inc. would be in no position to provide funds for a foundation to sponsor the needed research. But he said he was willing to help raise funds to support such a foundation and he got Miss Fowler to volunteer to help me set up the foundation."

The vote that fall day to establish the Buddy Foundation also named Mark as president, Dr. Allison as vice president and Louise as secretary-treasurer. Those three, along with Agnes Fowler, also were named directors, or trustees. In short weeks—on October 22, 1948—Judge Kalteissen and Mark concluded the deal with Hill Packing Co. for production of Prescription Diets. A clause inserted in the contract at Mark's request specified that a portion of Mark's royalty on each can produced and sold—exactly one-half cent per tin—would be accumulated in a separate fund and sent monthly without restrictions to the Buddy Foundation to help finance research.

That one-half cent royalty per can would provide the Buddy Foundation with "seed money" during its earliest days. Later, as production of Prescription Diets found an ever-wider market, the half-cent royalty in 20 years would amount to as much as $10,000 per month. At one-half cent per can, it took sales of 200 cans of k/d and p/d to bring $1 into the foundation's coffers. Revenues of $10,000 a month meant sales of 2,000,000 cans every 30 to 31 days of a product which initially had one blind man and his guide dog on the customer list.

Mark's seemingly impromptu speech from handwritten notes to his handpicked group on that fall day in Stelton (now Edison), New Jersey, had been carefully thought out. It laid the framework, with only minor changes down through the years in the interests of modernization and growing size, for what was to become the Morris Animal Foundation, an organization which in 1982 had its goal of $1 million a year in research grants in sight.

"Money for actual research into animal diseases is very slim and very hard to come by," Mark had told his small audience. "Federal funds, largely through the U.S. Department of Agriculture, mostly are spent on food animal research. The goal is to build up America's beef, pork, poultry and other key parts of the food supply. And other federal monies handled by the National Institute of Health are spent largely on investigations into disease in humans."

"The general agreement, even though there is no formal census, is that there are between 60 million and 70 million dogs, cats, non-working horses and zoo animals kept in this country as pets or companion animals. Something like 45 percent of all families have one or more dogs, and cat owners number at least one out of five in our population."

Pets, or rather, companion animals, serve a vital human need, Mark said. Pets contribute to good mental health for many thousands and help fill the emotional needs of many more. Pets serve as a surrogate family for the elderly and countless childless couples. In an impersonal, crime-ridden society, they are close companions and guardians of property and life.

Mark warmed to his subject: "Pets are the unique and perfect companions of growing children, and they provide not only companionship and learning for the young but unforgettable lessons in responsibility, humaneness and gentleness. Children learn biological realities from their pets. There can be no doubt that companion animals fill deep psychological needs for millions of persons. Their health, injuries and illnesses are of real and lasting human importance."

From the outset, the Foundation was dedicated to providing funds for research into companion animal ailments, their causes and cures, by qualified advanced students at the nation's veterinary colleges. Over a period of years, its aim was condensed to these words:

"A Credo: Clinical veterinary medicine can be no better than the research which supports it, and research can be no better than its personnel. The most important element in veterinary research is people, and the Foundation can make its greatest contribution to veterinary medicine by providing opportunities for students to become skilled in veterinary research."

In dedicating a portion of his income from Prescription Diets to the Foundation, Mark felt he was repaying at least in part, the persons and their advice and research, who had made contributions during his years of work on the formulas.

Years later, in an interview, Mark had these words of explanation about the birth of Prescription Diets and his work:

"The image that I wish to leave, is that the program which has emerged as Prescription Diets isn't something that happened in any one year. It isn't the product of my thinking alone. Far from it. There was an input of information and experience from many different sources. They all tied together to create the basic foundation—the knowledge, the expertise, the know-how and the marketing skill that was vital. I was very fortunate. I had support, and it was the experience and knowledge of many capable persons in various disciplines. They made the major contributions to the program."

The early history of the Buddy Foundation was not one of instant success and acceptance. On November 5, 1949, a year and a month after the original articles of incorporation for the non-profit organization were filed, the trustees formalized a grant of $1,000 in cash to the department of veterinary anatomy at Iowa State College. The document specified that the money would be used to finance "a study of the effects of methionine deficient diet upon wound healing and upon endocrine and other organs of the dog."

After some negotiations, the Buddy Foundation's check for $1,000 cleared the bank on February 20, 1950.

Files and records of the Buddy Foundation are somewhat vague about precisely what happened to the $1,000 grant. There are mentions of "personnel difficulties and conflicts." One entry points to "an unfortunate choice of personnel." No exact blame on any individual is ascribed. The final report to the Foundation from an official of Iowa State College reads in part: ". . . It is unfortunate that the situation is such that it has been impossible to reclaim any of the material, but I think you will agree with me that information gained from what was done would be on rather flimsy ground and would be quite vulnerable to criticism.''

The report concluded: "However, it is the opinion of the anatomy staff that the original experiment is most challenging and worthwhile. The problem presents many facets which involve not only anatomy and histology, but also surgery, physiology, chemistry and pathology.''

On April 11, 1950, the name of the Buddy Foundation was changed by a vote of the trustees to "The Mark L. Morris Nutrition Foundation.'' On that same date, a grant-in-aid in the amount of $1,000 was made to the Bureau of Biological Research of Rutgers University. It was earmarked to aid in an ongoing study of protein metabolism "especially as it applies to the utilization of protein by the sick dog.'' The check was dated May 4, 1950.

Less than a year later, on March 31, 1951, the Mark L. Morris Nutrition Foundation was legally dissolved and its funds were transferred to the account of the newly-incorporated Mark L. Morris Animal Memorial Foundation. Officers were unchanged, but an added trustee named to the board was Judge Klemmer Kalteissen of New Brunswick.

By now, income was higher, and so was outgo. On October 31, 1951, at the first meeting of the Board of Trustees of the new Mark L. Morris Animal Memorial Foundation a grant of $3,166 was made to the then Colorado Agricultural and Mechanical College of Fort Collins, Colorado, (Mark's alma mater and now Colorado State University). It was made to support a study entitled "a study of the effect in the beagle of two dietary levels of calcium and phosphorus.''

The initial trustee board meetings of the Foundation under its succession of names were very informal. Several were held in an automobile parked on the campus of Rutgers University, where board member Dr. James Allison was employed. Always in attendance, early days minutes reveal, were Dr. Morris, his wife and Agnes Fowler, as well as Dr. Allison. In 1952, Mark and Louise acquired a summer cabin on Coyote Mountain, near the resort village of Allenspark in the Colorado Rockies. Summer board meetings in years that followed often were held there and one meeting was conducted beside a lake in nearby Loveland, Colorado.

The word "Memorial" was dropped from the title in 1956 and the organization became the Morris Animal Foundation. Mark explained that the "Memorial" part of the name had become a burden.

"People wondered about a memorial foundation being named for a man who was very much alive," he said. "It became too involved to explain that the word was included originally to help inspire bequests in wills in memory of departed loved ones and gifts from owners of deceased pets."

An audited report dated December 31, 1955 showed a cash balance of $71,463.72 "on hand at the present time" in the Foundation's treasury. That was a far cry from the first royalty check in 1948 for $222.92. The early scrambling years were beginning to end and the Foundation was able now to extend its research grants program.

It was at this point that Mark began to believe that his early dreams in launching the Foundation were indeed based on a solid premise.

"The Morris Animal Foundation was organized to carry on research which would provide better methods of diagnosis and treatment of ailing animals," he wrote to a friend. "But at first, the average veterinarian just yawned, agreed that the goal was good and decided, in effect, that it was okay for us to try but they wanted no active part."

In that same letter of the late 1950s to a friend, Mark went on to explain that veterinarians in general during the Foundation's early period could see the need for more research.

"They knew we needed to know a lot more about how to diagnose skin diseases in dogs and cats," he said. "They knew we needed a better method of vaccinating dogs against distemper. But when we asked them to put in some of their own money to help in the research effort it became instantly another ballgame. They thought that was the job of pharmaceutical houses, a chemical firm or the American Kennel Club. Anything, so long as it was somebody else putting up the money. As for investing some of their funds in a tax-free foundation to do research for the improvement of animal medicine, they wanted no part of it. They simply would not buy the concept.

"They looked upon our work as—'Thank you, Dr. Morris, it was nice of you to do this, but don't try to get me involved.' And that attitude, in many cases, applied also when we suggested they put us in contact with some of their wealthy clients with a real interest in animals who might be willing to invest some tax-free money in bettering animal health. They were very reticent."

The letter continued on a brighter note:

"It turned out that the one thing that broke through all of this opposition and general apathy was the fact that we were donating a royalty of one-half cent a can on all Prescription Diets sold to further the research cause," Mark wrote. "Veterinarians who began recommending the special diet foods did so because they were beginning to get good clinical results. They could see that these foods were doing a good job of treating sick animals. The fact that the Foundation was receiving some income from these products began to encourage the veterinarians across the country and in Canada to use them in their practices and to encourage pet owners to keep their animals on that kind of diet to insure further good health.

"We were getting clinical results for the veterinarians and it was making them a profit in their business. The fact that the money spent on Prescription Diets was providing funds for research in veterinary schools—research which would give them information they could use—suddenly became a big plus in a happy picture. With this approach, we began to get veterinary cooperation, and it spread. Veterinarians in general began to realize that it was to their advantage to help support the Morris Animal Foundation."

As grants to veterinary schools by the growing Foundation increased in both size and scope, Mark wrote, numerous veterinarians began to give added support "because they felt it was helping make it possible for young veterinarians to become better educated. Knowledgeable men in the field of veterinary medicine knew that it was mandatory that veterinarians in general have more training, more experience in order to command the respect they must have in dealing with an ever more educated clientele and in filling the many positions that were beginning to open to them in research and pharmaceutical laboratories and government agencies.

"We began to evaluate proposals for research grants on the basis of whether they presented an opportunity for the further education of an undergraduate veterinary student, or whether they offered an opportunity for a graduate student to get a higher degree. If a project came through from a university which was essentially faculty oriented, it began to get shoved down to the bottom of the list.

"Until the Morris Animal Foundation began operation, it was very difficult for most veterinary schools to get money for basic research into companion animal diseases. It was very difficult, also, for young students to arrange for finances for studies leading to higher degrees.

"It always has been a requirement on government grants that a study have some application to human medicine before a university can receive funds. We were providing money to support graduate work on diseases which had an impact on animal health alone. This was an important consideration. I think that one of the really great aspects of the Morris Animal Foundation is not only so much the vital information that has been developed but it is also the fact that we are contributing to the training of people who now are holding responsible positions all over the country in government services, in our armed services, in laboratories and especially in veterinary teaching."

A milestone year in development of the Morris Animal Foundation was 1956. A summary of that year's highlights was outlined on December 5, 1981 at the annual meeting of Foundation trustees in Honolulu. The speaker was Claude Ramsey, longtime Foundation executive director, who put his memories is these words:

"I attended my first trustee's meeting on December 14-15, 1956. Although there were only four trustees, the meeting lasted two full days. The place was Plainfield, New Jersey.

"Present: Mark L. Morris; James B. Allison of the Rutgers University Bureau of Biological Research; Agnes Fowler, a trustee of The Seeing Eye, Inc., and Louise W. Morris. Attorney Robert J. Johnson and I also participated.

"Dr. Morris read a waiver of notice of the meeting, Mrs. Morris read the minutes and gave the treasurer's report. The first order of business was a motion that all research grants run no longer than one year, that the Foundation would not commit to anything more than a year. Then the attorney announced the Internal Revenue Service had granted tax exemption to the Foundation. That was the first of many tax exemption letters which opened the doors to tax-free contributions by the public. Another report indicated difficulty in securing project reports from universities on grants in progress. Nothing changed there.

"The president summarized the various projects, one on the aging dog at Cornell University, one at Rutgers to determine the nutritive requirements of cats, and a final report on a project about sheep.

"The trustees considered six proposals, many of them generated by the president, and in most cases additional information was asked of the prospective investigators. A year or so later, we were to outline in detail to investigators the information desired. That eliminated much of the need, but not all of it, to go back to the prospective investigator for more information.

"The trustees in 1956 created a couple of new programs: one was the Small Animal Award for the veterinary profession, with a $500 honorarium. This award was tried for eight or ten years, and when politics developed in selection of the recipient, the program was discontinued. The other new creation at the meeting was the 'Scientific Advisory Board.' That board, with very few changes in structure, has continued and today is one of the Foundation's greatest assets.

"Oh yes, there was a name change in 1956. From Mark L. Morris Animal Memorial Foundation to plain Mark L. Morris Animal Foundation.

"The trustees in 1956 also named Mark's daughter, Ruth, as treasurer and elected her as a trustee. It was decided to move the annual meeting to July. Previously, the annual meeting of the Foundation was held in December, as near Christmas day as Dr. Morris could get them. He always said school professors had time off during the holiday season; things weren't too busy for veterinarians, so Christmas was a good time for a meeting.

"The proposed budget in 1956 anticipated an income of $45,000 for the next year, all of it from royalties of Prescription Diet foods. The trustees indicated funds might be solicited from outside sources such as animal owners, but no one really viewed it as a very likely source of income. There was one other companion animal foundation in existence, Grayson, but the trustees didn't know about it.

"The trustees in 1956 decided to budget $400 a month for operating expenses: telephone service, postage and part-time executive director (Ramsey). They also authorized publication of a brochure, and approved payments of $10 an hour to the attorney.

"The Foundation has undergone peaks and valleys. That meeting in 1956 was one peak, when the decision was made to create a scientific advisory board, to secure a tax-exempt certificate, to hire an executive director and to employ an attorney. Another peak occurred twelve years later in 1968, when the decision was made to 'go public' and become a public, rather than a private, family foundation.

"The growth of Morris Animal Foundation is a tribute to its volunteer leadership which the Foundation has enjoyed over the years."

The scientific advisory board, which reviews all research work financed through grants to the Morris Animal Foundation, has been composed from the outset in 1956 of experts with D.V.M., V.M.D., Ph.D., and M.D. degrees, chosen for their scientific knowledge to serve as advisors. Investigators across the U.S. must appear in person and explain their work to the advisory board members.

The Foundation's original emphasis on research into the ailments of dogs has never slackened, but with growth in the 1950s came a gradual broadening into other divisions of the companion animal world.

By 1956, the Foundation ranked as one of the first sponsors of scientific research into feline health problems and was sponsor of a basic study into protein requirements of cats at Rutgers University.

In another major expansion move, General Wayne O. "Sage" Kester, D.V.M., joined the Foundation staff in 1959. The retired general had served as chief of the veterinary service of the U.S. Air Force from 1949 to 1957. Working on a part-time basis as a retired Air Force officer, he was to serve the Foundation in varied capacities for some 20 years.

In a 1979 report, General Kester outlined his experiences with the Morris Animal Foundation this way:

"As chief of the U.S. Air Force veterinary service, I saw the need for trained doctors of veterinary medicine. For example, we had to have men who understood the management of nuclear energy to work out the hazards of radiation exposure. We had to have people who understood and could work out the problems of biological and chemical warfare defense, the use of toxic fuels in our jet aircraft, the feeding of in-flight personnel and later astronauts, and the effect of space, high altitude, gravity and compression.

"All this required the use of many different kinds of laboratory animals. We used everything from donkeys to pigs, dogs, cats, mice, rats, monkeys and chimpanzees. It was obvious that many veterinarians qualified in laboratory animal medicine would be needed.

"When I moved from Washington, D.C., to the Denver area in 1958, I didn't have much idea what I would do in retirement, and it had never occurred to me to join the Morris Animal Foundation. I had known Mark Morris for many years, and, in a discussion with him at a veterinary meeting at Colorado State University in the fall of 1959, I mentioned that I was to receive the Zeta Award from the student chapter at Auburn University.

"Mark showed interest, and said he had two research grants in operation at Auburn and asked me to look into them while I was there. I did the checking and reported at the next meeting of the Morris Animal Foundation. At the end of the meeting I agreed to join the Foundation staff as director of research on a part-time basis."

General Kester served in that capacity for several years, lending professional guidance to projects at the various veterinary schools. But soon he was attracted also into a field the young Foundation had not yet penetrated.

"My special areas of interest, beyond a desire to help provide trained veterinary personnel through the Foundation, was in the equine field," General Kester wrote in this 1979 report. "The lack of equine research on a national basis was quite obvious to me. It was obvious also that the equine industry was going to come back in the 1960s. The population in the 1940s was about four million horses. It since has climbed to more than eight million—and the need was clear in 1960 for research and for the veterinary profession to get ready to handle expansion in equine medicine. At the American Quarter Horse Association meeting in 1960, I pointed out the need for research in the equine area, and as a result, a research committee was established by the association.

"We first tried to work through the Grayson Foundation, but this didn't seem to materialize. Then the thought was to establish a new foundation, an idea which I opposed, knowing the problems of establishing a new tax-exempt foundation. I was already with the Morris Animal Foundation and knew how it worked. The problem there was that it was known as a cat and dog foundation and it was kind of hard to get horse people and dog people mixed, especially when racing is involved, because of the competition between horse and dog racing factions.

"I look back on my association with the Foundation with a great deal of satisfaction. It has been wonderful to associate with so many fine and dedicated people over the years, and it's rewarding to know that we started so many young veterinarians in research, and that they have carried on in that field. In the area of horse research, none was being done when we started. Now every veterinary college in the country has a horse research program and many private institutions also are carrying on this type of research.

In 1960 while Claude Ramsey was acting as executive director on a part-time basis for the Morris Animal Foundation, the first informational booklet was published.

The booklet listed 12 current research projects then underway with Foundation financing. They ranged from a study of aging processes of dogs in various parts of the country to research on lead poisoning as a common cause of canine disease and a study of the relation of nutrition to obesity in spayed female dogs.

The booklet listed members of the then pioneering scientific advisory board. The five serving in 1960 were Charles W. Bower, Topeka, Kansas, veterinarian; William D. Carlson, D.V.M., M.S., Ph.D., College of Veterinary Medicine, Colorado State University; Clarence R. Cole, D.V.M., M.S., Ph.D., College of Veterinary Medicine, Ohio State University; Dean E. C. Stone, B.S., M.S., D.V.M., College of Veterinary Medicine, Washington State University; and Dr. W. J. Zontine, Lancaster, California, veterinarian.

Universities involved in ongoing Morris Animal Foundation research projects in 1960 were Auburn, Cornell, Illinois, Kansas State, Michigan State, Missouri, Oklahoma State and Washington State.

A year later, in 1961, the Foundation's annual booklet had grown to 32 pages and included a detailed technical report on the Foundation's research findings on subjects ranging from dermatology and nutrition to the raising of germ-free dogs, canine surgery, pathology and obesity.

A brief foreword said: "The Morris Animal Foundation attempts to fill the gap between the research institution and the veterinary clinician by providing new information about the diagnosis and management of diseases in animals."

"The veterinary practitioners will, we believe, find the report of these studies not only of interest, but of real clinical value."

Mailings went out to veterinarians everywhere in the nation.

The 1961 booklet also listed nineteen ongoing research projects in universities stretching from coast to coast.

And it listed for the first time the names and affiliations of forty-four persons who had achieved the title of Foundation Fellow by successfully completing scientific research projects financed by the Morris Animal Foundation.

By the early 1980s, the list of Foundation Fellows would swell to beyond the 400 mark.

Mark and Louise carved a cake at the 25th annual meeting of the Morris
Animal Foundation in Denver in 1973

11

A New Product Parade

The slow but steady growth of the national market for k/d and p/d, first in what was to become an ever-broadening line of Prescription Diets for companion animals, did not turn Dr. Mark L. Morris into a contented man.

As an inventor, marketer and researcher, Mark was convinced as the 1950s unfolded that his work had only begun. True, his original concept that proper nutrition is a key instrument in providing and maintaining good health in dogs and cats had been proven beyond challenge.

Thanks to the Morris-developed k/d, dogs stricken by kidney ailments or failure and formerly sentenced to a short and distressful life were enjoying an extended span by being fed the biologically complete k/d diet. It had been designed to relieve the stress on the damaged organs of elimination.

Similarly, p/d was booming in sales across the nation. Stunted, anemic pups placed on the diet were turning into healthy animals. Their mothers, fed p/d from earliest pregnancy, were prospering too.

"That's not enough," Mark told Louise one evening after reviewing the latest sales success reports. "We've only scratched the surface. It's true that today sick animals are being benefited by diet therapy as much or even more than from the so-called wonder drugs. But the war against animal disease we've started still is limited to a very narrow front. We've got to open up some new fronts if we expect to make a meaningful contribution to scientific research. We must develop new products."

To Mark, the course ahead was marked clearly. But economic considerations—the matter of money—dictated that he move slowly. And before he could tackle the big job of developing new products—

new diet foods to solve additional canine health problems—Mark was faced with the problem of working out effective quality control for the two products then being mass produced at the Hill Packing Co. plant in Topeka.

"Quality control is our only means of avoiding customer complaints," Mark told his staff. "Chemical testing of the food here in Topeka, using cans selected at random from the packing line, is working out well. But the basic problem now involves palatability and some biological angles."

One of the problems involved k/d. From time to time, complaints would come in from various parts of the country. The latest shipment of k/d was sticky. It was sticking inside the mouths of dog patients and they had problems swallowing it.

It took days of frantic labor to solve that one. In the product k/d, the amount of meat was held down to keep the protein level low and reduce strain on ailing kidneys. This meant using more cereal grains, especially wheat.

"It took a long time and a lot of laboratory work to discover that the gluten in wheat is not a constant thing but varies with different strains of wheat and even with the locale in which the wheat is grown," Mark explained later in a speech on the subject to a group of veterinarians.

"We learned that some kinds of Kansas wheat, when cooked, become super sticky. That means a pasty shipment of k/d—and a lot of unhappy dogs and dog owners. We solved the problem by using hard red winter wheat from Minnesota, but before we identified the cause the situation was a classic in public relations."

Another colossal problem was that of constant palatability. The cause, it turned out, was that production methods were not yet fully standardized. But, before the culprits were identified and removed, the problem was king-sized.

"We were sending products for biological testing back to the Raritan Laboratories in New Jersey," Mark explained. "While the test results were pending—it took a lot of travel time between Kansas and New Brunswick—it was necessary to hold production in storage at the Hill warehouse in Topeka. Nothing could be shipped out to distributors without our formal authorization. And we couldn't grant a release until the laboratory in New Jersey put its stamp of approval on samples from each day's production in Topeka."

It became obvious that the Kansas-New Jersey shuttle was a major bottleneck. So Mark made arrangements with his friend, Topeka veterinarian Dr. C. W. Bower, to set up a special kennel section of his clinic, for six dogs to be fed nothing but samples of each day's production from the Hill plant. They would serve, along with local laboratory analysis, as palatability control agents.

"The Bower Clinic quickly ran out of extra space," Mark was to recall. "In addition, there was the constant problem of sick animals being kept at the clinic always in close proximity to our test dogs. It became urgent that we work out something else. And, in addition, we needed the services of a food technician trained in the field who could deal with the blending of ingredients and determine such key factors as changes in color and consistency."

It was then, through one of the lucky coincidences that kept popping up in his life, that Mark learned from a chance conversation of a new research institute which had opened in nearby Kansas City, Missouri.

A telephone call and a two-hour drive into Kansas City put Mark in the office of Dr. Charles Kimball, president and director of the Midwest Research Institute. The institute gained world-wide renown in engineering and allied fields, but under the direction of Dr. Kimball it maintained a department of biological chemistry involving foods. It was this specialty that interested Mark in the institute.

Minutes into his interview with Dr. Kimball, Mark determined that the institute staff included Dr. Harrison Newlin, a food technologist with a Ph.D. degree earned at Cornell University and years of experience in the research and development laboratories of General Foods Corporation.

"Before the hour was ended, I had signed a contract as an individual to employ the services of the institute, with Dr. Newlin as the assigned staff specialist," Mark recalled. "Under the terms of the contract, Dr. Newlin would assist me personally in a broad program of food technology research, product development and quality control as it related to my line of Prescription Diets for companion animals."

Files of Midwest Research Institute show a steady series of contracts from early 1951 to 1972 between the institute and both Dr. Mark L. Morris and Hill Packing Co.

Nearly all of the research efforts, the institute files show was directed toward "research development of diets for dogs and cats."

A report by William B. House, a senior scientist on the MRI staff, said three types of projects were carried out for Dr. Mark L. Morris "in a continuing program that ran for many years." They included, he said, continuing quality control "on the Hill Packing Co. canned and dry products produced for dogs and cats"; fundamental research on animal foods for nutritive requirements, and "consulting services for domestic animal research."

The House report in some of its finer detail, clearly shows the depth of the research efforts directed by Mark which resulted in the broadening of the Prescription Diet line beyond the original k/d and p/d.

One of the detailed House reports dealt with early stages in the development of r/d—a dietary food for obese and overweight animals:

"In early production stages, a problem arose in the fact that consistency of the food to be canned began to vary from day to day." House wrote, "The variation in texture ranged from an unacceptable soft and sticky substance to a reasonably firm product which was easy to can. There was no assurance from day to day."

"It was decided that these variations in texture could be smoothed out by the addition of an acceptable thickening agent. This project involved the selection and testing of thirteen distinct types of thickening agents representing twenty-eight commercial products. All of these agents were tested in an r/d mix base. The tests showed that all of the vegetable gums, as a class, were ineffective. The thickeners methocel and agar produced an appreciable increase in water absorption when used at levels up to 0.35 percent of the canned diet. The texture characteristics imported by these thickeners were acceptable and produced an acceptable product." The tests took months and many dollars.

Another extensive research project by Midwest Research Institute involved Mark's development of a diet called i/d—a bland, low-residue and easily digestible food designed primarily to help control diseases of the gastrointestinal tract in dogs.

Mark called on the institute for studies on how much fat should be added to experimental i/d for feeding to growing fox terrier puppies. The House report:

"The objective was to determine the optimum level of fat in the diet that would not interfere with the growth, fat absorption, appetite and general well-being of the puppy terriers."

"The puppies were raised through the range of eleven to twenty-three weeks on i/d with an adjusted fat content of 4.3 percent, 9.4 percent and 14.4 percent fat. The control diet, which consisted of unsupplemented i/d from the production line, contained 0.82 percent fat. The puppies that consumed 4.3 percent fat in their diet had no adverse growth effect and the absorption of fat increased to 97.5 percent, in contrast to 88.8 percent fat absorption by the puppies on the control diet. The puppies that were maintained on the i/d diet with 9.4 percent and 14.4 percent fat levels were markedly inhibited in growth and their fat absorption was reduced.''

That report gave Mark the clues he needed to make i/d an all-purpose diet food for animals with intestinal ailments.

The House report included other details:

"There was a range of fundamental studies that went on from year to year. Two examples of these types of investigation are: (1) Maintenance of senile dogs on a k/d diet; (2) Physiological effects of maintaining cats on commercial diets high in fish products. It was determined that senile dogs maintained with k/d for six months were in excellent condition throughout the test period. During the period, tests were made to compare the absorption by senile dogs of fiber, ash, calcium and phosphorus as compared to that of one-year-old dogs fed the same diet.

"The results of these tests showed that the absorption of the senile dogs was not significantly different than that of the young dogs.''

This was a major piece of proof that ailing and aged canine could live contented lives for extra years on a k/d diet.

The House report also detailed results of tests on c/d, Mark's first special diet in the Prescription line for felines:

"The test cats were maintained for a year on four different commercial canned cat foods selected from grocery stores. The foods were consumed at will and at a high level, but the test cats remained thin and in a poor condition. The cats were placed in metabolism cages for six day periods and all of their urine was collected and studied. It was clearly indicated that the cats maintained on fish-based commercial diets excreted much higher levels of minerals than control cats maintained on c/d, a diet that contains less than two percent ash. At the end of the experiment the surviving cats were sacrificed and examined by pathologists. The cats that died before the end of the experiment all had indications of general starvation (on commercial cat foods selected from grocery shelves.) Observations of the pathologists listed urinary system damage due to high ash content in the commercial diets and indications of vitamin A and thiamin deficiencies.''

As thorough and complete as they were, the research projects by Midwest Research Institute were only a supplement to the work being done personally by Mark in the new product development field.

"I owe a debt of gratitude to the institute for the help it provided," Mark was to say years later. "They provided an extra set of arms for me, and they gave me support when I needed it. My association with the Midwest Research Institute was one of the nicer things about those busy years of the 1950s and 1960s."

Mark served on the board of trustees of Midwest Research Institute from 1963 until 1978. His fellow trustees included such men as Dr. Vernon Alden, president of Ohio University; Richard H. Amberg, publisher of the *St. Louis Globe-Democrat*; Harold Boeschenstein, president of Owens-Corning Fiberglass Corp; E. F. Bullard, chairman of Pan American Petroleum Corp.; Howard J. Carey, chairman of Carey Salt Co.; George H. Clay, president of the Federal Reserve Bank of Kansas City; Cris Dobbins, chairman of Ideal Cement Co., Potash Co. of America and Denver's Boettcher Foundation; Joyce C. Hall, president of Hallmark Cards, Inc.; E.S. Marsh, president of the Santa Fe Railroad; Dr. Franklin D. Murphy, chancellor of the University of California at Los Angeles; Charles C. Tillinghast, Jr., president of Trans World Airlines, and Robert Wagstaff, chairman of Coca Cola Bottling Co. of Mid-America. Dr. Newlin of Midwest Research Institute became a Kansas City-Topeka commuter in the months immediately following start of the research contract on Prescription Diets. And Mark found himself spending more and more time at the crowded Bower Animal Clinic in Topeka as work on new products began to accelerate.

At this point in Mark's career another quirk of chance came to his rescue. Fred Weber, brother of Louise, announced from New Jersey that he was looking for "something to do." Mark added him to the staff in Topeka and sent him on a search for land on which to build a fully equipped laboratory and kennel area to replace the Raritan Laboratories complex in New Jersey. In short order Weber located a 100-acre tract about five miles north of Topeka near the main highway route to Kansas City. The tract was purchased and it quickly was converted into Weber Food Testing Co., a headquarters for development of new Prescription Diet products. Jim Hahn, the farmer who sold the land, stayed on as a member of the original staff.

As the Prescription Diet line burgeoned in both products and sales, the farm operation was expanded. It became headquarters for Morris

Research Laboratories, Inc., with the Webers and Mark and his wife as shareholders, and finally in 1965 was renamed as Theracon, Inc. (for therapeutic consultants) to become a major force in food testing.

The new Topeka center gradually grew into a pivot point of Mark's operation. Kennels on the 100-acre expanse began to hold scores of dogs and cats. Their controlled diets were the key to acceptance or rejection of each lot of Prescription Diets rolling off the Hill Packing Co. line. They also were the key to new product development and to ongoing research into diseases and other health problems with nutritional relationships.

With his base in Topeka well established, Mark decided to rid himself of the time and travel necessary to maintaining his former operation in New Jersey. The hospital and practice were sold and Raritan Laboratories was closed. The buildings were sold, one by one, and moved off the property. Mark held the property until the construction of the interstate highway through New Jersey suddenly gave the acreage new value. It was sold to a New York investor for industrial development.

The first new member of the Prescription Diet line developed by Mark during the hurly-burly early days of his campaign to expand the line was r/d—in simple language, a special diet designed to reduce the weight of fat dogs while keeping them healthy and happy.

Mark decided that obesity in companion animals was as great a health problem as kidney trouble or distemper and determined that a special diet to combat the problem was badly needed.

"Many owners think a fat dog or cat is a symbol of good food and easy living," Mark explained to Louise as he began the research and development task. "Fatness has become sort of a status symbol, and that's not as it should be. Obesity in companion animals, as in humans, is mostly the result of a higher than necessary caloric intake. And what most people don't realize is that obesity hinders general health and actually interferes with normal body functions."

In routine tests, Mark had established that fat dogs usually have trouble breathing properly and suffer intensely on hot summer days. Tests showed dangerous fat deposits around the heart, pancreas and intestinal walls of overweight dogs. Other tests established that portly animals tend to exercise very little, setting up a vicious circle leading to diseases of the skin, respiratory tract, joints, and even the digestive system.

Another key point in Mark's decision to proceed with development of r/d was a study by Dr. Charles Bower of Topeka, which showed a growing epidemic of overweight dogs taken to veterinary clinics for care "with no way to control the problem."

Dr. Bower speculated, and Mark agreed, that heavy coast-to-coast advertising of dog foods as a "convenience" by dog food manufacturing companies was part of the growing problem of canine portliness.

"There are dogs which are naturally susceptible to obesity, like cocker spaniels and the English bulldog and some of the small terriers. These dogs are around the house a lot and are often fed bits of candy and other sweets as a snack or reward. Fatness is a natural result.

"This presented a real research problem: How to create a diet that would be palatable, fill up the stomach, provide very little real nourishment—and still not create a diet deficiency disease. That is a real puzzle. It sounds easy, I suppose, but it gets real rough when you are faced with the task of choosing the ingredients to perform this magic."

The first thing Mark ruled out was a diet of very lean meat. He decided a diet based on that alone would end in disaster. But after extensive shopping, he located from a distributor in the Chicago area a product called celluflour.

"It actually is a pulverized form of cellulose, which is wood pulp," Mark explained. "We knew that cows, through the bacteria contained in the rumen or their first stomach, can digestively break down cellulose. But not so the dog or cat. Their digestive juices strike out on that.

"So we decided to start with celluflour as a base. It holds water and makes a high bulk in the stomach and the intestines, but provides no energy. Basically, it just makes the animal feel like it's had a good meal and passes through the digestive system largely unchanged.

"With the base established, we started to add real food to the new r/d diet. And we immediately ran into a problem: The solids would separate from the moisture in the mixture and we ended up with a can of food with solids on the top and water on the bottom. Well, we couldn't sell a thing like that. So we called on Dr. Newlin of Midwest Research Institute. This was his field of food technology. He worked out a series of additives which held the whole mixture together and turned a mess into an attractive, palatable product which worked.

"But before we put r/d on the market, we ran it through a whole series of kennel feeding tests. At one point we discovered we had cut down too severely on the fat content. The test dogs on the ration got so constipated after a few weeks that their feces were like limestone rocks. This had to be worked out, along with the problem that a lot of fat dogs actually are finicky eaters. They turned up their noses at what essentially was a can of cellulose and water, but some liver, which is very nutritious but low in calories, solved that problem.''

All of which left Mark with the major problem of how to convince veterinarians—the key in the sales chain—to persuade owners of obese pets to put them on a special diet.

"It was a major educational program and it's still going on today," Mark said. "We developed an entire training program for reducing dogs and how to keep the owner happy during those first weeks when the animal seems to be losing no weight at all and he is putting out extra dollars for expensive diet food. The physiology of the problem must be explained in simple language so the owners know a weight loss is inevitable—even when his dog gains a pound during the first three weeks. This is because fat is lighter than water and is last to be eliminated.''

With problems of the content of r/d largely worked out, Mark ran into production trouble at the Hill Packing Co. plant.

"The first batches had to be nursed through the production process every step of the way," he recalled. "There were clogged filters and clogged canners and a host of other problems, but gradually r/d was on its way.''

The fourth member of the growing Prescription Diet family was called i/d. It got its name for "intestinal diet" but actually is a semi-synthetic ration low in fat and fiber, but rich in all other digestible nutrients. It was designed as a therapeutic instrument with a wide range of potential applications.

"Everything an animal eats must pass through the intestinal tract to be digested," Mark said in introducing the new product. "The type of diet eaten can control the efficiency of the intestinal function. The ingredients of i/d are cottage cheese, whole egg, wheat, horse meat, corn grits, dried yeast, corn starch, sugar, animal fat, pectin, salt, vitamins and minerals. There is a reason for each ingredient.''

Mark started his research and development work on i/d by employing the principles of a "purified diet" he had worked on years earlier.

"When Dr. Allison at Rutgers and I worked on the nutritive requirements of dogs in order to establish the basic requirements for proteins, it was necessary to create a synthetic diet," Mark explained. "This is a diet in which every component can be chemically identified so one component at a time can be removed to study the basal requirements of animals. But the problem we faced as work started on i/d was that a purified diet or synthetic diet would have cost at least $3 a pound at mid-20th century price levels. Our chore was to modify the expensive diet into a price range of a lot less than a dollar a pound so pet owners could afford it."

"The first thing we did was discard the use of vitamin-free casein as a source of protein. It was much too expensive. So we decided to substitute cottage cheese and eggs as a protein base—and it worked. At first we used no meat at all, but we adjusted the mineral and vitamin balances. The problem: The test dogs wouldn't eat the product. So we added bone broth and finally a controlled amount of horse meat. That did the trick."

Finally, after endless months of effort, i/d was coming smoothly out of the laboratory and it was time to try a pilot run at the Hill Packing Co. plant so the new product could be offered to veterinarians across the country.

"I'll never forget the night of the first pilot run in the Hill plant," Mark recalled. "It was a nightmare. We used the same equipment at the identical settings which had been turning out k/d and p/d all day. But it didn't work. All was well when we brought the first batch up to 180 degrees and put the cooker on pre-cook. That started the product flow into the line and onto the can filling equipment. But it didn't last long. Once the can-fillers began operation the whole line backed up. The upshot was that the crew had to tear down the whole cooker line and clean the i/d out of it so the plant would be operational the next day. That took all night. The stuff turned into a substance more like chewing gum than dog food. It was a monumental mess."

It was back to the drawing boards, with Dr. Newlin, the Midwest Research Institute's food technologist, as a consultant. Mark was fully satisfied with his new formula, but something had to be changed so it could be canned.

"We tried a dozen different things, and finally hit on the right formula," Mark said. "At long last, i/d was running through the Hill plant and cases of the product were coming out at the end of the line."

As i/d made its way to veterinary clinics in all parts of the United States and Canada, complaints began pouring in.

"The dogs wouldn't eat it," Mark recalled with a shrug and a very slight smile. "The kennel workers treated i/d just like they had been handling k/d and p/d. They opened the cans, cut the contents into chunks or merely cut the ration in two and put it in the cage. If they put the entire contents of the can, or even a half-chunk into a pan and placed it in the cage, the dog would take a bite and choke on it, or the food would stick in the dog's mouth and it couldn't swallow."

"We were getting i/d through the lines at the Hill plant, and now we had the problem of getting it through the dog."

The problem lay in the fact that i/d was not meaty in texture, like p/d or k/d, but more resembled a block of solid cheese. But hours more of laboratory work solved the difficulty and i/d was turned out into the market once more.

"All was well for more than a month, then new complaints came in," Mark said. "After sitting around in storage for several weeks, the sugar in the product would produce a carmelizing effect and the i/d would turn brown in the can. The brown streaks discouraged kennel operators, veterinarians and dog owners. The i/d was perfectly good, but anyone seeing the brown streaks would immediately decide it was spoiled."

"We knew then that it's not enough to make a product that is good for a dog or cat. You have to make one the owner will buy."

An indefinite number of attempts to solve the problem resulted in a steady flow of i/d with a uniform light cheese color. Sales resumed.

Then complaints started coming directly to Mark from officials of Hill Packing Co. Although veterinarians and distributors were ordering i/d at an ever-increasing rate, the sum total of the orders still was small.

"We're being forced, as an example, to put in ten cases of i/d to round out an order for a thousand cases of p/d and a thousand cases of k/d," said one Hill complaint letter. "This is a nuisance. We ask that we be relieved of responsibility for the production of i/d as of the first of next month."

Mark was stubbornly reluctant to give up on i/d. He was convinced of its merit, pointed out that sales were growing steadily if slowly and said the profession was gradually learning "the excellent and numerous potential benefits of this new diet." He predicted that "soon it will be one of the best therapeutic diets in our line: stay with me, please."

Mark's professional opinion that i/d, a slow starter, was destined for sales glory was bolstered initially by a lone supporter, Dr. Lawrence Goodman. He was a former Cornell classmate who, by the early 1950s, was operating one of the highest-rated animal hospitals in the New York City area.

"He was the type of dedicated veterinarian who always wanted to feed the dogs in his hospital personally so he could check on their condition," Mark recalled. "He kept writing us to say that dogs fed on i/d had saved him thousands of dollars in expense of cleaning up the hospital. He kept insisting that i/d could replace just about everything in the diet line, as far as he was concerned. And he rapidly became the biggest buyer of i/d in America. He also kept telling other veterinarians about his success.

"The real value of i/d gradually became apparent in sales figures. It took more than ten years, but it was worth it."

With four products for dogs firmly established in the Prescription Diet line (k/d, p/d, r/d, and i/d), Mark and his staff turned their attention to the task of perfecting a proper diet for household cats.

"We discovered from the outset that the feline diet field is a large, complicated and difficult area," Mark recalled. "Why? Largely because of the wide individual variation among pet cats. The cat, by nature, is inclined to develop fixed habits which are difficult if not impossible to break. A cat, especially a pampered pet, develops some very unusual eating habits. They live close to the family. Some almost never venture out-of-doors, preferring a personal litter box and safety to adventure.

"Pet cats are very unlike pet dogs. They usually develop a strong preference for one kind of food—tuna fish, chicken livers, salmon or sardines, for instance—and they eat that with a purr day after day after week after month ad nauseam, turning up their noses at anything else.

"To complicate things, we discovered that cats are difficult to house under research conditions. Very little laboratory work specifically on behalf of cats had been done by the early 1950s, but we quickly learned that cats are prone to contagious diseases when kept in colonies under research conditions. It is not unusual to lose a whole colony of a hundred or more cats in a couple of weeks, usually to upper respiratory diseases or ailments of the urinary tract."

Mark's original goal was to develop a c/d or cat diet capable of nourishing an animal properly without exposing it to the high mineral levels contained in commercial cat food based on fish products.

"It's well known that cats love fish," Mark explained. "The most reasonable source of fish is the so-called trash fish which comes in on the ocean fishing boats intermingled with tuna and the other prize parts of a catch, but which under law can not be sold for human consumption in any form. At the typical cat food manufacturing operation, the trash fish were being dumped into big grinders and turned into mush—bones and all.

"The routine was to pipe the mush into cans, seal the cans, slap on a cat food label and send the cases off to market. If there were too few trash fish in the catch, the mixture was supplemented with the ground-up bones of better fish which had been turned into filets. That included the heads, tails, skeletons and insides of a lot of fish."

"When all of this, ground finely, is cooked and canned, the end product is very high in mineral content. In laboratory work, we burn down food samples with high heat and the end product is ash. The cat food based on trash fish was very high in mineral ash. If the animal had a choice, a cat meal would consist of the soft tissue of the fish—the same choice humans would make. With no choice, cats fed commercial food were ending up with urinary tract blockages caused by deposits of the mineral, known medically as uroliths or calculi (hard pebbles as in gall bladder trouble)."

Mark's goal was to create a dietary food for both mature and growing cats. A secondary target was elimination of most of the mineral-based ingredients which seemed to be the basic cause of the mineral crystals which formed in the urinary tracts of fish-fed cats. Later research has indicated that Mark was correct and that it is the magnesium in the diet that actually causes the stones.

C/d has a long success record as the key in dietary management of many feline diseases and, in recent years, surpassed k/d as the largest seller in the Prescription Diet line.

The final new entry into the Prescription Diet line accomplished in the 1950s was f/d—an all purpose foundation diet for dogs. It emerged as a dream-come-true in answer to repeated demands from veterinary customers across the country. This group of vocal practitioners kept insisting that in many cases of pet-owner feeding of dogs which had been released to home care after a bout of illness, the cost of specialized formula diets like k/d, p/d and i/d was "a little too steep." They kept demanding that Mark and his staff develop some sort of prescription dry food to which could be added, depending on the condition and ailment of the pet involved, a little fat or cottage cheese, or perhaps some fresh meat to adjust the animal protein as required by each case.

"They wanted to concoct the special diets for special patients they had been treating," Mark explained. "They demanded a way to avoid the expensive fixed formulas we had worked out and they insisted they were anxious to make up diets for their canine patients to their own specifications.

"At first, we resisted these demands. But then it began to dawn on me that there might be a secondary market for some sort of foundation diet in the feeding of large colonies of dogs, like the research animals around the country and the canines used in serum production who require a very high degree of protein. We finally decided to move ahead and develop a flexible diet food which could be adjusted to fit each individual need. It turned out to be a mistake.

The first problem in the early development stages of f/d was the form the product should take. A dry food of some type was indicated, but Mark quickly learned from his research that there were perils involved.

"In the 1920s and early 1930s, dry dog food was the most popular type," he explained. "There was very little canned dog food on the market until later in the 1930s. A pioneer in the dry dog food field was Spratts of Great Britain. For a long time they dominated the market.

"Then National Biscuit Co. got into the field and came up with a product called Milk Bone, which still is on the market. They made a biscuit of flour, milk and yeast—the same ingredients you would use in making biscuits at home—then added extra milk and called it Milk Bone. Then came a company in Fairfield, Connecticut known as Kennel Food Supply, Co. They started producing a line of dried, biscuit-type dog food. The basic ingredient was No. 2 white flour to which yeast, salt, powdered skim milk, bone meal and a small amount of animal meat supplement were added. This was mixed in large quantities, rolled into sheets, baked in large ovens then exposed in a wind tunnel to dry it quickly. After that it was broken into what became known as the kibble biscuit and run over a screen to produce the varying sizes for different sizes of dogs."

Mark's research showed that the heat drying process used in the manufacture of dog biscuits posed a threat to the effectiveness of such vital ingredients as thiamine, or Vitamin B$_1$, and Vitamin A.

"We learned that the Vitamin A especially would oxidize away almost completely in biscuits exposed to heat and then packed in a pasteboard box without a liner to sit on a shelf somewhere for weeks before it was fed," Mark said. "We wanted no part of that."

Working with scientists of Midwest Research Institute, Mark and his staff finally settled on a then new to the market process called expansion-type.

"Under this process, the dry food was placed under pressure during the formulation period and literally was exploded," he explained. "This method was used to rupture the starch cells so they would be more easily digested. We decided this process offered the possibilities we were searching for in providing a basic diet which would be nutritionally sound."

In its final form, f/d had the appearance of a broken biscuit, a sharp contrast to the pellets of other manufacturers. To speed its acceptance, Mark and his research staff prepared an entire list of special menus for distribution with f/d. They ranged from one designed for the clinical management of surgical patients (add one-half cup of fresh lean meat, 2 tablespoons of liquid fat and one teaspoon of cod liver oil) to another for growing puppies in the hospital for surgery, fracture repair, wounds or other trauma, (add one egg, one cup of canned meat, 44 cc of raw liver and two teaspoons of cod liver oil).

"Almost from the outset, despite all of the requests we had received, it became obvious that veterinarians across the country were not willing to accept a flexible product," Mark reported.

"It eventually boiled down to the fact that veterinarians, in the main, did not want to take the time to use our charts and menus and convert f/d into an individual diet for each animal under their care. The 1950s, in retrospect, were the beginning of the current era of convenience when the housewife, and everyone else it seems, wants everything done for them in advance. Today the meat is trimmed and wrapped in see-through cellophane in the markets and even the cakes to be baked at home come in a cardboard box to which you add this or that, pop it into a preheated oven and reach in a few minutes later to find a perfect product. Sooner or later they'll figure out a way to add the icing while the cake is in the oven."

To Mark's dismay, veterinarians began asking if it might be possible to add something to make f/d a complete dog food requiring no mixing in of additives.

"We worked out a formula for a simple-to-add supplement and we called it ez/d—for simple diet. And before we knew what had happened the veterinarians were discovering that ez/d was a very palatable food for dogs and were feeding it alone.

"All they had to do was toss a dish of it into a cage and the dogs would gobble it up. That's what too many of them started to do instead of following directions and adding one cup of ez/d to four cups of f/d and mixing them together with two cups of warm water. The end result was too many dogs ended up with an unbalanced diet.

"After much discussion and thought we discontinued the products f/d and ez/d. It was a temporary setback—but in a few years we used the concept of the f/d-ez/d feeding program as the basis of a whole new line of products called Science Diets. The ingredients that had been in each one of the f/d-ez/d mixture were put together in one pellet and packaged as separate products. The 4:1 f/d-ez/d mixture became Science Diet Canine Maintenance; the 70:30 mixture—Canine Growth, etc. So what at first appeared to be a failure turned out to be a roaring success after some additional research and fine tuning."

While he worked during the 1950s to expand the Prescription Diet line, Mark—with Louise by his side when she could spare the time from her duties of handling business affairs of the laboratory in Topeka—"hit the road" whenever possible to continue his one-man campaign to convince veterinarians everywhere that dietary animal food could be a major force in their careers.

"It should be realized that the Hill Packing Co. did not have the personnel who could assemble groups of veterinarians in all parts of the country," Mark explained. "This was my obligation."

Snatching a week or two weeks at a time from laboratory work, Mark would get out the family car and follow itineraries carefully worked out in advance by Louise.

"We toured the northeast, the northwest, all of California, and Texas, and most of the South," Mark recalled. "We would arrange in advance for me to be on the program of veterinary meetings in areas we were visiting. And if there were no meetings we'd arrange in the various cities and towns for a veterinarian we knew (usually one met at a meeting of the American Veterinary Medical Association) to call several other veterinarians in the area and invite them to dinner.

"These dinner meetings always ended up as roundtable discussions on the use of diet foods in the practices of the professionals who were our guests for the evening. It was from the answers to the myriad questions they would ask me that we later fashioned the many brochures used in promoting Prescription Diets.''

On all of his tours, Mark was finding a real and growing interest among veterinarians on the subject of diet foods and their role in managing animal disease. But there were, from time to time, incidents of resistance from persons who claimed that Mark's appearance as a speaker at professional meetings was ''commercial and self-serving.''

Mark avoided arguments on such occasions.

''Through the years, I concentrated carefully on bringing only a message about nutrition and dietary foods in general and their potential impact on disease management,'' he often said. ''Nothing ever was said about Prescription Diets per se unless someone asked a direct question. My goal was simply to sell a concept.''

A case in point was a regular meeting of the Oklahoma Veterinary Medical Association held at the Mayo Hotel in Tulsa in early February of 1952. Details were provided by Dr. J.F. Alberson, D.V.M., who attended the regular meeting and the special session which followed:

''Dr. William Irwin, a nationally known small animal veterinarian, who practiced in Tulsa and on whose staff I was employed attempted to place Dr. Morris on the scientific program to speak on nutrition and dietary management. He failed because the program committee said his appearance would 'be too commercial, amounting to actually selling.' During the final afternoon of the convention, Dr. Irwin circulated among those veterinarians he knew and told them that Dr. Morris would visit with interested persons at Dr. Irwin's home after the sessions ended. He told them that the topic would include 'some new and exciting ways to manage some clinical problems in dogs and cats.'

''So many veterinarians showed up at Dr. Irwin's house at the appointed hour that they overflowed the living room. The Irwins borrowed folding chairs from the neighbors and set them up in the unheated two-car garage and on the driveway. Coffee was brewed and the audience kept on their overcoats. They sat happily through about three hours of what I regarded as pure evangelism on dietary management of canine and feline ailments ranging from gastroenteritis and hookworm to dry skin and obesity.''

The only touch of commercialism was an unobtrusive box of postcard order forms for Prescription Diets addressed to the Hill Packing Co. in Topeka. Mark concedes that the box was almost empty later when he picked it up.

"It's interesting," said Mark. "Those order forms, I discovered on looking it up in my files, listed k/d, p/d, i/d and r/d at about $3 per case. That was 1952. Some 30 years later, thanks to inflation, those same products are listed at around $15 per case. And they're still selling."

12

Dr. Morris: Mr. President

Early in 1960, Mark announced formally that he was a candidate for election as president-elect of the American Veterinary Medical Association. The formal announcement was a climax of months, even years, of weighing by Mark of the pros and cons of seeking a national elective office as titular head of his profession.

"Friends of mine in the association's organization had been urging me to run for president-elect for months," Mark recalled. "They kept telling me the association needed new leadership of the type I could provide. They told me it was my duty."

Mark conceded that the prospect of being elected president of his profession's national organization was appealing. But he spent hours in private debate with friends in the A.V.M.A.—and with himself—over the fact that his main business was developing dietary animal foods for veterinarians.

"I knew that any competition which developed if I ran for national office could claim that my interest in the position was a commercial one," Mark said. "I wanted to avoid that if at all possible."

The arguments of Mark's friends finally prevailed. They insisted that the creation of the Morris Animal Foundation years earlier, plus Mark's assignment in 1948—a full twelve years before the election—of a portion of the royalties from sale of Prescription Diets to the foundation for use in research erased any commercialism from his candidacy.

The national post was a three-year job—one year as president-elect, one year as president, and a final year as immediate past-president of the association.

The annual convention of the American Veterinary Medical Association in 1960 was held from August 14-17 in Denver, Colorado.

The convention site was the venerable Denver City Auditorium. The convention in Denver drew a record attendance of practicing veterinarians, college professors, researchers and supply company representatives.

On Monday, August 15, as the convention got underway, an announcement was made on the floor that the House of Delegates in official session had nominated two men for the office of president-elect of A.V.M.A. and "one will now be selected by ballot of the membership."

The announcement said the polls would be open from 8:30 a.m. on Monday until noon on Tuesday. The winner would be announced on Tuesday "as soon as the tellers have counted the votes."

One of those nominated was Mark L. Morris, D.V.M., of Topeka, Kansas. His opponent was William W. Putney, D.V.M., of Los Angeles, California. At stake were more votes than ever before had been cast in a presidential election of the American Veterinary Medical Association.

Backers of Dr. Putney's candidacy stressed their candidate was a practitioner and cited his brilliant record in World War II as they circulated among delegates in a search for votes. The polls were open, but electioneering was rampant on both sides.

Dr. Putney indeed possessed a war record. He had volunteered twice for service in the U. S. Marine Corps in late 1942 and, after a tour in officer's training school, had been commissioned as a second lieutenant in February, 1943—just weeks before he was awarded a D.V.M. degree from Alabama Polytechnic Institute. He had gone to the War Dog Training School in Camp Lejeune, North Carolina, after receiving his commission and his degree as a veterinarian. He organized, trained and commanded the U. S. Marine Corps 2nd and 3rd war dog platoons and organized the first veterinary hospital section of the Marine Corps for duty in the Pacific.

The success of Dr. Putney's war dog platoons in heavy Marine engagements in the battle of Guam led to the addition of war dog units to all Marine divisions in the Pacific War Zone and to Dr. Putney's nomination for the Silver Star, one of the nation's highest combat decorations when the war ended.

Following the war, Dr. Putney entered small animal practice in the Los Angeles area. He was second vice president of the California Veterinary Medical Association as the national convention opened and had held every elective office in the Southern California chapter, including the presidency in 1956. He was 40 years old.

Campaign literature on Mark circulated at the convention stressed his role as a researcher and as developer of the Prescription Diet line of dietary foods. It also touched on his formation of the Morris Animal Foundation and cited the foundation's 1959 report card on research financing. It said he had "helped to educate 29 veterinarians in 16 different schools."

The literature also stressed Mark's membership and service in a host of scientific organizations, his first-year presidency of the American Animal Hospital Association and his service with the Surgeon General and the War Food Administration in World War II.

The Putney campaign repeatedly emphasized their man was a practitioner and Mark no longer was.

Other factors not mentioned in the literature were to help decide the outcome of the Morris-Putney race for the presidency.

For Mark the 1960 convention of the A.V.M.A. was a time to renew a lot of old acquaintances. In the decade of the 1950s he and Louise had traveled by automobile across most of America to meet and talk with veterinary groups in small towns and large cities everywhere on the subject of proper animal nutrition.

That fact alone gave the candidate from Topeka an edge. He was known personally to more voting delegates than almost any person among the nearly 5,000 in attendance.

In addition, Mark had spent much time during the 1950s visiting the nation's veterinary schools and encouraging the development of seminars on the impact of nutrition. He also had worked tirelessly on a national scale to promote better care of dogs, cats and other animals used in veterinary research. He had been a pioneer in the development of the Animal Care Panel composed of veterinarians, biochemists, physicians and other professionals. This organization encouraged educational programs to bring about improved facilities in research institutions and college laboratories.

Most of Mark's work in this field had been carried out through the American Animal Hospital Association. It had brought positive results in research facilities across the nation and had extended into the government, involving the U.S. Army, the Air Force and the U.S. Navy, the U.S. Public Health Services and the agricultural colleges.

Another quiet strength of Mark's candidacy was the fact that he had taken time during the 1950s to fill speaking engagements at seminars and professional meetings in all parts of the country. Most of these were devoted to what Dr. J. F. Alberson of Tulsa, Oklahoma, had described as "pure evangelism on dietary management of canine and feline ailments."

A perusal of Mark's engagement books of the 1950s shows the extent of his travels on nutrition-oriented speaking and conference engagements.

1953: 1/20/53—Seminars at Illinois Veterinary School, then to Boston for industrial meeting, followed by trips to New York City and Metuchen, New Jersey, on feline diet research; 2/11/53—Detroit, Southern Michigan Veterinary Medical Association meeting; 2/23/53—St. Louis, seminars and conference; 5/23/53—A.A.H.A. meeting, Minneapolis; 7/15/53—Newark and Metuchen, New Jersey; 7/16/53—Conference, Bureau of Biological Research, Rutgers University; 7/16/53—Toronto, Canada Veterinary Association; 7/24/53—Midwest Research Institute conference, Kansas City; 10/15/53—Daytona Beach, Florida, veterinary meeting; 12/7/53—veterinary meetings, Cleveland, Toronto and Ithaca, New York; 12/18/53—veterinary meeting, Buffalo, New York.

It went on like that, year after year. In 1958, highlights were speeches in Puerto Rico; Washington, D.C.; Ithaca, New York; Newark; Westchester; New York City; Chicago and Miami, Florida.

In 1959, highlights were 1/14/59—Michigan State University short course; 2/22/59—A.A.H.A. meeting, Colorado Springs; 4/18-20/59—veterinary association meetings, Topeka; 4/24/59—University of Minnesota, Minneapolis; 7/20/59—Morris Animal Foundation meeting, Denver. 8/15/59—A.V.M.A. meeting, Kansas City; 8/20/59—Colorado State University Research Foundation meeting, Ft. Collins, Colorado; 10/24/59—New York City and Fort Detrick, Frederick, Maryland; 10/31/59—Central Virginia Veterinary Medical Association meeting;11/2/59—Southern district veterinary meeting, Baltimore, Maryland; 11/7/59—New England Veterinary Medical Association meeting.

A campaign factor that no one had considered moved into the foreground as the 1960 convention vote drew near. It was the fact that old friend Dr. J.V. LaCroix had sold his NORTH AMERICAN VETERINARIAN, and new publisher, Harry Costello, had taken over with headquarters in Santa Barbara, California.

Costello had been devoting the facilities of his widely read journal to electing a California veterinary practitioner as president of the A.V.M.A. and had thrown his support behind Dr. Putney, the ex-Marine. His magazine was conducting a national straw poll among veterinarians, hopefully to prove the popularity of the California candidate.

Friends of Mark charged openly that the Costello poll was "rigged in favor of Dr. Putney." Then, they took action. They duplicated the Costello postcard and sent out the cards to friends from coast to coast.

Publisher Costello's plan had been to announce as voting began in Denver that an unbiased, impartial straw vote of veterinarians showed overwhelming support for Dr. Putney of California.

That announcement was not made. "I got back more postcard ballots than we mailed out," Costello told friends. "They came in from cities and towns we didn't have on our list. And most of them favored Dr. Morris."

Still another election factor was an incident involving publisher Harry Costello and several of his friends which took place in the lobby of the Denver Auditorium.

"California is going to win," Costello told the group in general. "Dr. Putney is the winner and he'll be certified when they count the votes tomorrow."

Dr. Olaf Norling Christensen, a veterinarian from Chicago and a friend of Mark, was in the listening group.

"Why don't you put your money where your mouth is?" Dr. Christensen demanded of Costello. "You want to back up that prediction with a bet?"

Costello rose to the challenge. "I'll bet you and your friends a thousand dollars that California and Dr. Putney win," he responded.

The two men were now the attention center of the delegate-packed gathering. Dr. Christensen shouted that "we'll take that bet" and fell into a friendly argument with nearby delegates over who was going to write the check and who was going to hold the bet. In minutes, the money was in hand and given to a neutral delegate for safekeeping until the votes were counted. It was $1,000 against $1,000 with the winner taking all.

The $1,000 bet touched off a round of open electioneering the likes of which the normally staid A.V.M.A. never had been exposed to before. Backers of Dr. Putney set up a reception room in the auditorium and collared delegates as they arrived to cast ballots. The reception room featured free California orange juice.

The Kansas delegation, largest at the convention, rose to this orange juice challenge. Led by Professor Marvin Twiehaus from the veterinary school at Kansas State University, they began an all-out electioneering drive of their own. Professor Twiehaus posted university alumni from Kansas at all doors of the Denver Auditorium. Anyone who arrived to vote was given the full case for candidate Morris before he received a ballot.

The polls closed on time at noon on Tuesday and association officials spent more time than usual counting ballots. The winner was Dr. Mark L. Morris. The victory margin was slender but both official and emphatic. Mark had won by just under 200 votes.

In the merrymaking that followed, Dr. Christensen announced that publisher Costello's check for $1,000 had been cashed "and we voted to make it a gift to the veterinary college of Ohio State University so there will be no bad feelings."

But the open electioneering that preceeded the final ballot count had left an impression on A.V.M.A. officials. The bylaws were changed and all presidents of the association chosen since the meeting in Denver have been elected by the House of Delegates, acting on behalf of a membership which otherwise might be lured into election day antics regarded by many as "not exactly dignified."

The hectic floor activity ended with the final ballot tally and Mark was certified officially by the Board of Governors as winner. The "Convention News" edition of Wednesday, August 17, gave Mark's victory top position on page one. But befitting a professional organization, the close vote drew no mention. The story simply stated that "Dr. Mark L. Morris, elected by ballot, is new president-elect of the American Veterinary Medical Association."

It added simply that Dr. Morris succeeded as president-elect Dr. E. E. Leasure, Manhattan, Kansas, who would be installed as the new president of the association that night during a banquet at the Denver Hilton Hotel.

With his election now official, Mark was swept immediately into a year-long round of meetings and speeches designed to both improve his knowledge of the association and its aims and to spotlight him as an emerging spokesman for a professional organization with at that time nearly 20,000 members nationwide.

Mark automatically became at once a member of the association's Board of Governors. The three-man board, consisting of the president, president-elect and chairman of the executive board, is charged with the responsibility of administering all association activities.

One of Mark's first official actions as president-elect was a personal tour of the association's headquarters office in Chicago. He spent days familiarizing himself with the association's work and its key personnel. Then it was on to Washington, D.C., for an inspection of the association's office in the nation's capital.

In Washington he met the men and women of A.V.M.A. whose task it is to represent the veterinary profession before the U.S. Congress, its myriad committees and the numerous federal boards and commissions.

Here he met the officials of the Food and Drug Administration, the U.S. Department of Agriculture, the National Institutes of Health and a host of other bureaucrats whose daily actions have a direct bearing on the work and fortunes of the nation's veterinarians. Here he learned that a profession without a strong voice in Washington, D.C., is like a new lawn without a fence. It's likely to be stepped on hard.

A full busy year later, on August 21, 1961, at the opening session of the 98th annual A.V.M.A. convention in Detroit, Michigan, Mark was sworn in as the association's new president.

"During the last 12 months I have spent most of my time preparing for the next 12 months," he told the convention in his inaugural address. "I will not belabor you with a report of meetings attended and mileage covered. But I did find that it takes a full year to get ready for the responsibilities of this office."

And with that, Mark outlined what he called "A Blueprint for Action." It was a carefully drawn list of improvements and changes within the operation of the A.V.M.A. designed to make it a more smoothly operating force in betterment of the veterinary profession.

More than 20 years later, in the spring of 1982, Mark outlined again some of the key points of his "Blueprint for Action" and listed the progress made since 1961 on each.

"You must remember that the A.V.M.A., like most organizations and many business operations, is an entity run by committee," he said. "Nothing happens quickly and few things are accomplished overnight. But if the cause is worthy and the pressure is constant and well-applied, things do get accomplished."

In 1961, a problem of the profession was that recruitment of veterinary students was poorly organized and there was little cooperation or coordination between the national and state association and the veterinary colleges.

"In my 'Blueprint for Action,' I told the convention that our recruitment program had become a veritable No Man's land in states where there are no veterinary colleges. I said the solution would involve a formal and intensified recruitment program backed by A.V.M.A. and including most importantly hard work by individual veterinarians to induce bright young people of both sexes to join their profession."

In the early 1980s, lines of applicants now seek admission to veterinary colleges across the U.S. and Canada. Figures compiled by the A.V.M.A. show that as of January 1, 1982 there were 2,216 newly admitted first-year veterinary students in U.S. colleges of veterinary medicine. They were selected in 1981 from among 7,638 qualified applicants.

Another part of Mark's Blueprint for Action involved biomedical research.

"The management of animal colonies used in research is a responsibility which our profession shares with scientists in genetics, nutrition and biochemisty, plus other disciplines," Mark told the convention. "Diagnosis of laboratory animal diseases and the care and treatment of laboratory animals needs to become a part of veterinary education. Students need to be made aware of this new field of specialization. It is estimated that 500 specially trained veterinarians are needed in the immediate future. Our association must assume its share of responsibility along with other scientific and medical associations and government agencies."

Mark's 1982 report on this: "Compared to 20 years ago, the changes in these areas are almost unbelievable. Many millions of dollars have been invested in facilities and in highly trained specialists to utilize laboratory animals to the highest degree of efficiency."

Mark's Blueprint for Action called also for the A.V.M.A. to take the lead in "establishing closer relations with the pharmaceutical, biological and feed industries for mutual benefit."

This program was placed in effect during Mark's term as president. Cooperation between the profession and allied industries now is routine.

Mark also called for relocation of the headquarters office of A.V.M.A. into its own permanent building.

His recommendation was implemented. The A.V.M.A. now is headquartered in its own complex in Schaumburg, Illinois, a suburb of Chicago just west of O'Hare International Airport, and for years has been aided by a top-ranking public relations director, another of Mark's 1961 recommendations.

Mark's years as president-elect and president of A.V.M.A. made the delivery of major speeches, mostly involving association policy, a routine for him. An example—in effect a measure of the man and the workings of his mind—was an address by Mark on April 11, 1962, at the Statler Hilton Hotel in Washington, D.C., before the American Health Institute. It was entitled "Why the Veterinarian?"

Speaking before scientists as an envoy of his profession, Mark told a packed general session audience in the hotel's ballroom that "the veterinarian today is probably the most versatile individual of all professional people."

Common to all veterinarians, he said are three basic objectives of the profession: to conserve man's major animal food sources; to control so-called zoonoses, the diseases which are transmissible from animals to man and to alleviate the suffering of individual animals.

Veterinarians are needed, Mark told the scientists, "because nature does not automatically provide mankind with a supply of animal food which is healthy, clean, in ample supply and ready for consumption. Animal food supply must be cultivated, it has to be guarded against possible decimation or obliteration through diseases, and it has to be protected against health hazards."

He said veterinarians are needed because animals "destined by nature to be man's servants and companions, may also become a curse for man through disease transmissible to their masters."

And he said veterinarians are needed "because man, recognizing a measure of kinship to animals and his dependence on them as beasts of burden, as food supply, or as companions, is not indifferent to their suffering and their ailments."

Mark pointed out that in the course of their professional training, veterinary students devote some 4,000 class hours to subjects such as anatomy, physiology, pharmacology, pathology, microbiology, biochemisty, surgery, medicine, public health, preventive medicine and parasitology.

Veterinarians, he said, are key forces in medical research, the development of pharmaceutical products, in nutritional research and in space flight experiments.

"Human and veterinary medicine are being drawn closer and closer together in the basic sciences to gain maximum health for man, pets and farm animals," he said. "The studies undertaken in a small group of animals may save the lives of a million men. And a surgical technique developed for man may be applicable for saving animal lives. Prevention of many diseases in man depends to a large extent on the eradication or control of those same diseases in animals."

The veterinarian, he added, also has long played a key role in boosting livestock production to meet the demands of fast-growing national and world populations.

Then he summed up his case: "I think we can justly say that the veterinarian, if he did not exist, would simply create himself—because he is an indispensable part of civilized society.''

The applause Mark customarily drew for his speeches was in contrast to the reception he received generally for another of the key points in his Blueprint for Action. He had called at the conclusion of his inaugural address for an increase in association dues.

"Your A.V.M.A. today operates with a budget of $800,000, a sizable portion of which is derived from publication of the *Journal of the American Veterinary Medical Association*," he said. "The Blueprint for Action I have outlined would require an estimated annual budget of $1.4 million. If we are going to increase our activities and carry out new programs, we are going to have to find new revenue. This means just one thing. Our membership dues must be increased."

As Mark had noted it takes time to move a national organization. Mark had to be content with his $800,000 budget in 1961-62. But dues were raised and the A.V.M.A. budget, by 1963-64, when Mark retired as immediate past-president, reached the $1 million mark. The A.V.M.A. budget for 1982 was nearly $5 million.

As his term as president entered its final phases, Mark began to return his attention to business affairs. With Louise at the controls in Topeka during Mark's numerous A.V.M.A. trips, production and sales of Prescription Diets and work at Theracon Laboratories had continued much as usual. But now it was time, in Mark's view, to pull all stops on stepped-up research to develop a special new diet aimed at helping to manage heart disease, the elusive-of-control killer of both humans and animals.

In the early 1960s, as Mark turned his attention to developing the new formula, a federal grant of $1.5 million had been made by the National Institutes of Health to the University of Pennsylvania. It called for extensive research by both the School of Medicine and the College of Veterinary Medicine at the University of Pennsylvania to gather new information on the various phases of human heart disease.

The bulk of the big research grant was earmarked for the screening of some 5,000 research dogs under the direction of Professor David K. Detweiller, a member of the staff of the veterinary school who also had an appointment from the cardiovascular section of the university's medical school. Dr. Detweiller's assignment was to determine through tests involving the research canines as much as possible about the incidence, diagnosis and potential management of all phases of heart disease. The goal was to establish the relationship existing between man and dog in heart ailments and to make the information available to specialists in human heart research.

The research work at the University of Pennsylvania was in cooperation with similar research at the Animal Medical Center in New York City and at the College of Veterinary Medicine at Ohio State University, under the direction of Dr. Robert Hamlin.

Shortly after he learned of the new federally financed research on heart disease, Mark was invited by the Colorado Medical Society to appear as a speaker at a special symposium in Denver.

Mark, caught up personally in the heart disease diet problem, decided that the relationship between management of heart ailments in humans and canines was a fitting subject for the medical symposium. He promptly arranged for Dr. Detweiller of the University of Pennsylvania to join him for the Denver program.

During the course of the Denver meeting, Mark and Dr. Detweiller had several conversations about the progress of the heart research projects at the university's laboratories in Philadelphia.

"It's not going well," Dr. Detweiller confided. "We've run into a blank wall."

He explained that the studies were centered on the role of sodium—notably salt intake—in cases of congestive heart failure, one of the well known cardiovascular phenomena.

Mark was well aware that congestive heart involvement or failure long since had been traced in both human and animal cases to the development of back pressure exerted on heart action. It involves the seeping of blood serum out into surrounding tissues with a result that fluids begin to fill the lungs, and swelling or edema, in medical jargon, occurs in the feet and legs. Breathing becomes more and more difficult and finally impossible as lungs fill with fluid.

Dr. Detweiller said his experiments involved trying to maintain the laboratory dogs on a reduced sodium intake.

"When the sodium level drops below a certain point, the animals refuse to eat their food," he reported to Mark. "No matter what we've tried, they just won't touch the stuff. They seem to prefer to starve."

The non-eating canines had thrown into disarray the series of electrocardiographic measurements planned as a key to the experiments. "We've hit a blank wall," Dr. Detweiller finally summed up. "Any ideas?"

Mark then announced calmly that he and his Theracon staff were at work on what they proposed to be a low-sodium diet for management of canine heart disease and that "we'll be pleased and honored to cooperate with you."

Before the two men left Denver, Dr. Detweiller had agreed to forward to Mark in Topeka all of the analytical data on foods including sodium levels collected to date in the research project. Mark had made it plain that the data would save him valuable time and serve as an aid in pinpointing the precise level of sodium content which showed promise of aiding in the management of heart congestion while still remaining palatable to the taste of dogs.

The invaluable data arrived in less than a week and Mark at once set up a series of meetings with Dr. Harrison Newlin of Midwest Research Institute, the scientist who had played a key supporting role in development of other special foods in the Prescription Diets line.

"We started out on paper," Mark recalled. "We listed the ingredients we knew would appeal to canine appetite and then aimed for a diet which would contain no more than 28 milligrams of sodium per pound. That was the level Dr. Detweiller said he was shooting for. When we came up with several possibilities, we then went over the work to make certain that the food we were developing was well balanced from a general health standpoint."

Mark and Dr. Newlin finally selected a handful of formulas and had them turned into food at Theracon Laboratories and then supervised a massive test, feeding the experimental food daily to a series of Theracon dogs in good health.

As the tests went on, Mark was strengthening his staff at Theracon to make certain no avenue leading to a palatable low-sodium canine heart diet was left uncovered. The Theracon team quickly grew to include, in addition to the veterinary staff, several nutritionists, a food technologist and a clinical pathologist.

"With all the brainpower behind it, our project finally came up with a couple of low-sodium recipes we were able to get the dogs to eat, although not exactly with relish," Mark recalled. "A few changes later, and we knew we were beginning to close in on what we had been seeking."

The new diet was prepared in the pilot plant facilities at Theracon and sent to Dr. Detweiller in Philadelphia. The University of Pennsylvania scientists had confirmed by telephone before the shipment left Topeka that "we're still on dead center here with all tests suspended because we can't find a low salt diet our dogs will eat."

Several weeks of silence followed the food shipment. And then the telephone call Mark had been hoping for came in from Philadelphia.

"We need more of that food," Dr. Detweiller said. "The dogs

are eating it and the electrical measurements we're now able to make are significant. Send more food.''

Within days another call came in to Mark, this one from Dr. Robert Hamlin, who was conducting heart disease tests at Ohio State University.

"Send me food and I'll send you data," he offered. Mark accepted. "Before long we were receiving invaluable data from two large and well-equipped laboratories," Mark said. "This helped to speed up the final phases of our research. The big remaining problem was whether reduction of the sodium level in the diet might interfere with other diet-essential ions such as potassium and magnesium. It took a lot of research, but we finally worked it all out."

Mark then tackled the considerable task of convincing the top executives of Hill Packing Co. that he had a new product worthy of mass production and mass promotion.

Dr. Hamlin of Ohio State University proved a valuable ally in Mark's campaign for mass production. He began a series of lectures to veterinary groups across the United States, telling the practitioners about the new low-sodium diet and assuring them "it's a lot better and more effective than any medicine you may have been using in heart cases."

Positive results on the test use of the new diet on patients in veterinary clinics across the country began flowing in to Topeka. In months, the label "For Experimental Use Only" was replaced by a formal label for "h/d® " or heart diet, the newest full-production member of the Prescription Diet line being turned out by the Hill plant in Topeka.

"There were some problems as mass production began," Mark recalled. "For one, we quickly discovered that we couldn't use regular city tap water in the formula—too much salt in that. It was distilled water only from then on."

Mark has frequently said that despite his role in creating it, h/d as a diet for dogs "never ceases to amaze me."

Before h/d was made available to the veterinarians in mid-1964, the usual veterinary practice in trying to control congestive heart failure in dogs was similar to the method employed in human treatment— the use of various glycosides—notably digitalis.

"Most veterinarians also used the mercurial diuretics, also employed in human cases, to rid the body of excess fluids via the urine," Mark said. "With h/d, the treatment was vastly more simple. I still take delight in seeing h/d used as an exclusive diet for canine patients so loaded with heart-threatening fluids they can hardly walk.

"After three to five days on h/d, those dogs begin to run around and exercise normally. It's as though something magic was taking over and eliminating the excess fluids from the tissues and the lungs."

A case in point which Mark has said "I'll always remember with delight," was that of a toy poodle he came upon one morning in Los Angeles while visiting the office of Don Mahan, executive of the Southern California Veterinary Medical Association.

"I watched the little dog stretched out under a bench in the office and commented to the lady at the nearby desk (the association's secretary, Marje Maiden), that the dog obviously didn't feel well.

"No, not very well at all," she said. "My dog has heart and kidney trouble and is very sick. That's why I bring him to work with me."

Mark identified himself, asked if he could examine the dog and promptly diagnosed the case as one of advanced heart congestion. He learned the little animal was under veterinary treatment and was on a k/d diet because of kidney damage.

"I got the veterinarian's name and gave him a call," Mark recalled. "I told him I had chanced upon his poodle patient and would like to suggest a diet change. I told him about h/d, which was new then, and suggested that k/d, even though low in salt and as good as it is, contained too much sodium for this particular patient.

"The veterinarian was very gracious about this stranger butting in on his patient routine. He said he valued my suggestion and would get on the phone and order a supply of h/d for the poodle right away."

As he left, Mark told the secretary he'd check back with her later that week.

"I called five days later from the Los Angeles airport, where I was changing planes," Mark recalled. "Her voice was smiling all over. She said the h/d had arrived the day I left, that she started her poodle on the new diet at once and that three days later the dog started running all around the place. Until then, she had to carry the poodle outdoors to let it limp around for exercise. She was one happy lady."

13

A Family Affair

In the view of Mark L. Morris, the most important event of his life was his marriage on the fourth day before Christmas in 1928. He gained a wife, a mother for his family-to-be and a knowledgeable business partner when he linked his life to that of Louise Weber of Stelton, New Jersey.

In later years, Louise was fond of recalling those early days of struggle as the new wife of a budding and ambitious young veterinarian with his eyes on a goal far beyond the daily treatment of the ailments of animal patients.

"I really hadn't programmed my life to becoming the wife of a veterinarian," she told friends. "But one thing led to another and he was a man of great persuasion.

"Naturally, Mark and his new practice in veterinary medicine needed someone to keep the office records, and I became the No. 1 record keeper. What I didn't know when I married a veterinarian was that I also was marrying a business, a research organization and a foundation. I wasn't too surprised at becoming a mother and a grandmother, but the other things I hadn't counted on."

To Louise W. Morris, Mark's career was her career and there never was doubt about that. She ran the office, handled the telephones and the appointments, managed the finances and supervised the raising of daughter Ruth and son Mark, Jr.

Louise was at Mark's side on the countless trips he took over the years he was building the Prescription Diet line and nurturing his young foundation. She was his manager, his hostess. She sat in on hundreds of business and scientific meetings, saying little and observing all and coming up later with observations that aided Mark in making some of the key decisions of his career.

169

Louise and Mark posed for an official photograph in Denver in the early seventies.

It was the fondest hope of both Mark and Louise—expressed often to each other and close friends in privacy, but never mentioned to their children—that both Ruth and young Mark would develop an interest in the family enterprise and join them in their work.

First to respond was daughter Ruth. Armed with a degree in journalism, she had moved to California shortly after graduation from the University of Colorado and had been working as a newspaper reporter. But the need of her father's expanding line of Prescription Diets and the new and still-struggling foundation for an effective public relations program intrigued her.

She volunteered to help, but stressed that she would need professional help and guidance at first to polish her innate and book-learning-aroused interest in shaping public opinion and building an aura of success and high class around her father's products.

Ruth and her father found the perfect starting combination in William Kostka & Associates, a Denver public relations firm headed by a former New York City newspaperman and bolstered by a young but highly qualified staff. A one-year contract with the Kostka firm specified that work on the account would center on Ruth Morris, who would be based in the Kostka office under the supervision of a Kostka executive.

Thus did Ruth join the family team as a working partner. The assignment was a broad one—in Mark's words "to disseminate knowledge about k/d, p/d and the foundation among veterinarians, to encourage a favorable image among them and to develop a whole new area of professional and public relations as it may relate to veterinarians."

Assigned to the account by Kostka was Claude Ramsey, former United Press International writer and bureau executive who had moved to Denver in the wake of wartime service in the Pacific on the staff of General MacArthur to begin a postwar career in the public relations field.

From the outset in November, 1954, the Claude Ramsey-Ruth Morris professional pairing was a success story. They learned quickly to function as a team. And the results of their public relations campaign were sufficiently on the positive side to impress even Mark L. Morris, who was maintaining a neutral and non-parental stance.

"Experience with the Kostka firm as an entity is not too satisfactory," Mark said in a letter to a laboratory associate in mid-1955. "Kostka and his staff, with the exception of Ramsey and Ruth, essentially

Daughter Ruth Keesling in 1981 photograph, organizing the veterinary student agent program

know nothing about the type of program we are involved in. About all they are providing is an office and a desk where Ruth can do the work with the help and supervision of Mr. Ramsey, who has several other accounts to handle.''

Claude Ramsey and Ruth Morris were not aware of her father's attitude. In due course, as the Kostka contract neared expiration, Ramsey asked for an audience with Mark on one of his visits to Denver.

"I've been thinking for some time about opening a public relations company of my own," Ramsey began. "I'm ready to do that now and we're going to call it Public Relations Incorporated."

Ruth Morris, said Ramsey, was ready to join him at Public Relations Incorporated, and she would be in charge of the Morris public relations efforts.

A deal was struck after some negotiating and in December, 1955, Public Relations Incorporated opened for business in 505 Mile High Center, the first of what now is a veritable forest of skyscraper office buildings rising in downtown Denver. As part of the new contract, Claude Ramsey became part-time executive director of the Morris Animal Foundation.

On June 30, 1956, Ruth Morris became Mrs. Thomas Keesling and, in the words of her father, "Tom became a very important member of our family." Tom Keesling, at the time of the marriage, was the head of a young but growing travel agency. He quickly would build it into a leader in its field, specializing in conducted tours of exotic and far-off places, but his new bride insisted on continuing with her public relations work for her father's enterprises and in her newly acquired post as a lifetime trustee of Morris Animal Foundation. After a honeymoon trip, Ruth Keesling was back at her desk at Public Relations Incorporated.

A steady flood of pamphlets and other carefully prepared literature, designed to increase understanding of and build support for both the Prescription Diets program (and nutrition as an aid in managing animal disease) and the Morris Animal Foundation, flowed from the outset from the new public relations office.

As the work progressed, into clear focus came a dazzling fact—the need for a definite program to impress on young veterinary students before they leave college the facts of animal nutritional needs, and the role proper diets can play in handling the ailments of canine and feline patients.

"It became quite obvious to Louise and me in our continuing travels to meet with veterinarians across the country that students coming out of veterinary schools in the late 1950s and early 1960s knew little or nothing about small animal nutrition," Mark has said. "We realized that, if our program was to be a success, we had to find a way to reach these young veterinarians before they got out into the field, while we still had them in the classroom."

Out of that came the Student Agent Program, an innovative, unique and almost instantly successful low-key public relations effort in which Ruth Keesling was to be a leading force for decades—despite travels around the world with husband Tom and the duties of a mother of three sons (Tom, Jim and Frank Keesling).

The need for a force like the Student Agent Program was outlined at length by Mark. The chore of putting it together and "getting it on the road" was taken over by Claude Ramsey and Ruth.

The initial Student Agent effort sponsored by the Morris interests began in the fall of 1957. The original model, like Henry Ford's first car, has undergone steady revisions and drastic changes at intervals down through the years of a quarter century. But the basics remain. The idea is to convert veterinary students into practicing users and advocates of dietary management, simply because years of experience have proven its worth in controlling animal diseases.

It all starts with annual selection of student agents, chosen now from members of sophomore and junior classes in the 29 colleges of veterinary medicine in the United States and Canada. (This represents a huge number of soon-to-be practicing veterinarians. In the 29 veterinary schools as of January 1, 1982, there were 8,354 professional students enrolled, along with 1,040 newly created veterinarians enrolled as graduate students and 540 non-veterinarian graduate students of various veterinary medicine disciplines).

The clockwork smoothness of the 24th annual indoctrination meeting of new Student Agents of Mark Morris Associates, which began on Friday, October 9, 1981 and concluded on Sunday morning two days later, was testimony to the professionalism of Ruth Keesling.

The new agents, both young women and men students, were chosen in advance for the 1981-82 college year, largely through recommendations of the graduating students they were to succeed and of faculty members. Their indoctrination at this point had been sketchy, but all were aware of the basic duties they would be expected to perform and of the rewards of their efforts they could count on receiving.

The first of those rewards was a letter on Mark Morris Associates stationery signed by Ruth Keesling. It confirmed each appointment as student agent and outlined plans for the annual conclave to be held as usual with a Kansas City, Missouri, International Airport Hotel as the initial gathering point.

"It is required that students planning to serve as agents attend," the letter said. "Please fill out and return the enclosed card as soon as possible. Your trip will acquaint you with Morris Associates personnel, will familiarize you with the role of nutritional management in veterinary medicine, will acquaint you with your assignment as a Student Agent, and will include a tour of various facilities.

"Please discuss past distribution techniques of agent material at your school with the previous agent and with your nutrition professor so you can tell us of your school's particular needs."

There followed a complete outline of the program set for the meeting and details on how to reach the session's headquarters, down to advice on using the courtesy phone at the Kansas City air terminal to summon a bus to the Marriott Airport Hotel.

Days before departure, each new agent received a letter from Travel Associates, Inc., the Keesling travel agency in Denver which is called on annually to arrange details of the complicated convergence at roughly the same hour on the Kansas City airport of students literally from all points in the United States and Canada. Inside each letter, along with detailed final instructions, was a complimentary round-trip airline ticket. The instructions included details on how to submit an expense account to cover any needed item en route in both directions.

The roll calls later, after each stop of the tour bus, which took the international group to Topeka, Kansas, and back on Saturday, sounded like nomination ballots at a national presidential election.

Each began with Auburn, followed by California and Colorado State. Each ended with Washington State. In between were Cornell, Florida, Georgia, Illinois, Iowa State, Kansas State, Louisiana State, Michigan State, Minnesota, Missouri, Ohio State, Oklahoma State, Ontario (Canada), Oregon State, Pennsylvania, Purdue, Saskatchewan (Canada), Tennessee, Texas A&M, Tufts, Tuskegee, and Virginia-Maryland.

A hospitality room on the mezzanine of the Marriott Hotel stayed open until the early hours Saturday so newly arrived student agents could meet each other. Wakeup calls sounded throughout the hotel at 6:15 a.m. Saturday and the entire group gathered in the hospitality room for breakfast and introductions.

Then it was off to Topeka by chartered bus with students changing seats every 5 minutes or so on a signal from Ruth Keesling. The idea was to give everyone a chance to greet everyone else and thus melt the ice which usually chills a gathering of strangers. It worked; by the time the bus pulled into the headquarters office of 100-acre Theracon Laboratories on the eastern edge of Topeka it was able to unload a cargo of chattering friends.

As a group, the students who attended the 1981 Student Agent meeting of Mark Morris Associates looked like a handpicked cadre of the upper 10 percent of the average college student body.

A few decades earlier, a group of veterinary students chosen at random from across the nation might have worn the unmistakable stamp of rural background. Not so these students of the 1980s who battle odds of higher than three-to-one even to win admission to the veterinary college. This was a group of dedicated youngsters with a bent toward science, medicine and human relations. They wore an all-American look.

Twelve were young women. Two of the smallest of these said they planned to specialize in treatment of large animals after graduation. None of the group smoked either a pipe or cigarettes. Ashtrays at all stops remained empty, but nobody commented about it. There was little idle chitchat among the students, except during a break for a picnic luncheon on the Theracon grounds and an "attitude adjustment hour" around 5 p.m. at the headquarters building of Mark Morris Associates after walking tours of the Hill plant on the banks of the Kansas River in Topeka and the Topeka Zoological Park, one of the finest small city zoos in the world.

The business trip aura was relaxed only during a dinner at the Topeka Country Club and on the 70 mile bus trip back to the Marriott Hotel and Kansas City International airport, where new friends parted for flights back to their own campuses.

As a commercial effort, the 1981 Student Agent meeting was distinctly low key, as is the entire Student Agent program under the direction of Ruth Keesling.

"We don't ever ask them to sell anything, not even our image," Ruth said. "Their job with us is limited to their college and it consists solely of assisting Mark Morris Associates, formed in 1962 as the business arm of my father's enterprises, to carry out its professional educational program on the application of nutrition in veterinary medicine.''

The job, Ruth told the students, involves relationships with other students, faculty and previous student agents. During each college year the agents will receive copies of eight or more specialized pamphlets or booklets. Each will deal with a separate aspect of the nutritional management of small animals. The subject will range from treatment of allergies and anorexia to diarrhea and heart failure. The material will be supplied by Mark Morris Associates and will include a series of ''Case of the Month'' capsulized summaries of symptoms, diagnosis and nutritional treatment. Coordinating shipments to the students are Mary Raines, Mark Morris Associates secretary and Eleanor Winrick.

''All of the literature must be coordinated with the proper professor to make sure it arrives in the hands of the students at the best time to tie in with ongoing courses,'' Ruth said. ''The new agents are urged to keep in close touch with the students they succeeded in the job for tips.''

Throughout the college year Ruth keeps in close touch with each agent by letter, helping to iron out problems as they arise and eventually exchanging notes on personal happenings like special trips, engagements, marriages and class honors.

''We become sort of a family,'' Ruth said. ''The information sent us by student agents on specific suggestions for improvements or changes from their classmates and the insight we get into the general feeling of students about our program has enabled us to fine-tune it over the years.''

The two-hour annual lecture on nutrition of the small animal is the highlight of the program. Participants from Theracon are Woodrow Nelson, Ph.D., food technologist; Harold Scheid, nutritionist; and Alvin Stuke, vice president of the company. Lecturers from the Morris Associates' staff are Mark Morris, Jr., D.V.M., Ph.D.; Dr. Stanley Teeter and Dr. George Doering who explain the literature to be distributed. Lon Lewis, D.V.M., Ph.D., has recently joined the staff and updates the agents on latest nutritional trends.

''Your job with us is not to sell a product,'' the lecturers said several times in varied ways. ''Your task will be to keep up on the latest in veterinary education on nutrition and act as our liaison. Our sole mission is the application of nutrition to the management of disease in animals.

Your chore is to convince your classmates that you have found a technique—and it's nutritional therapy.''

While touring some of the facilities of Theracon, Mark, Jr., presented a list of some of the valuable employees: Dan Manning supervises all animal care, while Jim Hahn, long-time employee, is now in charge of the pilot plant and general maintenance; Jake Bowser oversees the metabolism animals and serves as veterinary assistant; Ken Delfelder is in charge of the important quality control program; Don Campbell cares for the cat colony; and Red Becker manages the dogs on palatability studies. Pat Miller serves as Theracon secretary.

Dr. Mark Morris, Jr., kept a running drumfire of commentary during the special tour of the Hill plant. He made it easy for the young student agents to grasp that the plant was a new and fully automated facility devoted entirely to the production of the Prescription Diet line of animal foods and the Science Diets developed in recent years. He explained details of the automatic mixing stations and cookers and the special areas where thousands of cans, manufactured on the spot out of ribbons of steel, meet the flow of cooked food and are filled and labeled automatically to flow on out for temporary storage in the warehouse area.

And he stressed areas where cans are removed from the line at intervals for separate quality checks by specialists on the Hill payroll and by experts at Theracon.

"No can may leave this plant for market until the entire batch from which it came is quality checked and rechecked by us," he said. "That is an unbreakable rule, even if an entire batch of up to 300,000 cans must be scrapped because of a flaw."

The secret of success for Prescription Diets, he said, is quality control. "Once you have achieved something really good, you must be certain that it is the same at all times. That's quality control," he said.

One detour on the plant tour had a special impact. It took the student agents into a room where labels for Prescription Diets are stored until they are needed in the plant. Many of the label stacks were written in foreign languages to handle the steadily increasing export business. Young Mark explained that Japan had become the biggest overseas customer for Prescription Diets. Close behind, he said, are Great Britain, West Germany and South Africa.

"The export business is growing fast," he told the students. "Our product has worldwide appeal. After all, a dog with heart failure is the same in Japan or the United States, and they both need a low salt diet."

The Topeka Zoo tour produced low-key but impressive testimonials for special diets developed by Mark Morris Associates. Zoo director Gary K. Clarke, who was to be that night's unforgettably good dinner speaker at the Student Agent gathering at the Topeka Country Club, led the tour. He guided the students through the elephant and ape exhibits, past the polar bears and into the zoo's remarkable tropical rain forest exhibit. Then on to the special area where eagles are on exhibit in giant woven wire forest glades.

A sign on one fence said the eagles on display there were the first American golden eagles to be hatched and reared in captivity in any zoo in the world. They had arrived via hatching on May 2, 1971, and now were raising a family of their own.

"As mankind asserts himself on who is Number One in the world, he keeps expanding into wild habitat," the zoo director said. "The only way to preserve some species is in zoos and that makes mankind's first duty to feed his captives a proper diet.

"The production of young under zoo conditions has been a major problem," Clarke continued. "The main problem has been finding a proper diet to support procreation and insure the arrival of succeeding generations. In the case of the golden American eagles, zoo experts believed somehow that eagles mated only in flight and had been feeding rabbits or similar food to captive eagles. They were producing no young.

"Then Dr. Morris, Jr., and his colleagues at Mark Morris Associates started research and came up with a line of balanced zoo diets they have started producing under the Zu-Preem® label. We credit his diet for carnivorous birds with the successful hatching of golden eagles in captivity. They had made certain this species will live on."

An informal poll of seven students on the bus ride back to Kansas City turned up seven self-styled "converts to the Morris message on small animal nutrition." The new believers said they planned to "work real hard" to spread that message among their fellow students. They represented campuses on both coasts, in the midwest and in the deep south.

Dr. Mark L. Morris, Sr., is proud of the Student Agent Program and of his daughter's leadership role in continuing and perfecting it.

"Our Student Agent Program has been recognized by people in the industry, and by leaders in the pharmaceutical and biological fields as one of the best in the country," he said. "A few companies maintain agents, but none carry out the extensive program we do. The job some of them assign is to pass out some samples of pills or vitamins

Son Mark Morris, D.V.M., Ph.D., in a 1977 photograph, overseeing the details of Mark Morris Associates' research, quality control and professional education programs

or what have you. The students feel that they are being brainwashed by a big corporation. Ruth makes them feel they are working for a cause and are part of a family.''

The arrival of Mark's son as a full-fledged partner in the family enterprises came some years after Ruth's role began. It was preceded by one of the best and most complete formal educations in veterinary science available in the land.

Young Mark had triumphed completely, in the manner of the young, over his uprooting from high school in New Jersey in the middle of his junior year in early 1951 and the sudden transfer to Topeka High School, a place with 2,000 students, all of them strangers.

By the time graduation day rolled around at Topeka High, young Mark ranked as director of the school's symphony orchestra, drum major of the marching band, and a good enough Thespian to rate a second lead in Brigadoon, the musical comedy staged by the senior class.

The bulk of his high school class was headed for the University of Kansas, and Mark decided to join them. He chose to specialize in the basic sciences as a prerequisite of medical school. Part-time work with Lattimore-Fink Laboratories in Topeka as an assistant in clinical pathology had stirred an interest in medicine in general.

The university campus at Lawrence was only 20 miles from Topeka, but young Mark joined the Phi Delta Gamma fraternity and moved into the fraternity house. All went smoothly until late in the fall semester of his sophomore year when Mark, Jr., arrived suddenly at home and asked for a private chat with his parents.

''I've made up my mind at last,'' he told them. ''I've decided that I want to be a veterinarian and that I want to apply to Cornell University. I think it's the best in the land, and besides, it's where Dad went.''

The potential barriers to admission at Cornell popped up quickly. One was the fact that the school in Ithaca, New York, officially known as the New York State College of Veterinary Medicine at Cornell University, accepted 80% of its student body from New York State. The bulk of the remaining 20% came from New Jersey, Pennsylvania and the New England states.

Potential barrier number two was the fact that Cornell insisted that all of its veterinary students prove actual working experience on a farm as one of the requirements for admission to the veterinary school. That had been no problem for his farm-reared father, but Mark, Jr.'s, total farming experience involved summer visits with his Uncle Lester, Mark, Sr.'s, younger brother.

The spring and summer of 1954 found Mark, Jr., at work in the Henderson, Colorado area—his father's birthplace—on farms operated by his uncle, Lester Morris, and his uncle's friendly neighbor, Gene Rucker.

The Rucker operation was a large garden farm, specializing in sweet corn, tomatoes and similar crops for the wholesale produce market. Mark, Jr., got his farm experience, documented by Rucker and Lester Morris, and the required papers were sent to Ithaca. Back came a request that he appear at Cornell for an interview with the Committee on Admissions.

After a nervous period of anxious waiting following the Ithaca interview, Mark, Jr., was accepted and in the fall of 1954 became one of only two non-eastern students in the Cornell University veterinary school. Two years later, in the fall of 1956, young Mark met the girl of his choice.

Mark, Jr., an upperclassman, met his bride-to-be as she came down the line of students taking their physical exams to enroll in Cornell's graduate school of nutrition in 1956.

She was dark-haired Bette McGehee of Canyon, Texas, holder of a bachelor's degree from Texas Tech and candidate for a master's degree in human nutrition. She and Mark, Jr., were friends from the first smile. A few dates followed the initial meeting. Then came wedding bells.

Mark, Jr., and Bette graduated from Cornell together in 1958 and the young couple headed for Topeka where Mark, Jr., had accepted a summer job at Theracon "until I can sort out what I want to do about further education and the draft."

All United States males of draft age were subject to call to military duty under conscription in 1958. But young Mark, as holder of a new degree as a Doctor of Veterinary Medicine, had a choice. His option to the draft, and possibly service as an infantry private, was to volunteer for a direct commission as a first lieutenant in the U.S. Army Veterinary Corps. But before he could make a choice, Mark, Jr., received a notice from his draft board ordering him to appear within five days at Fort Leonard Wood in Missouri for induction into the army.

"The draft board had no official notice that young Mark held a D.V.M. degree and had the option. Something had to be done quickly and I took the first route that occurred to me," Mark, Sr., recalled.

The Morrises, father, mother and son, caught a plane for

Washington, D.C., and minutes after landing were in the office of General James A. McCallum, a retired brigadier general in the Veterinary Corps, who was heading the office of the American Veterinary Medical Association in the nation's capital and who ranked as a personal friend of Mark Morris, Sr., from his A.V.M.A. days.

The general confirmed a mixup at the Topeka draft board, and personally accompanied them to the office of General Hershey, director of Selective Service. The next morning, following a hurriedly arranged physical examination at the Pentagon, Mark, Jr., left Washington with a commission as a first lieutenant and an assignment to introductory training at the Army Medical Service School at Fort Sam Houston, Texas. The order to report as a draft inductee at Fort Leonard Wood had been canceled.

Joined by Bette, his wife, Mark, Jr., reported five weeks later for permanent assignment at the U.S. Army Biological Warfare Laboratories, Fort Detrick, Maryland.

Mark, Jr., drew the pathology division at Fort Detrick, and it developed into a perfect assignment for the young and ambitious holder of a new degree in veterinary medicine. Head of the division was Dr. James Rooney, also a graduate of the veterinary college at Cornell University who had returned recently from graduate studies in animal pathology in Sweden. (Dr. Rooney later was to serve on the Scientific Advisory Board of Morris Animal Foundation.)

The assignment called for regular work sessions in slide-reading at the Armed Forces Institute of Pathology at Walter Reed Army Medical Center. This opened new vistas for the young veterinarian—the study of disease slides from all over the world.

"We learned about almost every disease anyone ever heard of," young Mark assured his father.

The duty also involved processing thousands of monkeys, flown to this country directly from jungles in Asia for use in research and in the making of polio vaccine. The death rate among the imported monkeys from dehydration en route, disease and parasites was high, and, for Mark, Jr., the experience was a crash course in handling the ailments of exotic animals. Out of this grew Mark, Jr.'s, ranking as an expert in zoo nutrition.

The tour at Fort Detrick also involved Mark, Jr., in research work destined to lead him into graduate studies and the pursuit of advanced degrees following his duty in the Veterinary Corps.

One research project young Mark tackled was the problem of a mysterious blindness among laboratory cats. His goal was to pinpoint the specific cause of the disease and to determine if the lack of Vitamin A or some other diet deficiency was leading to dilated pupils and the loss of retina function among felines. The research resulted in the first published description of the lesions involved in the disease and of indication, later confirmed, that they were the result of an amino acid deficiency. Mark, Jr., later was to base his masters thesis at the University of Wisconsin on the cat blindness problem.

Another of his research projects at Fort Detrick involved skeletal diseases of larger breeds of dogs. Scientifically, he was studying possible causes of foot distortion—flat fleet, splayed toes—developing among pups of breeds like Great Danes and German shepherds.

Mark, Jr., was deeply involved in pathological studies when his tour of duty with the Army Veterinary Corps drew to a close in 1960. He promptly decided to continue his studies and, after consultation with Dr. James Allison, a friend from his boyhood days in New Jersey, chose the University of Wisconsin for graduate studies.

Mark, Jr., took reports of his Fort Detrick work on feline eye problems and canine bone distortion to the University of Wisconsin. His professors looked over the material, quizzed him at length on his background in pathology and came to a conclusion which delighted him. If Mark could pass a required course in comparative pathology at the University of Wisconsin medical school, spend a specified number of weeks in the autopsy laboratory and then expand his army work of feline eye problems and turn it into an acceptable thesis, he would at the end of one year of slave-like work receive from the university a master's degree in veterinary science with a specialty in pathology.

Young Mark did just that, but the new M.S. degree did not fully satisfy his desire for further education. He was filled with a burning curiosity to delve into the mysteries of mineral deficiencies in animal foods and their relation to disease and bone malformation. The challenge of solving these problems of flat feet and splayed toes among Great Danes and German shepherds he had researched at Fort Detrick in Maryland still bothered him.

In Mark, Jr.'s, view, the climate of the moment at the University of Wisconsin was ideal for his pursuit of a Ph.D. degree. He took the M.S. degree in stride and went in search of higher pursuits.

His graduate professor was Dr. Paul Phillips, rated at the time as one of the world's best in the field of canine nutrition, especially mineral nutrition. Dr. Phillips had been doing research on nutritional requirements of dogs and was co-author of numerous scientific papers outlining the role of dietary nutrients in human and animal disease.

Mark signed up to do his Ph.D. thesis with Paul Phillips and counted himself fortunate to be accepted. Dr. Phillips was in poor health and nearing the end of his academic career. Mark, Jr., was to be among his final students.

The Ph.D. work centered on the entire problem of mineral metabolism, ranging from calcium and phosphorous to magnesium and potassium, and it took two full years of steady work for Mark, Jr., to produce his completed thesis.

The coveted degree was awarded by the University of Wisconsin in 1963, and Mark L. Morris, Jr., D.V.M., M.S., Ph.D., was ready for a professional career. Specifically, he was faced with a vital decision—whether to join his father in the family business or accept promising offers which had been made to him for an academic career.

The choice was a difficult one, its complexity made even more difficult by the fact that Mark, Jr.'s, wife, Bette Morris, held a masters degree in human nutrition and had remained both active and interested in the field. While the couple was stationed at Fort Detrick, Bette had worked as a teacher of nutrition, and also had been employed by the Maryland Health Department. She had invitations for full-time appointments to the staff of several universities.

Another factor which had to be considered was that Mark, Jr., and Bette had become parents while he worked on his advanced degrees. Two sons—Mark Lee Morris and David Russell Morris—had arrived and daughter Lynn was on the way.

Lynn Morris was born in December, 1963, in Topeka, Kansas. The decision had been made. Mark, Jr., joined the family business.

Dr. Mark L. Morris, Sr., and Louise carefully avoided any intervention while their son worked out his decision on how to spend the rest of his life.

"Louise and I felt it was a decision that Mark, Jr., and Bette had to make for themselves," the father has said often. "We prayed that he would decide to join us. And it's a plain fact that if he had decided to seek a career elsewhere we would have been forced to put our entire business on the market for sale somewhere down the line. It was growing too large for us to handle by ourselves."

The threat of "too big to handle" did not materialize. Starting in the fall of 1963, the Morris operation became a family affair.

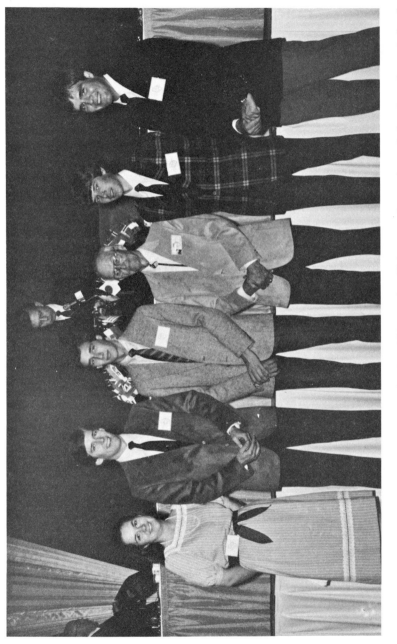

Mark and his grandchildren met on March 13, 1983, at the 50th annual meeting of the American Animal Hospital Association. Left to right: Lynn Morris, Tom Keesling, Jr., Jim Keesling, Mark Morris, Frank Keesling and David Morris. Not shown: grandson Mark Lee Morris.

14

The Surging Sixties

Mark and Louise threaded their way along downtown Denver's busy 17th Street, famed as the "Wall Street of the Rockies." They paused at the corner to wait for the "Walk" light to flash on, then hurried across the street and into the imposing building which housed Boettcher & Co., the investment banking and stock brokerage arm of the fabled Boettcher financial empire.

"We have an appointment with Mr. David Lawrence," Mark told the attractive young woman presiding over a reception desk. "The name is Dr. Mark Morris."

It was the fall of 1965, just weeks short of Mark's 65th birthday, the one that would bring him to the age when retirement was customary for hardworking American males. But retirement and birthdays were far from the minds of Mark and Louise as they greeted senior vice president of Boettcher & Co., David Lawrence, and were ushered into his office.

"Your attorneys have briefed me fully on your situation," said Lawrence, after a few ice-breaking moments of chitchat about the lovely Denver weather and assurances that the couple's trip from Allenspark had been an enjoyable one.

Lawrence fingered some papers stacked neatly on the otherwise clear and gleaming expanse of his walnut desk. Then he smiled and leaned slightly forward to continue:

"I've studied the background material which Winston Howard was kind enough to turn over to me," said Lawrence. "This is an unusual situation, but I feel certain that we'll be able to work it out to the satisfaction of everyone involved. You have nothing to worry about, as I see it."

It would take nearly three years of hard work and sometimes tough negotiating on the part of David Lawrence to make those sanguine words come true, but Mark and Louise felt better at once. The largest investment banking firm in the Rockies had agreed to tackle their problem and the man in charge said it could be solved and he would work on it.

The fateful—as it turned out—meeting with David Lawrence of Boettcher & Co. had been arranged by the attorney Mark had retained nearly six years earlier to handle legal affairs of the Morris Animal Foundation after its permanent headquarters had been established in Denver with Claude Ramsey, initially the part-time director, now in charge as executive director. Ramsey had recommended Winston Howard, and Mark and Louise, over a short span of years, had come to rely on him as well as fellow attorney, Hover Lentz, for personal legal advice apart from the matters he handled for the foundation.

It was Howard, by then a senior partner in the Denver law firm of Dawson, Nagle, Sherman & Howard, who had set up an estate management plan for Mark and Louise in the early 1960s. And it was Howard who had pointed out that the Morris arrangement as of 1965 with Hill Packing Co. had certain flaws which could prove ruinous in years to come unless some sort of reorganization could be worked out.

"It's my belief that you should sell the entire Prescription Diet program as it now stands," Winston Howard had said. "Your goal should be to turn your holdings into either cash or a bloc of stock in a recognized national company—or both."

Out of that comment had come the meeting with David Lawrence of Boettcher & Co. And out of that, nearly three years later, would come a multimillion-dollar solution with a major impact on all the members of the Morris family.

But on that fall afternoon in 1965, the nagging worries of Mark and Louise were only partly soothed by the assurances of David Lawrence.

Three years earlier, in 1962, Burton Hill had died while Mark and Louise were visiting England, attending a meeting of the British Veterinary Medical Association as president and first lady of the American Veterinary Medical Association.

"Mr. Hill's death was a personal shock, but it had even sharper impact on the business," Mark was to recall. "He had run his operation as Mr. Hill, Inc. and over the years our relationship had become one of trust and mutual respect. Then suddenly this old-style industrialist who ran the shop, made all of the decisions and was top man without challenge was gone. There was a terrific void in the Hill operation.''

Burton Hill had been the father of three daughters. One of them, Floy Hill Hancock, wanted to sell her stock in the company and Mark and Louise agreed to buy the Hancock stock and then sell it immediately to the other two daughters at no profit.

The Hancock stock transfer was finalized shortly after Burton Hill's death. The reorganization was completed when husbands of the other two daughers took over management of Hill Packing Co. Richard Davis, who had married Fay Hill, became president and Fern Hill Hogue, the remaining daughter, took over as treasurer. She held a degree in chemistry from the University of Kansas and her husband, Donald Hogue, was a graduate chemical engineer destined to play a major executive role in the reorganized firm.

By 1965, the new office building for Hill Packing Co. had been built in Topeka and non-profitable branch operations had been closed and sold. Plans were underway for a modern new packing plant to match the air-conditioned headquarters building, but Mark was not content with the arrangement.

"Our original contract with the Hill Packing Co. was due to run out in 1968 after 20 years," he pointed out. "And my lawyer in Denver had been warning me that unless something different could be worked out, my family would be faced with heavy estate taxes. Winston Howard kept telling me the government would be in a position to make arbitrary decisions on the value of my holdings. He said we had to take action soon to peg the price, to determine through a sale the actual value of an enterprise that had started from zero. Was it worth $1,000, or a hundred times that? Or was it worth a million dollars or more? There was only one way to find out and after that meeting with David Lawrence in Denver the answer was up to Boettcher & Co."

There was no warning on that fall afternoon in 1966 that the solution was nearly three years in the future. Nor did Mark worry about it. He was a busy man with no thought of retirement and there was much to be done while waiting for something he was confident would happen.

Back in Topeka, Mark found his son hard at work at the family research facility and its headquarters for testing and development of new small animal diet lines. Mark, Jr., had added several specialists to the Theracon payroll, including Dr. Woodrow Nelson, a food technologist with a Ph.D. degree from the University of Wisconsin. Dr. Nelson acted as chief aid to Mark, Jr., in the development over ensuring years of a host of new products.

The development work was done in the name of Mark Morris Associates, Inc., a corporation which Mark, Sr., had formed in April, 1962. Mark, Sr., had assigned all trademarks and copyrights of the Prescription Diet line to the new corporation, along with his license agreement contract with Hill Packing Co. to the new corporation. He served Mark Morris Associates, Inc., as president and Louise was treasurer. The only other shareholders were Mark, Jr., and daughter Ruth Keesling. Financial watchdog for the Morrises' interests, in addition to the ever-alert Louise, was accountant, Adrian Richel of Topeka.

In 1963, on his return to Topeka to join the family business, Mark, Jr., had established offices of Mark Morris Associates, Inc., in a new office building. He now was firmly committed to carrying on and expanding the unique business founded by his father and his new credentials included a lifetime appointment as a trustee of Morris Animal Foundation.

The middle 1960s also saw dramatic changes in the structure of the foundation. In 1962, the trustees voted to formally establish three divisions of Morris Animal Foundation—canine, feline and equine. It was an initial step to broadening the foundation's role and three veterinarians with national reputations were chosen to head the three new divisions as chairmen. They were William J. Zontine, D.V.M., Lancaster, California, head of the canine division; Lester E. Fisher, D.V.M., director of the Lincoln Park Zoological Gardens in Chicago, head of the feline division, and Fred D. Maurer, D.V.M., associate dean of the College of Veterinary Medicine, Texas A & M University, head of the equine division.

In 1964, Claude Ramsey, executive director of the foundation on a part-time basis since 1956, closed down his Denver-based Public Relations, Incorporated firm and became full-time director of the foundation with offices in the Guaranty Bank Building on Denver's 17th Street.

It was Ramsey, with the full blessing of Dr. Mark L. Morris, Sr., who launched a successful campaign to broaden the foundation's base and give the general public a major role in its direction and funding.

Ramsey opened his campaign at an annual meeting of foundation trustees in Denver. In a formal speech as executive director, he listed foundation achievements and called them "a job well done."

He also called attention to the fact that the Morris family down through the years has been the main and sometimes the only contributor to the foundation through royalties from the sale of Dr. Morris's Prescription Diet foods.

"I suggest we may be overlooking personnel in other walks of life," Ramsey said. "Let us shift attention to the American Cancer Society. That organization, founded in 1921, collects funds for research on and treatment of cancer. Its original governing body and administrators were physicians, and the society enjoyed a solid, praiseworthy growth—just like the Morris Animal Foundation. In the year 1943, when the society was 22 years old, the income was $336,000. That year became crucial in the society's history, because 1943 was the year that laity invaded the American Cancer Society. The laity was uninformed, but dedicated.

"That year, the society—not without a lot of soul-searching and some pressure—added to its board such lay persons as the president of Standard Brands, the president of Braniff Airways, the president of Aetna Life and others of similar business stature. That was accomplished with considerable grumbling from the physicians. They wondered aloud what such men knew about cancer. They soon found out that what such men lacked in technical knowledge was more than offset in other areas.

"The next year, the American Cancer Society raised a record $4,292,000. Since then, it has been governed jointly by physicians representing research and treatment, and businessmen representing the general public. Strangely enough, and especially surprising to the physicians, the two groups get along fine. And today, they raise a budget of $145 million yearly.

"I wonder if it isn't time we brought in the animal owners and gave them a voice. Our personnel today—like that of the American Cancer Society 20 years ago—is highly technical, interested in research and treatment. But do we have anyone representing the end product— the animal? It would appear to me that we can little afford to ignore the companion animal owners of the country."

In 1964, the trustees added to the board of Morris Animal Foundation its first public representative.

The initial public member of the board of trustees, whose election opened a new era of public participation in the foundation's financing and decision-making, was Ed. H. Honnen of Englewood, Colorado. He was to serve for two decades as a foundation trustee, president or chairman and his credentials were suited to the task.

Honnen won business fame as a heavy construction contractor and as Colorado distributor of products of Caterpillar Co. He was known as "the biggest dam builder" in the region. His interest in horses had led to posts as president of the Rocky Mountain and American Quarter Horse Associations, and as an advisory committee member on equine affairs for both the U.S. Internal Revenue Service and Colorado State University. He had served as a director of Colorado National Bank in Denver and First National Bank of Colorado Springs and as president of the Colorado Contractors Association.

Joining Honnen on the board of Morris Animal Foundation in 1967 and destined to succeed him as president and board chairman, was Burr Betts, Denver financier, head of Security Life and Accident Co. and past president of the International Arabian Horse Association. A new era of public participation in the foundation's decision-making process had begun. Both Honnen and Betts believed that the public—people like themselves—would provide the foundation with money and support to help solve animal health problems. Time has proven them correct.

As the newcomers began to demonstrate their genuine interest and willingness to work for the foundation, the trustees in 1966 voted to increase their own number from eight members to 25 and additional animal-oriented individuals and businessmen became trustees.

The "new look" of Morris Animal Foundation quickly drew a major benefit. The Internal Revenue Service ruled it no longer was a private foundation and in fact had become a public foundation offering tax advantages and deductions to contributors.

The first contribution from the public at large was a $1 bill donated "In Memory of Patsy," a pet dog owned by Mildred Pine of Cincinnati, Ohio. The bill was framed and remains in the foundation office "as a reminder that all contributions, no matter the size, are important since they represent pet owners who realize the value of research" in solving the health problems of companion animals.

In the wake of "going public," the foundation's expanded board of trustees turned the investment portfolio over to a finance committee of its own members charged with seeking sufficient revenue each year from investments to pay the foundation's overhead costs. This in most years has made it possible for all contributions from animal enthusiasts to be used for research without dilution.

Also established was a policy under which persons who have served the foundation as trustees or members of the advisory board become consultants after their elected terms expire. The names of those who continue indefinitely to lend expertise and guidance reads like "Who's Who."

Another innovation of the late 1960s was establishment through the efforts of the then newly-elected trustee Burr Betts of a legacy committee. This ongoing committee has adopted as its motto the phrase: "Where There's a Will, There's a Way to Help Companion Animals." The committee operates nationally, seeking funds through and bequests from animal lovers. One of its initial successes was a bequest from Mrs. Emory Ford, Grosse Point, Michigan.

By early 1967, well embarked on its new direction, the Morris Animal Foundation was able to report—in the words of executive director Claude Ramsey—that it felt like a late teenager (at 18, going on 19) now approaching adulthood. Over its relatively short span, the foundation by then had financially supported a total of 93 research projects involving animal health at 20 veterinary schools in North America. It had reached the stature of sponsoring from 15 to 25 additional research projects annually at a cost of more than $100,000 a year.

For the upcoming year, it had requests for funding of 31 new projects for a total of $196,000 (more money than was available) and it had passed the 112-person mark in the number of young veterinary students who had conducted its research efforts and become Fellows of the foundation.

"By our standards at that time, those were impressive figures," Mark was to comment years later. "We knew we were on the right track and we were pleased."

Added executive director Ramsey: "Pleased, yes. Satisfied, no."

In his address to the annual meeting of foundation trustees that year, Ramsey told of a grade school youngster who once was asked at the start of a psychological test what he would ask for if he were granted the fulfillment of two special wishes. The youngster quickly decided he wanted a million dollars with his first wish. Then, after some thought, he came up with the second request: "A million more wishes."

Ramsey wondered if it wasn't time for the Morris Animal Foundation to "think some new thoughts, look into great unplowed fields of animal research."

"We have shone some light into veterinary research," he said. "Is it time to look for more darkness? Is it time to wish for a million more wishes?''

A big wish-come-true materialized for both Dr. Mark L. Morris, Sr., and his Morris Animal Foundation in the fall of 1968. It began with a long-awaited telephone call from Boettcher & Co. in Denver.

"I've found the right buyer," said David Lawrence, senior partner of the investment banking firm. "It has taken a long time, but I'm sure you will agree that the wait was worth it."

Early in his search for a buyer for Mark's holdings, which began in 1965, Lawrence made a trip to Topeka for conferences with the surviving heirs of Burton Hill of Hill Packing Co. An agreement had been reached under which Boettcher & Co. would seek to find a single buyer for both Mark's line of Prescription Diets and for the Hill Packing Co. which manufactured and distributed the line.

Over the ensuing months, numerous contacts had been made with national firms in the field of both food and pharmaceuticals, among them such giants as American Home Products, Sterling Drugs, Inc., Smith, Kline & French, Beatrice Foods and Quaker Oats Co. Several offers had been rejected. But this new offer seemed to have no flaws. And in September 1968, papers were signed under which, for stock, all interests of the Hill and Morris families in both the packing company and the diet line were acquired by Riviana Food Inc. of Houston, Texas. The well written contract had the genius touch of Hover Lentz, Denver attorney.

Riviana had been founded and was backed by the Godchaux family of Abbeyville, Louisiana, pioneers in the U.S. rice business. Its stock traded on the American Stock Exchange and later at the New York Stock Exchange at the time it was diversifying into specialty food lines.

As part of the complicated transaction, Riviana Foods acquired all stock and assets (Prescription Diet line) of Mark Morris Associates, Inc.

The management of Riviana Foods, in return for its continued use of the Mark Morris name which had become synonymous with Prescription Diets, granted the Morris Family the right to continue in business under the abbreviated name of Mark Morris Associates (minus the Inc.), as a partnership. And it signed with the new independent partnership headed by Mark and his son, Dr. Mark L. Morris, Jr., a contract for ongoing technical services.

The technical services agreement, still in full effect as this is written in mid-1982, grants to Mark Morris Associates full responsibility for quality control of all Prescription Diets and allied animal food lines produced by Hill. This means, in essence, that the Morrises retained full control over manufacturing and no Prescription Diet products can be placed on the market until and unless cleared by Mark Morris Associates.

The new contract (signed just a month before the expiration date of Mark's original 20-year contract with Burton Hill) also specified that Mark Morris Associates could proceed with the development of new products which must be offered first to Riviana Foods for manufacture and sale under a royalty arrangement. This has been the green light in the years since 1968 for development of a host of new products.

One section of the new contract named Mark Morris Associates as Riviana's consultant in the total field of animal nutrition. It had Dr. Morris and his son responsible also for the production of education material which is used in numerous languages to tell veterinarians about therapeutic nutrition around the world—the new marketplace for Prescription Diets under Riviana Foods.

One hint of the magnitude of the 1968 transaction is contained in an on-the-record listing of benefits to the Morris Animal Foundation.

When he formed Mark Morris Associates, Inc. in 1962 to handle his holdings for tax and estate purposes, Mark had made a family gift of 20 percent of the firm to the foundation. That one-fifth interest resulted in an endowment to the foundation in late 1968 of more than $800,000 after expenses of the transaction. The royalties to the foundation were not included in the new contract and the foundation became, in fact, a "public" foundation dependent upon the public for its very existence.

15

The View Ahead

Dr. Mark L. Morris, Sr., sat on the screened-in, glassed-in terrace of his apartment reading a newspaper account of blizzard weather conditions sweeping most of the northern half of the country. It was mid-February of 1982 and Chicago was caught in one of the worst cold waves on record with a wind chill factor of some 45 degrees below zero in the gale blowing off snow-hidden Lake Michigan. Maine and Buffalo, New York, were held in an icy grip. Snowdrifts paralyzed traffic in New York City. It was snowing hard in the Rockies.

A gentle breeze was blowing in off the Gulf of Mexico which spread out in shimmering blue with white wave frosting under an azure sky at Mark's feet. His terrace, on the west side of a beach-hugging high rise condominium apartment complex in Naples, Florida, was at penthouse level. The view included a strip of white beach stretching off into the distance along the surf line. The white sails of pleasure craft dotted the blue of the Gulf. Far out, a pair of freighters were steaming north-northwest, probably headed for Galveston on the Texas coastline.

Mark glanced at his watch. It was nearly 10 a.m., about time for the arrival of the writer who would be responsible for turning out his biography. They were doing a series of final interviews, putting the finishing touches on a research effort which had taken many months.

The buzzer sounded from the securely locked hallway at the entry to the palm-fringed building which held Mark's apartment and 20 others like it, owned mostly by retirees seeking winter refuge from the weather up north Mark had been reading about. Mark rose to answer, clad in Palm Beach-weight slacks and a sport shirt open at the throat. He was tanned and carried with style a leanness almost

unchanged from his college days at Cornell University. His hair was
graying now, but there were no other signs that this man had celebrated
Birthday No. 81 the fall before and was looking forward to Birthday
No. 82 a few months ahead.

"I'm feeling just great," he replied to a question as he led his
guest into the living room. "I've been reading through some old correspondence and I'm raring to go. Get ready with your questions."

Mark and Louise had found Naples on Florida's western Gulf coast
during the winter of 1969-1970, a year after completion of their sale
to Riviana Foods. The own-your-own-unit apartment building on
North Gulfshore Boulevard was nearing completion and one of three
units on the top floor still was available. It was, in their view, by far
the best they'd seen during a lengthy tour of offerings in the booming condominium market on both coasts of the southern Florida
peninsula.

Louise had lovingly supervised the job of furnishing the new apartment and in the winters that followed the couple had enjoyed "hiding
out" from the harsh northern weather.

Naples is far down on the Florida peninsula, more than a hundred miles south of Tampa Bay and due west across the "Alligator
Alley" route of State Highway 84 across the Everglades from Miami.
In February it was a garden in bloom under a sunny sky with afternoon temperatures nudging 80 degrees and falling back only to the
low 70s with little rain. It was, Mark agreed, a perfect place for a
man to relax in winter in the semi-retirement that goes with 80-plus
years of active life.

In 1982, Mark was entering his fourth year as a widower. On
Oct, 2, 1978, Louise had passed away at Swedish Memorial Hospital
in Denver after a hospitalization of six months in Naples, Topeka,
and finally near her daughter Ruth in Denver.

"She is remembered as invincible, practical, gracious and always
the lady," said an in-memoriam pamphlet. "Her interests were many,
but the No. 1 was her family. Dr. Morris viewed her as an integral
part of his many activities, whether business or professional. Her ap-
praisal of people and her balanced judgment were important ingredients of the family enterprises. She was tenacious, but always fair,
and few persons who explained a bill to her ever forgot the experience.
The fun for her often was in the contest itself, not in the victory."

Louise W. Morris had written before her death that "I guess we're
semi-retired now, spending our winters in Naples, Florida." But she

had added that "I can't seem to escape the record keeping and I still handle the books for some of the activities.

"Mark is still vigorous, coming up with a fresh idea every few days to improve the profession or the country."

For months the vigor left Mark after the death of Louise. The June 1979 meeting of trustees of Morris Animal Foundation was the first ever not attended by the original founder.

But gradually, as always in human life, the vigor would not stay tucked away with his memories and Mark resumed an active life.

The summer home of many years on Coyote Mountain near Rocky Mountain National Park in Colorado had been closed and sold when the final diabetes-complicated illness of Louise made high altitude living dangerous for her. Mark and Louise had spent much of their time in Naples, with summer visits to Topeka and the Colorado Rockies.

In this new world of life without Louise, Mark decided to make Naples his headquarters. But his legal address and his office remain in Topeka. His automobile carries Kansas plates and his summers include long visits to a condominium apartment his daughter owns on the shores of Dillon Reservoir about 100 miles due west of Denver in resort and ski country.

Between travels, Mark makes it a point to stay in touch on a regular basis with events at both the Morris Animal Foundation headquarters and the office of Mark Morris Associates in Topeka. His personal impact remains at both organizations.

His winters in Florida are crammed with interest and excitement, Mark says with sparkling eyes.

"I'm a member of the Collier County Conservancy," he recited with obvious pride. "Our job is to help conserve the natural resources of Florida and a recent project involved a purchase by the Conservancy of 536,000 acres of swamp land. It was deeded to the National Audubon Society in perpetuity for one dollar and that land can never be used for anything except the alligators and what else God put there."

Still on the subject of the Conservancy: "They needed a new building to educate the children about what lived in the Everglades. Their old building wasn't large enough. So at a meeting one afternoon two and half million dollars were raised to build a new building. That's the Conservancy and I'm proud to be part of it."

Mark's office at the new headquarters of Mark Morris Associates in Topeka, built in the campus-like setting of a new business park, is crammed with evidence of a busy working life. The new two-level brick building sits idyllically on a gentle rise overlooking busy Interstate Highway 70, far enough away to the north that traffic can be seen but not heard. The setting is more like tree-studded Connecticut countryside than Kansas, but the plains and miles of wheat fields begin west of Topeka.

On a hill to the north beyond I-70 sits the Governor's Mansion of Kansas and the manicured lawns and trees of the famed Menninger Foundation. On the walls of Mark's ample office are certificates and diplomas attesting to his achievements.

There are diplomas from Henderson Grade School, Brighton High School, Denver University, Colorado A. & M. College and Cornell University. Beside these, dated July 9, 1926, is a certificate from the Board of Veterinary Medical Examiners, State of New Jersey, attesting that Mark Loren Morris, D.V.M., had passed a satisfactory examination before the board "and is hereby licensed to practice veterinary medicine, surgery and dentistry in the State of New Jersey."

There is also a certificate bearing the imprint of the New York Academy of Sciences noting the election of Mark as a Fellow of the Academy "in outstanding recognition for scientific achievement and promotion of science." Beside this are certificates noting Mark's election as president of the American Veterinary Medical Association and as president (its first) of the American Animal Hospital Association.

There also are certificates bestowing on Mark the Zeta Award of Omega Tau Sigma Fraternity at Auburn, Alabama, in 1962, and the Gamma Award of Omega Tau Sigma Fraternity at the Ohio State University in 1966 "for meritorious service to science."

One certificate, gleaming in a frame, bears the imprint of National Science Fair International and was awarded, with a replica of the 1962 gold and silver medal, "in recognition of service." Near it are a "Veterinarian of the Year" certificate dated February 19, 1963 from the Colorado Veterinary Medical Association and a certificate awarded on April 21, 1978 by the American Animal Hospital Association "in recognition of his vision in the formation and development of this association and his continuing interest in its growth and improvement."

Mark L. Morris, the man who won those honors and many more, is confident about the future of both Mark Morris Associates and the Morris Animal Foundation.

"They are in very good hands," he said. "My son is a highly capable man and he will make certain things go well."

The Foundation since early 1979 has been headquartered in its own attractive building beside a golf fairway in Inverness Business Park, just southeast of downtown Denver along Interstate 25.

It now boasts more than 400 Fellows who have directed research projects into animal health problems under its sponsorship and its plans for the future are glowing.

Late in 1981 the now greatly enlarged board of trustees voted in favor of a proposal that the national fund-raising firm of Brakeley, John Price Jones, Inc., of New York City be authorized to launch a four-year campaign to raise $9.5 million in donations to insure the Foundation's future success.

The $5 million mark in funds raised was in sight as the Foundation held its mid-1982 annual meeting in New York City. The money would form an investment base certain in future years to provide a million-dollars-a-year pace of research.

Mark Morris Associates, under the guidance of Dr. Mark L. Morris, Jr., has expanded steadily over the years. More than 40 different labels of therapeutic animal diets—including new lines of Science Diets and specialized foods for zoo animals ranging from flightless birds to polar bears, tamarins and marmosets—are being turned out in the modern Hill's Pet Products plant in Topeka. Riviana Foods now is a subsidiary of Colgate-Palmolive Co., but the arrangement with Mark Morris Associates remains unchanged.

Over the years, since those early day board meetings in a parked automobile on a New Jersey college campus, the Morris Animal Foundation has matured into a unique one-of-a-kind organization.

It is recognized as the only organization in the United States that represents the interests of companion animals and zoo animals, the animal owner, the veterinarian, the scientist and the breeder. Its mission is to provide leadership in improving the health of animals through research and education. It seeks out the best qualified individual at the best institution to investigate disease and animal health problems, and it educates both the practicing veterinarian and the animal owner through professional publications, seminars, newsletters, animal publications and the general news media.

Accomplishments of the Morris Animal Foundation through its ongoing financed research have been myriad. Here are a few highlights of those medical milestones in the four fields involved:

CANINE: From wide-ranging research came proof which destroyed the long-standing myth that spaying of female dogs causes obesity.

Other studies established that nuclear radiation and fallout do not result in sterilization of exposed canines and made it a scientific fact that female dogs exposed to large doses of radiation still can bear normal litters of puppies.

Also in the canine field various foundation-sponsored research projects have made progress in establishing a new method of canine birth control. The goal is a vaccine to prevent conception in female dogs, which could be reversible and generally free of side effects.

Foundation-sponsored researchers have successsfully frozen canine semen to preserve it. Progress continues in this field with a goal of perfecting artificial breeding with use of stored semen. In other areas, they have doubled the storage life of canine blood used in transfusions and have developed a new diagnostic test for the canine-killer known as parvovirus. Further studies are underway to develop a more effective parvo vaccine.

EQUINE: Foundation-financed studies have determined the needed priorities for research into the ailments of horses, and thus have laid the groundwork for the beginning of a planned national research program in this field.

Other Foundation-financed studies have determined that horses develop physiological immunity to internal parasites and that development of a vaccine-type immunity agent was feasible, and have uncovered agents leading to development of efficient medicines to destroy bloodworms in horses.

Basic nutritional studies by the Foundation's fellows have outlined the basic nutritional requirements of horses and established for the first time the proper levels of zinc, calcium and phosphorus. Foundation research also has determined guidelines for gauging the physical fitness of endurance horses, established methods of preventing colic deaths and perfected a system for testing the uniformity of racetracks and detecting soft spots which might cause mishaps.

FELINE: Foundation-financed studies have outlined the nutritional requirement of cats and led to development of a purified diet allowing accurate analysis of the cat's food intake and waste output. This in turn established that cats have a faster rate of protein metabolism than dogs and that diets high in protein are needed for their proper growth and maintenance.

Other studies established that interferon, a virus destroyer, is produced naturally in the cat and have identified several feline viruses, leading to development of several vaccines. Foundation fellows also learned that urinary obstruction, technically called urolithiasis, is a disease dangerous to male cats and can be caused by certain viruses and even by diets high in magnesium and phosphorus. Other results indicated that wet cat food or canned food may be better than dry foods in avoiding urinary stones among male cats.

ZOO ANIMALS: The Foundation has gathered information on infectious diseases among zoo animals and investigated the wide field of viruses and tumors. It also has gathered evidence of ulcers in sea lions and other captive animals, with indications of similarity to the stress-induced ulcers of mankind.

A milestone accomplishment has been publication of the first English language zoological text with material contributed by some 90 veterinarians and zoo specialists. The 940-page text was edited by 18 knowledgeable veterinarians under Foundation supervision and a second printing was ordered when the first 5,000 copies were sold.

On the drawing board at the Foundation are detailed plans for establishment of a computerized data bank for zoo medicine for use around the world.

Matching its research achievement, the Foundation has been blessed since its inception by a wealth of volunteer human talent. When Mark Morris stepped down as president in the late 1960s, his successor was Ed Honnen, Colorado businessman, heavy construction contractor, and horse fancier, who served from 1969 to 1971. He was followed by Burr Betts, insurance executive and prominent Arabian horse breeder. The fourth president was Rollin Barnard, Denver financier. He doubled as both president and board chairman until 1978, when Richard Newman took over as chairman and Joe Ballard of Fort Worth, Texas, became president.

Newman, a Denver businessman, is a past president of both the International Arabian Horse Association and the Colorado Arabian Horse Association. He became active in the Foundation's fund raising program, serving as first chairman of its capital campaign. As such he solicited the other trustees and, at one weekend meeting, directed efforts which resulted in more than $3 million in gifts, pledges and bequests. At the end of his chairmanship the total was $5.5 million.

Ballard's family was a co-founder of Southland Corp., owner of 7-11 Stores. Ballard brought a lot of Texans to the Foundation with him, particularly veterinarians. He served in a leadership capacity longer than any individual, other than Mark, going five years as president and then becoming chairman of the board in 1982.

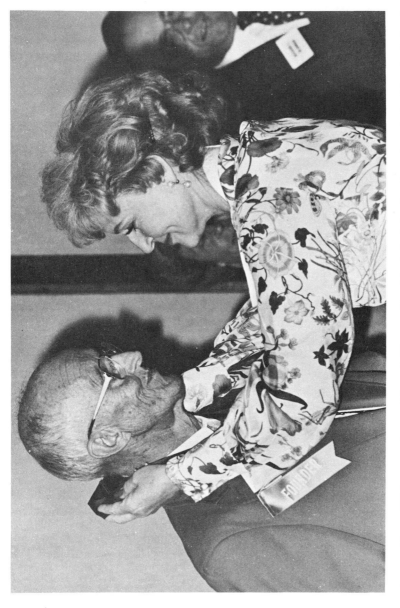

Actress Betty White awards a gold medallion to Dr. Mark L. Morris, founder of the Morris Animal Foundation, during the Foundation's annual meeting in Denver in 1980. Betty White Ludden was canine vice president and a trustee who later became president of the Foundation.

Betty White Ludden took over as Foundation president in 1982. She is the Betty White who co-starred in the Mary Tyler Moore television series, in several TV game shows, and in her own TV series. Betty was not a figurehead officer, but worked in the trenches with other trustees. She, as president, made numerous speeches around the country on behalf of the Foundation, as well as numerous television appearances, and often popped in unexpectedly on routine committee meetings.

Mary Tyler Moore, a longtime animal enthusiast and star of the long-running and high-rated television series which bore her name, joined the Morris Animal Foundation team at its 1982 annual meeting as national honorary chairwoman for the capital campaign.

In early 1983, J. Robert Fluor of Irvine, California, became chairman of the Foundation's capital funds campaign. He is chairman and chief executive officer of Fluor Corp., a world-class engineering, construction and natural resources company with 43,000 employees. He took over from Newman the job of boosting contributions for the capital campaign to 9.5 million.

The list of the Foundation's trustees, past and present, sparkles with notable names. Among them:

Mrs. Kenyon (Gradie) Bevan of Los Alamos, California, operator of Bevan's Arabian Ranch, trustee of the Arabian Horse Trust, who for years was the Foundation voice for the Arabian Breeders and Club.

Mrs. William (Patricia) Hewitt of East Moline, Illinois, now a resident of Jamaica where her husband is U. S. Ambassador. She is owner of the 500-acre Friendship Farm in Illinois, and is one of the staunchest supporters of the Foundation.

John M. Olin of New York City and St. Louis, Missouri, deceased industrialist who founded and funded the Olin Foundation, Inc., and was a leading thoroughbred horse owner and breeder. Olin himself invested considerable sums into animal research, particularly at Cornell University, and for canine hip displasia at the University of Missouri.

Eve Anderson of Waimanalo and Dora Singlehurst of Waialua, Hawaii, joined Foundation efforts through an Edith Head fashion show which Betty White narrated as a benefit. The enthusiasm generated provided a base for further support for the Foundation in Hawaii where there is a strong sentiment for a better method of canine birth control which the Foundation seeks.

Also Penny Chenery, breeder of famed racehorses Secretariat and

Riva Ridge and active in thoroughbred breeder circles; James Stewart, executive vice president and general manager of Hollywood Park race-track for many years; George Werntz, executive director of Seeing Eye, Inc., of Morristown, New Jersey; and John Pirie of Chicago, deceased breeder of English cocker spaniels.

It is volunteer leaders of this caliber, said Dr. Mark Morris, who will insure that the Foundation's future will be bright.

Mark, in his biography-related interview in Naples, was asked the customary question about advice he might have for would-be young veterinarians of the 1980s.

"Over the years, it has been my opportunity to provide career guidance for quite a number of young people," he said. "I often hear reasons for their choosing a career in veterinary medicine such as 'I like animals,' or 'I love horses' or even 'I want to spend my working time outdoors.' I always regard those reasons as poor guides to whether an individual will make a good veterinarian.

"In my own instance, I did not enter the veterinary profession because I particularly liked animals. Oh, we had a pet collie-shepherd when I was a kid, but in general I don't like dogs or cats as companions in the home. But just show me a sick one! I love the science of animal medicine and I love what can be done to control or eradicate diseases that make animals very uncomfortable or dead.

"What do I consider when talking to a young prospective veterinary student? Well, first I want to know what their capabilities are in mathematics and science. Do they have a science bent? Do they have a low verbal rating? If they do, they are headed for trouble because of the tremendous amounts of reading and studying that must be done with rapid retention.

"I don't believe in reasons like 'I love horses.' Would-be veterinarians who say that may flunk out. They would rather be out riding than boring into biochemistry."

In the interview, Mark had a definite view of what it takes to create a worthwhile life:

"What I've done will live after me, and I'm certain that what will be accomplished will have a good impact on both animal health and human health. I believe I have proven a definite relation between human and animal ailments and their management. I have established that people can learn from their pets how to take better care of themselves.

"I've known men who made millions of dollars, only to discover that they can't buy happiness or health with their money. I wouldn't trade places with anyone. You can't buy the kind of associations I have enjoyed for many years. I have friends, people. I have collected them and they have helped me."

His wish for the foundation: "We have helped to train more than 400 remarkable people. We have made progress against animal disease and through that effort have made contributions also to human health.

"My wish, and I don't need a million of them, is for the foundation to continue its good work—but on an expanded basis."

Almost overlooked in a stack of papers which had been taken from Mark's files in Topeka for possible background use in writing his biography was a copy of a poem written by Walt Whitman (1819-92), the New Jersey poet who wrote about a great America and great Americans.

The poem, which bore no title, was written years before Mark was born, but it seemed to fit him:

There's a man in the world who is never
turned down, wherever he chances to stray;
He gets the glad hand in the populous town,
or out where the farmers make hay;

He's greeted with pleasure on deserts of sand
and deep in the aisles of the woods;
Wherever he goes there's a welcoming hand—
He's the man who delivers the goods.

AUTHOR'S NOTE: During an interview in the course of research for this book, Dr. Mark L. Morris was asked what single force could be credited for his success. His answer came spontaneously: "My library."

The library, he explained, was as close as his telephone. It consisted of scores of educators and professional associates, personal friends and experts in a myriad of fields with whom he maintained close contact during his working years. When he needed an answer or felt the need for conversation about a problem, Dr. Morris used his library.

Following are excerpts from interviews and letters about their personal contacts with Dr. Morris from a sampling of the people who made up "my library":

ALLISON, James B. (deceased)
Rutgers University, New Brunswick, New Jersey
Bureau of Biological Research, Director

Letter dated May 23, 1963: "I have enjoyed the meetings of the Foundation very much and I admire the work that you are doing. It has been a great pleasure to take part in it and to watch the Foundation grow in service and influence over the years. Those of us who have been fortunate to be Trustees have had a great sense of satisfaction in being a part of the Foundation."

ARMISTEAD, William W., D.V.M.
Former Dean, University of Tennessee,
College of Veterinary Medicine, Knoxville

Telephone interview May 24, 1979: "My picture of Dr. Morris has been one of a very effective pioneer leader in many areas. It is obvious that he was a pioneer in the research on clinical nutritional problems of small animals. Dr. Morris was the leader and forerunner of much of the work that has been done to clarify the needs of small animals that were not agriculture related. He made a distinctive contribution to organized veterinary medicine through the A.A.H.A. and the Morris Animal Foundation by beginning to support young promising researchers in veterinary medicine. It may sound like I am a Mark Morris fan. Well, I am! He is a very remarkable man!"

ATKINSON, LeRoy, D.V.M.
Small animal practitioner, St. Louis, Missouri

Telephone interview April 26, 1979: "I went to work for Dr. Morris in July of 1942 at Raritan Hospital for Animals in Stelton, New Jersey. I quickly entered into the scientific practice that Dr. Morris conducted there and, while he was not full-time at the hospital, he found time to help a young veterinarian like myself. Dr. Morris's other venture at that time was as Executive Secretary of the Joint Committee on Foods of the A.V.M.A. and A.A.H.A. He spent a great deal of his time on this because this committee was giving the stamp of approval to foods that could pass the standards for adequate nutrition for the dog and cat.

"Through his association with other professional men, Dr. Morris was able to contribute much to the present day information that is known about dogs, and much of it applies to human medicine.

209

"One individual who I think did more for Raritan Hospital than anyone else was Louise Morris. It was Louise who took care of the business end, kept the employees going, and took care of the books and the financial part of the business."

BAGANZ, Herbert M., B.S.
Retired, Pharmaceutical Salesman, Lafayette, Indiana

Letter dated December 22, 1981: "Your research on distemper and blood analysis has revolutionized the veterinary profession. You pioneered blood diagnosis and, like other scientific men, you were generally criticized."

BRACKETT, Benjamin G., D.V.M.
Professor and Head, Department of Physiology and Pharmacology
College of Veterinary Medicine
University of Georgia

Telephone interview March 3, 1980: "It was through Dr. Morris's efforts that I was able to launch my career and continue graduate work after veterinary school. I was a Foundation Fellow for two years at the University of Pennsylvania, under Professor W. L. Williams, and I received my master's degree. It was the Morris Animal Foundation's grant that enabled me to develop and take the next step toward my degree.

"My first impression of Dr. Morris was of a very well-organized, business-like person, very vigorous, and abounding with contagious enthusiasm—emphasizing the latter.

"Through the Morris Animal Foundation Fellows the impact of the efforts of Dr. Morris is—and will continue to be—felt. This is in all the aspects of medicine and research. He is one of a dozen men who have had a great influence on my own life."

CARLSON, Dr. William
Past President of the University of Wyoming
Department of Radiology and Radiation Biology
    Colorado State University
Morris Animal Foundation Advisory Board 1958—1961.

Telephone interview February 15, 1980: "My first impression of Dr. Morris was that he was a person who knew what he wanted to accomplish. He was unique in trying to develop research for the companion animal—the dog and cat. He was probably the first one to encourage this—where one could get support for research on this type of animal. It went beyond that—it was an idea conceived and carried out by him."

CLARKSON, Myron R., D.V.M.
1930-1964—U.S. Department of Agriculture (Administrative Director) Past President of A.V.M.A.
First Director of Bureau of Veterinary Medicine of Federal Drug Administration
1966-1972—Executive Vice President of A.V.M.A.

Telephone interview June 26, 1980: "I first met Dr. Morris personally (although I had heard of him and his work) in 1960 when he was one of the candidates for President of the A.V.M.A. I heard him speak several times and was very impressed with his knowledge and with his sincerity. He has always been a person of innovative ways of approach to a problem. In that respect he has done a lot of good in his term as a veterinarian. He was sometimes involved in some controversy, but that is inevitable when someone has new ideas. If I remember correctly, he is the only individual in our profession who was president of the A.V.M.A. and the A.A.H.A."

COLE, Clarence R., D.V.M.
Former Dean, College of Veterinary Medicine, The Ohio State University (1967-71)
Present: Department of Veterinary Pathology, The Ohio State University

Letter dated April 2, 1968 to Dr. Morris: "Congratulations upon your special citation from *Who's Who In America*, who recognized your generous educational philanthropy extending over a long period of years.

"I also wish to congratulate you and all the members of the staff of the Morris Animal Foundation upon your very excellent 1967 Annual Report. Many of my colleagues agree with my frequent statement that Dr. Mark Morris has done more for graduate training of veterinarians than any other veterinarian. It must be a great satisfaction to you to see the success of the increasing number of Mark Morris Fellows."

CORNELIUS, Charles, D.V.M.
Dean, College of Veterinary Medicine, University of Florida (1971-1983)
Dean, Kansas State University, 1966

Telephone interview May 22, 1979: "When I arrived at Kansas State University as Dean in 1966, my job was to develop a program for new buildings. Dr. Morris was instrumental in helping make the proper contacts with the office of the Governor and other influential people in the Topeka area. His support was always there; his understanding was always there; and needless to say, it was greatly appreciated.

"I would like to comment on the visionary outlook Dr. Morris has had in the area of animal nutrition. Of course, and even more important to me as a researcher, is his understanding that things are only done in research when research funds are available to do them. With this background and understanding of Dr. Morris, the establishment of the Foundation filled one of the real critical needs. At the time the Foundation was created, there were practically no other resources for performing critical small animal research, so for one to establish such an idea was really miraculous."

CRAWFORD, John, D.V.M.
Small animal practitioner, retired
Cornell University, Class of 1926

Telephone interview March 18, 1980: "I have known Dr. Morris since he transferred to Cornell in 1925. We were in the same class. We were all young, of course, at that time, and did all the usual things—dances, etc.—but Morris was always close to the books. He was a very dedicated student. I remember him well after he was established in New Jersey. He started with the diet foods there. In fact, we used to think sometimes that he was a little "touched"—but it turned out that he was right, and we were wrong! Without a doubt, those diet foods that he originated were the greatest Godsend we ever had in the veterinary profession. The benefits he rendered to the veterinary profession were tremendous. He is a real credit to the profession. He ought to go down in veterinary history as one of its leading lights."

CUMMINGS, Fred C., D.V.M.
Small animal practitioner, Seattle, Washington

Letter dated January 23, 1953 from Dr. Cummings to Dean E.C. Stone, College of Veterinary Medicine, Washington State College, Pullman, Washington, referring to the work of Mark L. Morris, D.V.M.: "It has been shown beyond the shadow of a doubt that the Prescription Diets hold as important a place in the everyday life of the small animal practitioner as do penicillin, Terramycin, or any other drug that you might name."

CURREY, J. Raymond, D.V.M.
Small animal practitioner, retired, Bethesda, Maryland

Telephone interview May 7, 1979: "My friendship with Dr. Morris goes back a long, long way. We were both involved very seriously with the original Joint Committee on Foods, A.V.M.A.-A.A.H.A. Morris practically lived in Washington when we were trying to get Federal legislation enacted to have some standard set for canned dog food.

"Dr. Morris was always interested in research. He was a pioneer in seeking and searching and developing comparable laboratory aids and tests as applied to small animals. He was one of the first, in my opinion, to recognize the value of injectable therapy over the oral therapy that was commonly used. He was always interested in nutrition, and his belief and concept was that it was better to maintain health by adequate diet and nutrition than depend on medication to cover up deficiencies that would develop later. Prevention of illness meant much to Dr. Morris.

"In my opinion I think Dr. Morris was one of our real pioneers in development of small animal practice as it is recognized today, developing laboratory aids as a means to diagnose, and therapy and treatment as well. The small animal profession owes Dr. Morris a real great vote of thanks and appreciation.

"Dr. Morris's Prescription Diets have been one of the most copied products in the canine nutrition field, because he got a head start on everybody. He had to work for everything he got—nothing was handed to him on a silver platter. He has had opposition by factions about his way of doing things. There was criticism in certain areas of the veterinary profession that it wasn't right for a veterinarian to sell pet food, accusing him of being an opportunist, etc."

EBERHART, George W., D.V.M.
Small animal practitioner, Moraga, California

Letter to Dr. Morris, December 20, 1980: "What a story you have to tell—80 years, mostly veterinary medical pioneering, which continues on through your fine heir, Mark, Jr., The rest of us in the profession owe you more gratitude than we can express. The concept of nutrition which I have learned from you and your research has been one of the most important parts of my practice. Thank you, old friend Mark Morris!"

ELLSWORTH, Dr. Ralph E.
Formerly Director of Libraries and Professor of Bibliographies, University of Colorado, Boulder, Colorado

Telephone interview November 28, 1979: "I first became acquainted with Dr. Morris about 20 years ago, when he purchased his cabin up near ours, at Allenspark, Colorado. When I first met him he was a very active individual in veterinary medicine and all kinds of international aspects connected with it.

"He was a very direct, positive thinking man, with very definite opinions. He liked to get right to the point of things. He had been an executive and was inclined to be impatient with people who fiddled around and didn't make definite decisions. He wanted to get a job finished and move on to the next problem.

"I would like to add something about the Morris Animal Foundation, which Dr. Morris established. He has done a lot with that and devoted a good many years to it. In my personal opinion, I think that is probably the most important aspect of his work. The Foundation has been very worthwhile."

FRANK, Eugene M.
Bishop-in-Residence, Central United Methodist Church, Kansas City, Missouri
Formerly in Candler School of Theology, Emory University, Atlanta, Georgia

Letter dated May 28, 1979: "We first met Mark and Louise Morris on a Wednesday evening at the regular church dinner. We sat across the table from them, immediately became acquainted and began a long, beautiful friendship.

"Mark's knowledge of animal husbandry and medicine had already expanded into dietary products for small animals and it wasn't long before his products were the largest piece of business for the Hill Packing Company of Topeka.

"His operation at the Hill Packing Company was fascinating as also was the research and experimentation farm he established north of the city.

"I have traveled rather widely around the United States and been in contact with many universities with veterinary schools. I have never found a Dean yet who did not know all about Dr. Mark Loren Morris.

"One simply can't say enough about the part Louise had in this marvelous development. She was one of the most remarkable women I have ever met. A strong, capable, efficient businessperson, with deep feelings and capacity for warm friendship.

"Mark and Louise leave a mark on the science and medicine of animal husbandry that will be recognized for years to come, and their two children and their families they have sent into the world are an even greater tribute to their lives."

FRANK, Morris
Blind man who had first Seeing Eye Dog in United States
Associated with The Seeing Eye, Inc.

Telephone interview with Mr. Frank, May 7, 1979: "My dog, who had been in the Army-Navy hospital and wasn't doing too well, was treated by Dr. Morris . . . and he worked out a diet. My wife made the first food under his direction right in our own kitchen. She got the stuff from the doctor, and the Red Cross got us the boilers and things, and the American Can Company provided the cans.

"A Foundation was formed to become the Buddy Foundation, and Dr. Morris gave one-half cent a can for research on diseases. The agreement was at that time that all Seeing Eye graduates could buy their dog food at cost."

GREEN, David F., Ph.D.
Formerly with Merck & Co., Rahway, New Jersey

Letter to Dr. Morris dated January 17, 1981: "After you established the Morris Animal Foundation, research support continued. I am pleased to learn that you have supported 300 Ph.D. candidates."

HAMNER, Charles E., Jr., D.V.M., Ph.D.
Associate Dean, College of Medicine, University of Virginia, Charlottesville, Virginia

Letter dated May 7, 1978: "My association with Mark Morris began in the fall of 1959, prior to my graduation from veterinary school in the spring of 1960. Dr. Morris gave a very interesting and challenging talk to our class and I knew from the start that he had a deep interest in advancing veterinary medicine and he realized the way to do it was through advanced training of veterinarians to specialize in various areas of pathology, nutrition, etc.

"Probably no one recognizes the true significance and tremendous impact the Foundation has had on the veterinary profession through its awarding of more than 300 fellowships to veterinarians who have been able to take advanced training and become specialists while looking at many facets of diseases in the canine, feline, equine as well as zoological species. It has been my great pleasure and benefit to have been associated with the Morris Animal Foundation and I shall look forward in the coming years to continue this association.''

HONNEN, Edward H.
Englewood, Colorado
Formerly Caterpillar Dealer and Contractor
Morris Animal Foundation president—1969-1971

Telephone interview December 17, 1979: "First got acquainted with Dr. Morris through General Wayne O. Kester. My first impression was that he was an extremely brilliant man. I've never met a man more on top of a subject than he is. He devoted his life to the veterinary profession and attained the greatest height that anyone could in that profession.

"I was with the Quarterhorse people, along about 1960, when I first met Dr. Morris. In my personal opinion, I think he is an extremely articulate, energetic individual, as a person and as a doctor of veterinary medicine. He is one of the most capable men I have ever run across. I don't think there is anybody that has done any more for the equine profession. I am very happy with my association with him. I know he eliminated many of the problems with dogs and cats, one of which was hip dysplasia in dogs.

"I knew his wife, Louise, also. She was a wonderful help to him.

"The Morris Foundation is well respected all over the world. Mark Morris has done a *world* of good!''

JENSEN, Harlan E., D.V.M
Former Professor of Veterinary Ophthalmology, University of Missouri, Columbia, Missouri

Letter from Dr. Jensen in April, 1981: "In 1943 I went to work with Dr. Morris at the Raritan Hospital. Dr. Morris was developing his first diet food, k/d. About four months after my arrival, Dr. Morris began enlarging and remodeling his hospital; he put in all stainless steel kennels.

"The more I learned about Dr. Morris's pioneer work in blood tests and nutrition, the more I marveled that, at that time, his own state ignored him as a speaker; yet he was on national programs.

"During my time in New Jersey, Louise Morris's mother had cataract surgery. Dr. Morris introduced me to Dr. Castroviejo, her surgeon, who invited me to audit his surgery whenever possible. This I did on every half day off. Dr. Castroviejo was most helpful. He explained the differences between the human and the dog eye. He was also more courteous to me than to his own residents. Dr. Morris allowed me to operate after hours on the eyes of dogs which were to be put to sleep. I feel greatly indebted to Mark for his encouragement which resulted in my ever-growing interest in ophthalmology.

"Mark took me with him to the monthly meetings of the New York City Veterinary Medical Association. It was there that I realized that Mark's diagnostic expertise was not really appreciated or recognized. Although I never knew whether Mark could tell whether a dog was sick by a cursory clinical examination, he always knew when he looked at the laboratory workup."

KESTER, Wayne O., Brig. General, U. S. Air Force
Former Chief of the U. S. Air Force Veterinary Service 1949-1957
Director of Research, Morris Animal Foundation

Tape recording received from General Kester dated August 20, 1979: "Moved from Washington, D.C., to the Denver area in 1958. Joined the Morris Animal Foundation staff on part-time basis. My special area of interest had always been the equine area, and the lack of research there was quite obvious. The need for trained personnel and the opportunity in research was quite apparent to me. I was aware of what needed to be done, who could do it, and where it could be done. So the Morris Foundation was an excellent opportunity.

"In looking back it intrigues me to review the people in the horse world who have joined the Foundation because of the Equine Division and possibly because of their acquaintance with me and knowledge of my background.

"I look back on my association with the Foundation with a great deal of satisfaction. It has been wonderful to associate with so many fine and dedicated people over the years, and it's rewarding to know that we started so many, many young veterinarians in research and that they carried on in that field and we've got a lot of good research done, started in many areas that otherwise would never have been taken on, particularly in the area of horse research. None was being done when we started. Now I think every veterinary college in the country has a horse research program and there are many private institutions also researching."

KINGMA, Dr. Fred, Fairfax, Virginia
Former Professor of Physiology and Pharmacology, Ohio State
Retired in 1980 as Deputy Director of the Bureau of Veterinary Medicine, Food and Drug Administration

Telephone interview April 3, 1980: "First became acquainted with Dr. Morris in the late 40s or early 50s. My first impression of him as an individual was, of course, his being an extremely intelligent man, and one of the early ones to realize the significance of small animal medicine as a big part of our profession. He had a real feeling of appreciation for nutrition when it comes to veterinary medicine. This was something that was unheard of before he came along, actually."

KIRK, Robert W.
Professor of Medicine at New York State College of Veterinary Medicine, Cornell University

Telephone interview on March 10, 1980: "The Foundation has been something that has impressed me. I have been involved with The Seeing Eye and helped evaluate the grants that the Seeing Eye was going to fund. The Morris family got into all of that.

"In the Foundation's principals, they wanted to get as many dollars as they could into animal research, mainly for companion animals. What impressed me was how little of that money stayed in the organization and how much of the money got down to the bench. The Morris family worked very hard for years to get the Foundation set up to be almost self-supporting. I think this speaks very clearly for the kind of contribution Mark Morris has made for the world.

"One of the things that Mark and his family did that I think was real outstanding was to establish Chairs of Nutrition at Colorado State and at Cornell. Those are valuable things that are helping to improve the status of nutrition therapy of sick animals.

"Another thing about Mark—he is one of the most loyal alumni that the Veterinary College has. He is an outstanding alumnus and certainly one of the best known veterinarians we have ever graduated. He has made a tremendous mark for himself in veterinary medicine. He has been a terrific success throughout his whole life—as a man, as a husband, and a father, as a benefactor, as a teacher—he has had a terrific life and I am very happy to acknowledge the effect he has had on me and what he has done for me. The best way I can show this, I guess, is by passing on to my students some of the qualities he has shown to me."

McCoy, John, V.M.D.
Professor of Comparative Pathology, College of Medicine and Dentistry of New Jersey, Rutgers University
Director of the Vivarium (Experimental Phase), Rutgers Medical School
Adjunct Research Professor, Bureau of Biological Research, Rutgers University

Telephone interview May 7, 1979: "After I returned from Army service I tried different positions, thinking we had such an open field in veterinary medicine that I would have no problems, but found them all pretty unchallenging. Went to work for Mark Morris at Raritan Hospital for Animals in 1948. I had the duties of running the hospital with Louise's help—she had all the accounting, the books, the appointments, etc. After my orientation there I took over the work at Raritan Laboratories at Metuchen and later a collection of materials regarding nutritional research; and then we went into the work for the A.A.H.A. in regard to the Certificate of Approval for the balanced diets for dogs primarily. Later we got into the cat nutrition and did some basic work on that.

"In working with Mark I found the area I became involved in basically was biomedical research. After a couple of years the research began in cancer as it naturally occurred in dogs. I was offered a position in biomedical research in Rutgers in December of 1950 and was trained at the National Cancer Institute for the purpose of learning everything I could about canine cancer, still working at the Raritan Hospital for Animals, where the physical facilities for keeping cats and dogs were available. Mark had a lot to do with the start of that work.

"We still are interested in nutrition in relation to cancer in dogs. I think the cancer work was the one most directly in line with my relationship with Dr. Morris."

McGINNIS, Clifford L., D.V.M.
Retired small animal practitioner, Peoria, Illinois

Telephone interview July 15, 1979: "We were just married on June 3rd, after graduating with the class of '33. I had struggled through financially, so we had no money. Then we had the phone call to replace Fred Schmitt at Far Hills, New Jersey, in Mark's practice. I was properly impressed to watch him doing differential blood counts, and he was just beginning to mix diets which he would dispense in 10-pound bags and instruct the client to add one tablespoon of lard or oil. I thought it was magic at first—but it did work!"

McKEOWN, Don, D.V.M
Director, Small Animal Surgery, University of Guelph, Ontario Veterinary College, Department
    of Clinical Studies

Letter dated May 12, 1978, to Dr. Mark Morris, Jr.,: "I had a grand one-hour-and-ten-minute conversation with your father, and was I impressed! He really is a bright, well-informed, and dedicated veterinarian. I thought that I was aware of what was going on in veterinary medicine, but he was two jumps ahead of me. I was flattered that we were on the same "wave length" about the future of the A.A.H.A. and veterinary medicine. I believe that he can influence the organization more than any other individual, due to the high regard in which he is held by the profession."

MAURER, Fred D., D.V.M.
Retired Colonel, U.S. Army
Associate Dean and Director, Institute of Tropical Veterinary Medicine, Texas A & M University,
    College Station, Texas

Telephone interview and notes dated November 16, 1979: "First became acquainted with Mark L. Morris about 1955 while I was head of Veterinary Pathology. The Foundation asked me to serve as a member of the Advisory Group which evaluates the research proposals, and I served until 1962.

"It took a man with unselfish vision and devotion to his profession to devote his time, effort and money to such a Foundation, and I have been pleased through the years to be associated.

"At a time when both animal and human medicine was almost entirely devoted to infectious diseases, he saw the merits and need for better nutrition, which is only now being appreciated in both fields. The Foundation filled a need for research on the diseases of companion animals which had received grossly inadequate support. From 1925 until about 1950 there were almost no funds available for equine research and little for dogs, cats, and zoo animals. Dr. Morris has put new tools and knowledge in the hands of all veterinarians on a worldwide basis so that his efforts are multiplied by the vast numbers who use the knowledge he sponsored."

MELBY, Edward
Dean, New York State College of Veterinary Medicine, Cornell University, Ithaca, New York

Telephone interview May 9, 1979: "I have known Dr. and the late Mrs. Morris as long as I have been associated with veterinary medicine. I knew of his work with the Seeing Eye Foundation, developing diets and the eventual Prescription Diets. I followed the course of his veterinary medicine through the A.V.M.A. also.

"When Dr. Morris started his work on nutrition, I would dare say certainly very little was known—in human medicine as well—about the use of full range pathology, and I can't help but think how perceptive, how much ahead of his time Dr. Morris was in the development of the Prescription Diets, as well as the production of them. He was certainly the earliest that I know of, and probably the first to set up laboratory standards with very well qualified men trained to run them, and began studies and investigations which we would now call cursory in nature, but at that time were well ahead of the profession.

"He had an inquisitive mind, searching out the reasons on an inquisitive basis, and I think that sets him apart. I have to include his wife as well—that sets *them* apart from most of their peers in that area of activity. I think since that time, because of his and Louise's efforts, friends and colleagues, Prescription Diets, the Morris Animal Foundation and its concerns and activities—again, he was a man well ahead of his time. He took the training he had received and, again looking back from the vantage point of 1979, his vision in the sciences—but he took that knowledge and continued to build on his educational background to incorporate it in his work and apply it to his practice. Without any question, he was one of the "firsts" in veterinary medicine."

MINER, Mrs. Eunice T., Boynton Beach, Florida
Formerly Executive Director of New York Academy of Sciences

Telephone interview May 5, 1979: "Mark and Louise are very vivid persons to me—I will never forget them. Mark participated in a number of conferences of the New York Academy of Sciences. He had a mind that was constantly active and alert. He was interested in what I was involved in, and I was interested in his work, with his great interest in nutrition, animal diseases, treatment, and research.

"Mark Morris is as solid as this planet, and I am sure his children and grandchildren are very like him.

"We need more Mark Morrises in this world today in the field of science."

MORGAN, William E., Dr.
President Emeritus, Colorado State University, Ft. Collins, Colorado

Telephone interview February 1, 1980: "My first involvement with Dr. Morris was in the late 50s or early 60s. If I were to use one word to describe my first impression of him, I would say—INTENSE. He was all business, gets quickly to the point; he doesn't beat around the bush.

"My personal opinion of Dr. Morris as a person: I would say that underneath the surface, which is all business, he is a warm, friendly, sincere person.

"Quite honestly, he would have to rank among the outstanding American leaders in his profession. Having identified a weak link in the professional training of veterinarians, he set out to correct it by more than the conventional method of urging it (which is usually done with somebody else's money). Instead, he provided financial support from his own resources. Believe me, this is unusual, especially in this day and time when people almost instinctively turn to the government for assistance in a matter of this kind.

"A sure way to multiply one's efforts is to work through the influence on others, and this is the key to what I call the "multiplier effect of teaching"—and his contribution, of course, was especially important in the teaching of practitioners, who in turn go out and put their teaching into operation. This is a kind of philosophical point, but it is a very real one in this case, because when one gets up in years and looks back and says "What did I do that had an effect beyond the immediate people that I touched?", he can be certain that what he did to activate others had a wide spread of application in what he was accomplishing."

MOSIER, Jacob E., D.V.M., M.S.
Professor and former Head of Dept. of Surgery and Medicine, Kansas State University College
    of Veterinary Medicine, Manhattan, Kansas
President of American Veterinary Medical Association—1982

Letter dated January 25, 1982: "With each passing year I am even more impressed with the leadership Dr. Morris provided the veterinary profession.

"I am aware of the tremendous contributions of the two Morris Chairs of Nutrition. Here again the Morris family has made a major contribution to the veterinary medical profession and to animal welfare. Mark Morris's foresight and generosity are legendary."

OBERST, Fayne H., D.V.M.
Head of Medicine and Surgery, College of Veterinary Medicine, Oklahoma State University,
    Stillwater, Oklahoma

Letter dated January 18, 1963: "The other day in Milwaukee when I said I believed you had done outstandingly as A.V.M.A. president, I really meant it. You have always been forthright, an admirable quality. You have expressed hope, have given direction and are inspirational in your accomplishments.

"For a long time I've known we share ideas and hopes for veterinary medicine. Even though our fellow veterinarians may be slow in accepting these, I'm confident of their validity. You have my respect and thanks."

POPPENSIEK, Dr. George C.
Retired Dean, New York State College of Veterinary Medicine, Cornell University, Ithaca, New
    York

Telephone interview June 6, 1979: "I think very much of Dr. Morris and his whole family. He has been an inspiration to many of us for many, many years.

"There are many examples of the impact of the Morris family—particularly Mark and his wife—and all of veterinary medicine has benefitted greatly. He is one of the greats of veterinary medicine—a truly great man.

"One more thing—he always works on eight cylinders. He is always charged up like a battery. I would never know when I might get a phone call from him. Sometimes he would call at 11 o'clock at night, after I was in bed—but I wouldn't care if he called me at 2 o'clock in the morning—that is part of his charm—a phone call from him is always welcome!"

PRICE, Dr. Donald A.
Executive Director, AVMA, Chicago, Illinois

Telephone interview January 31, 1980: "My acquaintance with Dr. Morris began in 1960, when he was President-Elect for the A.V.M.A. The term of his Presidency was characterized by his aggressiveness. He was as active as any president we have ever had."

PULLEN, Gretchen Swanson
Daughter of Carl A. Swanson, founder of C. A. Swanson & Sons and the Swanson Center
   for Nutrition, Inc., Omaha, Nebraska

Telephone interview of November 2, 1979: "When Dr. Morris was in Omaha and working with my father and my brothers, at that time I was just enough younger so that business didn't enter my thinking at all. I was about 18 years younger than my brothers. I do remember overhearing their conversations. I do remember when he was there, and they always spoke of him with the greatest respect and admiration. He was such an attractive man, very dignified, and carried himself so well.

"Of course, since then our paths have crossed again, through my son, Kurt Bucholz, D.V.M. He reveres Dr. Morris as the supreme being in the veterinary world!"

RILEY, Dr. Charles, D.V.M.
Small animal practitioner, Ft. Worth, Texas

Personal note in December 1980: "My son, Dr. Douglas Riley, is very interested in the work of the Foundation. He has a client who is very impressed with the ideals and motives of the Morris Animal Foundation.

"Mark, I think of you so often and again I want to thank you and Louise for all you have done for our mutual profession."

RUST, Dr. John H., D.V.M., Ph.D.
Formerly with the University of Chicago, College of Medicine

Tape recording made by Dr. Rust: "In 1932 or 1933 I arrived at the Raritan Hospital in New Jersey and met a most exciting man—Mark Morris. He, with his wife, were operating a veterinary hospital on the highest scientific levels that I had ever seen. We discussed something new, to me at least, that Mark was conducting and that was a study of the blood picture in canine distemper. Here was a man in obscure Stelton, New Jersey, who was making forward steps that I felt were quite important. To do a blood count on a dog; to do a urinalysis on a dog, was unheard of at the veterinary school at Kansas State at the time but this man was doing just that. So I left Stelton with a great admiration for Mark Morris and Louise.

"Louise and Mark have shown many of us the importance of sharing your resources with others."

SCHROEDER, Dr. Charles R.
San Diego Wild Animal Park, Escondido, California
Former Director of San Diego Zoo

Personal letter dated January 24, 1982: "I recall so well meeting with you at Stelton, New Jersey and seeing your kennels housing your FDA project dogs. Most interesting was your unique floor radiant heating which I subsequently used at the zoo for Primates and Hippos, and believe it or not Okapis successfully.

"At that time, in the 40s, you were hot on the trail of better nutrition for dogs. As secretary of the New York Veterinary Association I was fortunate to have you give papers at our meetings on your early findings, of enormous interest to our members—the forerunner of companion animal nutrition today.

"Your extraordinary energy in the field of nutrition and the establishment of the Morris Animal Foundation and subsequent support of companion animal disease research places you in the forefront of veterinary medical research and development."

SCRIMSHAW, Dr. Nevin S.
Institute Professor, Dept. of Nutrition and Food Science, Massachusetts Institute of Technology, International Nutrition Program, Cambridge, Massachusetts

Dr. Scrimshaw met Dr. Morris at a Protein Conference. Scrimshaw was selected by the Committee that was establishing the World Nutrition Laboratories at M.I.T. Dr. Morris located Paul Newberne for him.

Letter from Dr. Scrimshaw dated 12/31/80: "Thank you for your letter of November 12, and the enclosed copy of your 1960 presentation on "Challenges in the Medical Sciences Facing the Food Industry." It is also hard to believe the obvious fact that this same talk could be appropriately given today, with the sole deletion of the references to President Eisenhower!

"It was a great pleasure to hear from you again and to know that you are working on a record of your experiences. Needless to say, we have been very happy with Paul Newberne and he has made an outstanding contribution.

"I stepped down as department head over a year ago, but with responsibilities for the International Nutrition Program and the Clinical Research Center, as well as the World Hunger Programme of the United Nations University, have not been idle."

SEVERINGHAUS, Elmer L., M.D. (retired)
Edmonds, Washington
Formerly with Hoffman-LaRoche

Telephone interview on March 27, 1980: "I first became acquainted with Dr. Morris when I had his help in developing a hybrid dog for laboratory use—about 1950. This dog was a cross between a smooth-haired bull terrier and a beagle. The purpose for this hybrid dog was to get a dog which would be available with good bones, good proportions in body, and easy to manage, for use in the pharmacology laboratory in testing drugs.

"Dr. Morris is highly intelligent and resourceful. I respect him for his professional ability and his personal approachability."

SHOCKLEY, Martin
Retired English Professor, North Texas State University, Denton, Texas

Telephone interview on June 17, 1979: "I will start in 1952, when the Morrises and the Shockleys both came to Coyote Hill (Allenspark, Colorado). The Morrises had bought a cabin, restored it, did it all over, making it into a very attractive mountain home. They added an office building from which they managed most or all the work they were doing at that time.

"Soon after we had moved there, I remember one of our neighbors, Ralph Ellsworth, told us that his new neighbor was not just an ordinary veterinarian. He said, 'Dr. Morris is one of the most distinguished scientists in the country.'

"We didn't know much about animal nutrition, but we gradually got to know the Morrises very well. We lived on the hill with them for some 25 years. I guess he knew I was a professor of English, so he asked me to be a sort of consultant on his books.

"When I talk about Mark I have to talk about Louise because they were very close and they really made quite a team. She was always helping him in everything he did. In my opinion he did more to upgrade his profession than any man I know in any other profession."

SMITH, Dr. C. Roger
Formerly Professor of Physiology and Dean, Ohio State University Columbus, Ohio

Telephone interview May 9, 1979: "My association with Dr. Morris began about the time shortly after I became a member of the faculty here, and I had attended an A.A.H.A. meeting. Dr. Morris was there and I was really impressed with his enthusiasm and excitement for the medical sciences. Not only that—but he was doing something about it! Even now everybody is talking about nutrition in connection with cancer, heart disease, etc. He was a forerunner of preventive medicine and treatment with diet, therapy, hormones, etc., before a lot of people gave any serious consideration to it.

"His interest in the support of research was very genuine—he realized the value of research before a lot of people did. He knew it was important both for the profession and the future of the profession. I always felt it was the real basis of progress—the way he set up the Foundation—setting aside a certain amount of his income to support the Foundation. That was remarkable and I always admired him for that. When that Foundation was established I had the privilege of working with them on the Advisory Board—from 1964-1967.

"As a person Mark has always been very nice. So was Mrs. Morris. She really was a fine person. I even considered one time going to work for him. They had a job opportunity and talked of a scientific research program, and I almost seriously considered that. I wanted to, but had been in academics for so long, it was a hard decision to make."

TERRELL, Charles
Former Assistant to the President of Colorado State University and Executive Secretary of Colorado State Board of Agriculture

Telephone interview of June 20, 1979: "My association with Mark and Louise has been to a large extent on a social, friendship basis. We found Mark and Louise to be a most unusual team. She was so supportive of Mark and so well informed in all he was doing. This was to me one of the great advantages he had. Mark is an unusual individual, in my judgment, in that his inquisitive mind and capacity to affiliate medical information and to structure research and experimental efforts is, to me, one of those things that is a great contribution to veterinary medicine, as well as to the medical profession itself.

"He has done an outstanding job, as well as starting a program at Colorado State University in the field of animal nutrition. The University has had programs in animal nutrition for many years, but those programs have been designed primarily for large animals, and not the type of nutrition that Mark had in mind and that he started here. As a result of his efforts and funding in starting the program in animal nutrition in veterinary medicine, he has opened up a whole new field for veterinarians in Colorado—and it seems to be national.

"The Morris Animal Foundation that they founded is one of those outstanding organizations that has the capacity to coordinate the efforts of many, many interests into the solution of mutual problems."

THIMMIG, John, D.V.M.
Retired Veterinarian, Brighton, Colorado
Former President of the State Board of Agriculture, Colorado

Telephone interview June 27, 1979: "We are very honored to have Mark as our very good friend. As far as the town of Brighton is concerned, Mark has always had a soft spot in his heart for that, and I have practiced here for 42 years. Mark's birthplace, Henderson, is about six miles south of here. He graduated from Brighton High School.

"When Mark began to expand with the Foundation to benefit the different veterinary research programs, etc., I happened to be serving as President of the State Board of Agriculture. When he decided to fund a Chair in Nutrition at Colorado State University I happened to be on the Board at the University. Mark honored the University by funding this particular chair and selected Dr. Lon Lewis to head that Chair.

"The Morris family, as a family, is one that we have thoroughly enjoyed. Mark is—well, there just aren't enough complimentary things you can say about that kind of man who is highly successful in his own right, perfectly willing to share his knowledge with others, and establishes institutions that carry on that type of work.

"As far as Colorado State University is concerned, we are certainly eternally grateful to the Morris family for the recognition they gave to the School of Veterinary Medicine and we will always be thankful that Mark was generous enough to return and do what he has at the University.

"Mark's life is certainly a wonderful story. It will be a great inspiration to many young men in the future."

WERNTZ, George, Jr.
Etna, New Hampshire
Retired—Executive Director, The Seeing Eye, Inc.

Telephone interview on May 8, 1979: "In 1946 Mark Morris started making food for the Seeing Eye, which was just about four years before I began my 25-year tenure there. If anything happens to a blind man's dog—because it is not only a way of getting there, but it is also psychological—they are completely dependent on them. And Mark was just wonderful. He always insisted we get all the medical facts and he handled it very professionally. His recommendations often involved a change of diet. He lived and prospered by the old saying, "You are what you eat." And he applied this to animals as well as to humans—and he has proved right many, many times in the field of animal nutrition.

"I think Mark is a visionary, has a lot of imagination, and is highly energetic. Also he is very persuasive. He had this single purpose of improving animal health by improving their diet. He had great contacts in the veterinary field. He worked with them all. I think some of them may have become a little jealous of his success, but when the chips were down, they had to admit he had done a damn good job. He has always been very generous of himself—he is a great fellow. He has great power for friendship, has great pride in his profession, and I think he has done a lot to enhance the prestige of the veterinary profession—they are not just "horse doctors" any more—they are scientists."

WHITLOCK, John H.
Professor Emeritus, Dept. of Preventive Medicine, New York State College of Veterinary
    Medicine, Cornell University, Ithaca, New York

Letter dated March 25, 1980: "I think Mark Morris demonstrates a number of things for our time: first, that a busy successful practitioner can do really independent, first-rate research; second, that applied research which really fits a need can be especially profitable financially; and third that a functioning social conscience can generate substantial funds for the society and profession that supported the researcher in his case through the Morris Animal Foundation and Mark Morris Professorship."

YOUNG, Wesley A., D.V.M.
Formerly Chief Veterinarian of the Animal Rescue League, and Managing Director of the Anti-
    Cruelty Society, Western Regional Director of the American Humane Association, Direc-
    tor of Los Angeles Zoo

Telephone interview on May 29, 1980: "Mark Morris's serious thinking about animal welfare—this business of food and diet—has really grown up to be the mountain top in animal care. I spent a lot of time with humane organizations and every time Mark and I met, it was with a warm feeling. I think he had a high regard for our humane work, and I had a great respect for him in the field of animal nutrition. Our animals (some people say) are better nourished than humans because Mark has given them some real solid information on nutrition and guidance.

"Here is a man who was a leader, pretty much a pioneer in the animal nutrition field, and he did something about it. The commercial angle was the financial means to really make something out of it—which he did!"

Index

225